INTO CHINA'S HEART

Into China's Heart

An Emigré's Journey Along the Yellow River

by Lynn Pan

New York • WEATHERHILL • *Tokyo*

First edition, 1985

Published by John Weatherhill, Inc., of New York and Tokyo, with editorial offices at 7-6-13 Roppongi, Minato-ku, Tokyo 106, Japan. Copyright © 1985 by Lynn Pan; all rights reserved. Printed and first published in Japan.

Library of Congress Cataloging in Publication Data: Pan, Lynn. / Into China's heart. / 1. Yellow River Valley (China)—Description and / travel. 2. Pan, Lynn—Journeys—China—Yellow River / Valley. I. Title. / DS793.Y45P36 1985 915.1'1 85-13020 / ISBN 0-8348-0205-8

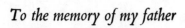
To the memory of my father

Contents

Map appears on pages 2 and 3.

INTO CHINA'S HEART

YELLOW RIVER BASIN

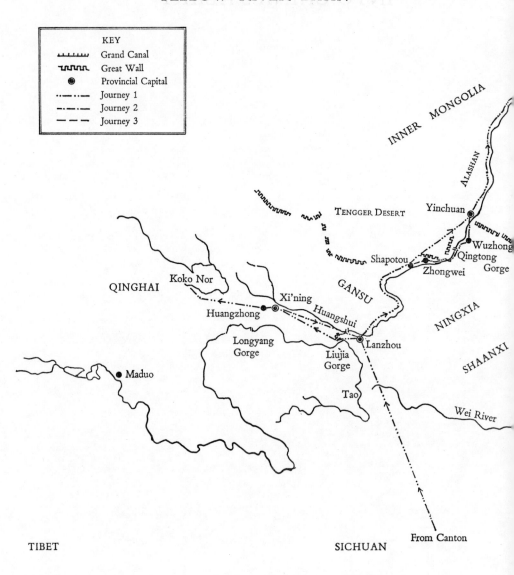

KEY

‡‡‡‡‡‡ Grand Canal

ᴜᴜᴜᴜᴜ Great Wall

◉ Provincial Capital

·—·—· Journey 1

·—·—· Journey 2

– – – Journey 3

INNER MONGOLIA

ALASHAN

Tengger Desert

Yinchuan

Wuzhong

Shapotou

Qingtong Gorge

Zhongwei

Koko Nor

QINGHAI

GANSU

NINGXIA

Xi'ning

Huangshui

SHAANXI

Huangzhong

Lanzhou

Longyang Gorge

Liujia Gorge

Maduo

Tao

Wei River

TIBET

SICHUAN

From Canton

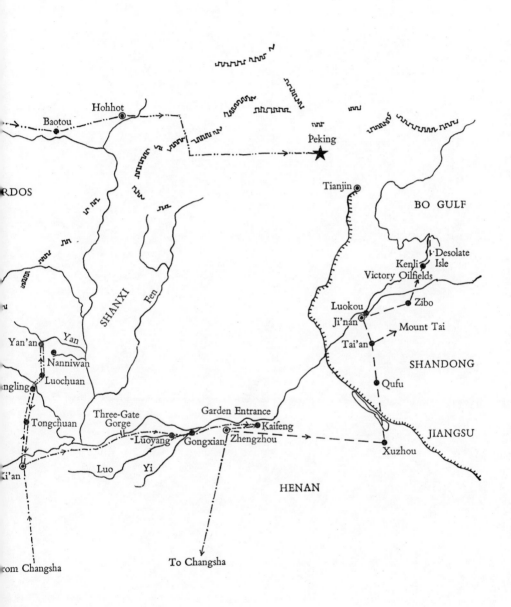

Hohhot

Baotou

RDOS

Peking

Tianjin

BO GULF

SHANXI

Fen

Desolate
Isle

Kenli
Victory Oilfields

Zibo

Luokou
Ji'nan

Mount Tai

Yan'an

Yan

Tai'an

SHANDONG

Nanniwan

Luochuan

ngling

Qufu

Tongchuan

Three-Gate
Gorge

Garden Entrance

Kaifeng

Luoyang

Gongxian

Zhengzhou

JIANGSU

Xi'an

Luo

Yi

Xuzhou

HENAN

om Changsha

To Changsha

Prologue

The valleys of the Yellow River, wrote the French explorer and thinker Pierre Teilhard de Chardin in 1923, struck him as "austere and desolate regions in which the mind, as well as the body, is exposed defenseless to all the great winds of the earth." He went on: "These immense expanses, grey and flat, out of all proportion to our plains of western Europe, and these completely bare and rocky mountains, provide no moral handhold. One feels lost in such undemarcated country."

It was for these valleys that, in three journeys undertaken between the summer of 1982 and the spring of 1983, I was bound. In such undemarcated country, I thought, I would see China in all its diversity. For between the two ends of the Yellow River stretches almost the whole range of Chinese life, from highland nomadism to offshore drilling, by way of hydroelectric power stations, irrigated rice fields, towns, communes, and places of worship, work, and rest. I thought, too, that I would see China at its source, and Chinese man against his earliest setting, for the yellow earth of the river valleys was Chinese civilization's very seedbed. And the special attributes of the river having since time immemorial provided the context for human struggle and enterprise in China, I thought I would see something of the transformation of society, as this is reflected by the transformation of the river itself.

What are these attributes? The first is simply that the Yellow River is the muddiest river in the world—and by far, its average silt concentration being thirty-four times higher, for example, than that of the Nile. The source of this silt is the world's largest area of loess, that loose yellow earth which, for all that its name is German, stands for the very setting of China. All of it is subject to erosion, and the appalling rate at which this happens—twenty-seven times greater than the world average—makes the lower Yellow what it is: a river whose bed rises from year to year, and is in some places fifteen to thirty feet higher than the surrounding terrain.

This terrible brown burden, besides being the fact on which the Yellow's fame and name rest, is also the reason for its epithet—China's Sorrow. For no river can carry one and a half billion tons of silt down to the sea every year without some disaster occurring, and floods and the Yellow River have indeed always gone together.

Continuous dykes keep the river in place downstream, but in the spring and summer, when melted snow pours into the water and torrential rain falls, floods can come upon the river like a cataclysm, swirling relentlessly over the land. Then, when the flood tide is staunched and the river level falls, the waters may go wandering in search of a new bed, causing the river to make one of those dramatic changes of course so familiar from Chinese history.

The Yellow River is history taking its course, wearing down an old people as its currents wear rocks on their way to the sea. In the last two thousand years history has recorded more than fifteen hundred dyke breaches and twenty-six major changes of course; and it was against this background of violence and havoc that much else in Chinese life was posed. Everything was a reverberation of this. From it had come famines, epidemics, destitution, death and the displacement of every instinct except that of survival. Out of it had sprung the need for organized river control and collective maintenance of irrigation systems which dictated the character of the kingdoms that arose by the banks of the river and indeed ushered in the political centralization in the first place. At the same time as the river's convulsions yielded up ruin, they yielded up civilization. For it was in the Yellow River basin that the earliest Chinese most densely clustered. Here were the earliest granaries, here the earliest irrigation works; here, at the confluence of the Yellow and the tributary Wei, was the center of the Chinese world at a time when the Great Wall bounded it to the north; here the imperial city of Chang'an rose in unparalleled splendor, its palaces fringed with parks and packed with beautiful women; here is the archaeologist's, historian's China.

For if the river is a destroyer, it is also more charitable than any human benefactor, providing water to lands otherwise too parched to support human life. It is to the massive organization needed to exploit and manage water, rather than any other natural resource, that some historians (Karl Wittfogel, for instance, in his influential work *Oriental Despotism*) attribute the tyrannies and elaborate bureaucracies that passed for state power in countries like China and ancient Egypt. For centuries just the state of the dykes and canals was enough to commend or condemn the Chinese imperial administration, and not to keep them in good repair was a black mark against the emperor, betokening dynastic collapse as surely as famines and uprisings and portents from heaven.

Not all of the river basin is open to the traveler from abroad, and for that reason I could not travel the entire length of the river, from source to mouth. Nor did I cover the distance in one lap: I wanted to see the country in different seasons, and rather than spend a whole year there and find my interest to keep on moving played out as the physical and emotional demands of traveling increased, I thought I would break my journey up into three sections, each beginning and ending in Hong Kong. This proved a good plan because, quite simply, I could not have endured unremitting travel in China, so often did it seem like an obstacle course, with the traveler having to work hard on several fronts at once—physical, practical, bureaucratic, and interpersonal.

My account is not nautical, for not much of the Yellow River is actually navigable. Unlike the Yangtze, it is not a great waterway. Nor is the account strictly chronological, in the way of a travel journal, for in the interests of geographical continuity I have rearranged some of my experiences so that they appear in the pages earlier or later in the sequence than they happened to occur. For the comfort of some of the people who appear in these pages, I have changed certain names and either suppressed or camouflaged any personal details which might identify them. These two inauthenticities apart, I believe the picture I have conjured up to be as true as anything which has been written about China, and probably a great deal truer than much that has been written about it.

Part of my advantage in this exercise lies certainly in my being Chinese; yet it cannot be said that I merged into the local scene without so much as a stare from anyone. It is true that in the remoter corners of the countryside I was sometimes taken for a local, but this was only because, with those for whom the world beyond China does not exist, for whom, indeed, there could be no other country on earth, one feels a strange compulsion to corroborate, almost to act out, their misunderstanding of one. I certainly never went out of my way to pass myself off as a local (I never, for example, dressed like one, though it would have been easy to do so); and in any case, the authorities always knew me for the outsider that I am. To them I was an Overseas Chinese, by virtue of my British nationality.

On two of my journeys my companion was Takia, a photographer living in Hong Kong. Though we are both Chinese by birth, the Chinese authorities regarded us differently. Whereas I was designated an Overseas Chinese, he is what they call a Hong Kong/Macao Compatriot, a category which makes him several shades less "foreign" than I. What is good about being a Chinese émigré in China is that you are allowed to travel to some places that are off limits to visitors of another racial descent, and you are charged less for your food, accommodation, and transport (though even here there are class distinctions: while Chinese from Taiwan pay least of all, followed by Chinese from Hong Kong and Macao, those like myself, holding distinctly foreign passports, have the dubious honor of occupying the topmost rung of the "compatriot" ladder). What is bad about being a Chinese émigré in China is that you are neither one thing nor the other, neither native nor alien, neither insider nor out-. While some Chinese I met felt they could be completely themselves with me, others were more wary, seeing me as part of that outside world from which their innermost thoughts must be withheld. And there were times when, just as I was beginning to think I counted for no more than the natives, sharing with them the comparative ease of unimportance, something would happen to make me feel that I was under special surveillance, and that my relations with people could not be entirely natural. At such times I had the impression of being sent right back to the beginning of a game I thought I had been playing according to the rules.

There was to my status as an outsider an element of privilege, and I was sometimes treated with greater courtesy than would be shown a native. But seeing Chinese émigrés enjoy privileges withheld from themselves has soured many a native's attitude toward the visitor, and from these I seemed to call up much resentment and envy. These Chinese wrongly suppose that I enjoy my privileged status unequivocally, and do not realize that it can close as many doors as open, impose as many limitations as remove.

I myself found some of China's characteristics all too familiar, from the heritage I share with its people, and others altogether strange and surprising; for while China is run by advocates of the socialist system, in the country I live in the very opposite is true. Of course I was drawn the more to the Chinese by my awareness of what we have in common, but at the same time I was acutely aware of our difference. Though I was born in Shanghai, and lived there to see it go communist, I have spent most of my adult life in Europe, and have long ceased to think of China as home. After all these years of living in the West I have grown remote enough from that country to see it with something of the detachment that I might feel, say, in India or Australia. Many other Chinese émigrés, I know, have gone to China to find their roots, seeking to rediscover their individual identities in an ideal of China, and now cannot give this up without losing themselves. Their wish to return to their own origins I attribute to their experience of studying or working or living for long periods in the West, where, sooner or later, they find themselves in a no-man's-land between East and West, and respond to their feeling of having come unmoored by a violent rejection of their host culture and a sentimental extolling of all things Chinese. But I am not glamorously split within myself, and do not need China for my self-identity. If this makes me a more impartial observer, it also lays me open to the often repeated criticism that enough books have been written about China by people who see it through Western eyes (as if a Westerner could see China other than through his own, Western eyes). I cannot judge if my view is all that different from theirs; I only know that, for all that I live among Europeans, and have done so for more than twenty years, I have never felt with them what I feel with the Chinese: the absolute conviction that I can get them right.

A Foreign Country

> *White bones scattered*
> *like tangled hemp,*
> *how soon before mulberry and catalpa*
> *turn to dragon-sands*
> *I only know north of the river*
> *there is no life:*
> *crumbled houses, scattered chimney smoke*
> *from a few houses*
>
> —— *Crossing the Yellow River*
> June 12, 1233
> by Yuan Haowen
> translated by Stephen West

Until I saw the Yellow River early Chinese history was a closed book to me, and northern China, the setting for that history, a foreign country, one that had nothing whatever to do with me. While I knew intellectually that Chinese civilization arose around the middle reaches of the Yellow, emotionally I felt it to be centered in the eastern stretches of the Yangtze.

This is because I am a southerner, and find empathy with Chinese history growing only from the twelfth century, after the Song dynasty emperors had retreated before the pursuing Tartars south to Hangzhou, and shifted the cultural node of China to the areas watered by the lower Yangtze. The cultivated valleys of that river, moistly clothed in green and neatly checkered in paddy, were far closer to my southern perceptions, and though I knew that nothing

11

could be more Chinese than the Great Wall and the Yellow River, yet they did not feel all that Chinese to me.

But I have come to recognize that, though many consider the Yangtze to be the greater river—it is certainly longer, and in geological time older—it cannot really be taken to stand for China. My travels revealed to me landscapes I had not seen before, traditions I could not grasp, people I could not even talk to; and for the first time I became alive to that other China.

And the first corrective I had to my earlier view I found in a simple, geographical fact—the fact that here in the northwestern part of the country, desert accounts for more acreage than is cultivated in the whole of China. Here, the fact that China ranks third in the world, after Australia and Saudi Arabia, in the extent of its desert area is not simply statistical, but very quickly palpable.

How false is the image of the Yangtze as the image of China you can deeply sense in Gansu Province, in the so-called Corridor West of the Yellow River. This is the eastern arm of that great transcontinental artery which the world knew as the Silk Route. Through it, along a string of oases running between the mountains to the south and the Gobi Desert to the north, travelers to Rome and silk caravans had passed, vulnerable to assaults by the Tanguts on one side and the Huns on the other. The place is brown and monotonous, and resonant with the romance of Central Asia and Samarkand. Here, before the pass of Jade Gate, the Great Wall straggles to a stop; and beyond, you feel, China itself comes to an end amid the "dragon-sands." But actually it doesn't, and here is another geographical fact to correct your perspective: Lanzhou, which is the provincial capital of Gansu and lies on the Yellow River not more than one hundred fifty miles from the Corridor, is, as a quick look at the map will tell you, the exact geographical center of China.

Lanzhou

I was more forcibly struck by the contrast between north and south China than by that between south China and the world from which

I had come. Imagining that things were going to be quite different over the border, I had arrived in Canton to find that it was half Hong Kong already: taxis you could flag down, girls in flowery dresses, a weakness for gambling. As my taxi drove into town, a girl in a pink dress and brown stiletto heels had flashed by on a bicycle. Not a block from our hotel, I had seen the frenzied traffic part to give a wide berth to a cyclist dismounting in the hurly-burly to pick up a scatter of mahjong tiles he'd dropped on the ground.

In Hong Kong, the approach to the airport—lying, as it happens, through some of the dearest real estate on earth—had been inexpressibly ugly, with the concrete facelessness of a boom town. But this was somehow worse; Canton has all the noise and congestion of a big city but not the dynamism. An inescapable fact of Hong Kong, standing on the edge of the hinterland, is the prospect of China unleashing socialism upon it one day; and Canton, its linguistic collateral but political antithesis, offers the closest vision of its future self. For the moment, though, the contagion is in the other direction, and Canton will be poised for a few awkward years between dialectical materialism and materialism of the Hong Kong sort. In a more fanciful moment one might envisage in Canton a sort of compromise—socialism and capitalism come to terms. In sober fact, however, it is more like a travesty of both. Though people are always saying how different things suddenly become when you pass behind the Bamboo Curtain, to me it felt more like crossing into a Hong Kong gone wrong.

I did not at all feel what many visitors from the West had felt—those Utopia seekers who, genuinely believing it was better to be poor and happy than to be rich and bored, had upon crossing the border into China been reassured by the immediate sense of difference, the absence of Coca-Cola and advertising billboards. I thought this as my eyes moved over the streets, taking in the undisciplined traffic and the hoardings splashed with political slogans. As I noted the current catch phrase, the Four Modernizations (meaning the upgrading of China's agriculture, industry, science and technology, and defense), it struck me that, judging from what I'd heard, there was something in common between the way China was going about this business and the way Canton's street traffic moved: too headlong for comfort, too slow for speed.

It was hot and steamy, but the real clammy heat of the south had yet to begin. I did not notice anything unusual about the weather, though I had been led to expect inclemency by newspaper reports of torrential rain hitting the province, causing floods and taking lives. The heavy downpours had disrupted the air traffic from Canton, and I felt more than a little anxious about my flight to Lanzhou the next day, though it would seem somehow appropriate to begin a journey to the flood-prone Yellow River with a delay caused by too much water. With that thought I began to imagine the journey ahead, the difficulties and frustrations to come. The excitement too—for there was bound to be some, in venturing into unknown places—and for a moment I knew that unreasonable happiness which comes to me at the mere thought of boarding an airplane.

Takia and I put up at the Overseas Chinese Hotel, where in the morning I woke at 4 a.m. to the sound of ablutions, doors opening and closing up and down the corridor. By five the sound of honking traffic was already inescapable. I staggered to the window, and when I looked down I saw, eddying round the courtyard, the morning shift fetching hot water for their breakfast. Clad in blue cotton trousers and a white shirt, each man carried an enamel mug and a thermos flask. I thought of my two months' supply of Nescafé and delved for it among my medicines, polythene bags, rolls of toilet paper, and other essentials of travel in China.

The morning was more than leisurely, it was sedate. We took a slow ride in a pedicab to Shamian Island, down by the southwestern edge of the Pearl River. The island, you would say at first sight, is an elegant Mediterranean suburb gone to seed—decaying villas with stucco balustrades and balconies with crumbling red tiled roofs. The place was a sandy flat before the first European settlers converted it into a sort of miniature Treaty Port after their victory in the second Opium War. British, French, and German interests were once represented here, but if the world of iced drinks and lawn bowls still lives, it lives only across the border in Hong Kong.

The five-star red flag now flies on the boats steaming up the Pearl River.

On the sidewalk edge a cluster of boys were playing a card game. Three or four middle-aged men and women stood about singly swinging their arms—a routine which passes for a constitutional in China. They were overlooked by political slogan boards, whose exhortations to work for the realization of the Four Modernizations seemed to strike a note too strident in this place where people sat silently with their backs to the sun as it climbed the sky, waiting for the evening breeze to come from the river.

All through lunch and the early afternoon that feeling persisted, of the unimportance of time when nothing could be accomplished by its economical use. It proved too much to expect the driver of the airport bus to curtail his siesta in the interest of prompt departure. I complained to the receptionist at the China Travel Service desk, and to mollify me he engaged in the make-believe of going to hurry up the driver. He must have thought: if the customer believes this will produce results, why destroy her illusions?

As it happened I needn't have worried, for if the bus was delayed the flight was even more so. The departure lounge was full of people with impassive faces. A mural reproducing in his own unruly calligraphy Mao Zedong's poem *The Long March* dominates the room, and was a sop to my impatience: you can't read lines like "The Red Army fears not that the long march is hard / Ten thousand rivers and a thousand mountains are as nothing" without being infected a little by their monumental heedlessness.

The plane when it finally took off was full, and not air-conditioned. The temperature, already high from the time of year and proximate body heat, rose further, to the point where even the eager air stewardesses wilted. We were fed dinner at Changsha, our first scheduled stop, at 4:40 in the afternoon. Shortly before eight the landscape showed, thousands of feet below, the brown of the Wei, the chief tributary of the Yellow River. The shadows of the plane crossed rectangles of ploughed loessland: an aged country, with one hopes its richest harvests still in the future. At Xi'an, the second stop, French, German, and American tourists confronted one another in rows in the transit lounge, their faces tired and baffled. As usual one could help oneself to tea. In another two hours we landed at Lanzhou.

Night had fallen some time ago. The temperature had dropped ten degrees and we were two hours away from the town center. A large bus bore us and scores of native Chinese into the darkness in a rattling rush. I couldn't see a thing and developed an excruciating headache. A whole hour passed in this way, infernally. Then, just as I was thinking nothing is as absorbing as pain, the sky suddenly reddened, and leaning forward to look out of the window I was stunned by as amazing a sight as I could ever hope to see: the dark glistening flow of the Yellow River holding within it the red glow of a flare that blazed away between it and the stars. It was an oil flare, taking its draft from the gaseous emissions of the petrochemical plants of Lanzhou's factory suburbs; and it burned and smoked there in the sky, a harbinger of hydrocarbon stench and pollution to come.

But on we bumped with no end in view. When another half hour had passed and several passengers had alighted, I thought to speak up and ask the driver if he would please put us down in front of the Friendship Hotel (the one I'd seen mentioned in the guidebooks).

We had already passed it, he said, and added that we had better put up at the Lanzhou Hotel, further up the road. It was midnight when we tumbled out of the bus, and though there was a porter at the gate, he was only there to tell us that the hotel was full and we'd do far better to go to the Friendship. A provincial-level conference on productivity was on, I learnt, and the delegates had occupied all the rooms.

I began to explain what he knew quite well, that we couldn't possibly go to the Friendship since transport was scarcely conceivable at that hour in Lanzhou. He agreed with sympathy, and then offered to telephone the Friendship to find out if there was a room.

I was in that advanced stage of fatigue where there is no longer any inhibition to thought or action and it takes little to push the inner frustrations to outward aggression. A volley sprang from my mouth; I spoke with the unhampered vehemence of one using her native tongue.

One comes to expect different strategies to work in different countries. In China getting your own way is often a matter of not taking no for an answer. There is always cause to do a lot of talking; obdurate as they are bound to be at the beginning, those who have it in their power to smooth your way or hinder it sometimes reward your efforts to talk them round by suddenly becoming the most obliging people imaginable. I put up some suggestions. Could we perhaps go inside the hotel to investigate the matter further? What were the chances of a room for tomorrow? Once he let us in he could be rid of us. We did not mind much where we slept, a sofa would do.

Then all of a sudden it became one of those nights that conspire for success, when everything goes as you wish. The porter waved us in; the hotel, which loomed up in the grounds in all its Soviet solidity, had a light burning inside and a cook, a receptionist, and a floor receptionist still up. (Only because they had decided to make a night of it with the bottle, as I was to learn from the cook, a fellow Shanghainese with whom I fell in at once, a common dialect being always a spur to camaraderie in China.) The receptionist said nothing but shook his head all the while, with that air of distraction that portended refusal, but I could tell from the way my fellow Shanghainese was nudging him that he was going to produce quite soon. He was bowed over his reservation charts for a long while, and when he looked up from them he brought forward for consideration not just one room but three.

It is not unusual for Chinese hotel rooms to make no concession whatsoever to the pleasure principle: no hot baths, no frills, no "atmosphere." What would be unusual would be if I minded this that night. Even the chambermaids, who are the scourge of early morning hours, clattering as they do into your room in the breaking light of dawn, never knocking, to whisk your thermos flask away to replace it with a fresh one, did not grate unduly. I slept as if in a coma. This was just as well, for the next day saw the closing of the productivity conference, and the delegates making the most of the last hours of that junket by roistering beneath my window until three o'clock in the morning.

Lanzhou is a dry, unlovely city, as I saw when I mounted the humble heights of White Pagoda Hill, getting there by walking across a steel structure which calls itself The First Bridge on the Yellow River. The bridge dates from the last years of the empire and owes its existence, so a memorial stone tells us, to German inspiration and American engineering. It is an easy enough climb to the top, and from any number of vantage points you can see the city lying wanly below.

Lanzhou stands at the point where the hills close in on the Yellow River—a junction of east-west traffic, the threshold of Turkestan and the outlet of Tibet. Once rafts of inflated goatskin and oxhide glided past, and ponies and camels ambled down the streets. King Leopold II of Belgium stationed his mining agents here, just in case there were coal or copper or silver concessions to be had, and Belgian missionaries ran the salt monopoly. Russian refugees and exiles would sometimes fetch up in these streets, delayed by a lack of money on their way to Shanghai or Peking.

Then the communist regime's First Five Year Plan in 1953, marking the place out for intensive development as an industrial base for the Northwestern Economic Region, changed all that. A bird's-eye view of Lanzhou will tell you that this is the city of Mao Zedong's short-lived Soviet phase, when he believed that China's drive to industrialization was to be fueled by imported machinery and technical help from the U.S.S.R. and Bloc countries. A belief translated into fractionating columns, storage tanks, factory workers' housing, and the opacity of polluted light. When Lanzhou's Soviet-designed oil refinery sprang up in the 1950s, it was the biggest and the most modern in the country.

The rush into industrialization was accompanied by a massive influx of people—the technicians, engineers, university professors, hairdressers, and tailors needed to man the new enterprises. The snatches of different dialects you sometimes hear on the buses are the liveliest reminder of that great displacement, away from the industrial northeast, Shanghai, Canton, and Hunan, into this far and unfamiliar city, where these migrants, or more appropriately, exiles, put down their roots. If there ever were times when it seemed possible they would be returned to where they came from, these people have given up hope of leaving now. They were wry about the city, the ones that I talked to, and, unable to put their disaffection down to anything specific—the standard of living is after all perfectly adequate—usually complained about the climate. It is in fact a tolerable, even congenial, climate—"a white man's climate," as Eric Teichman, an Englishman in His Majesty's consular service, described it in 1917: "no mosquitoes and the wearing of European clothing all year round."

But I can quite well understand why these migrants feel so cut off. For though it is bang in the middle of China, Lanzhou still has about it the feel of an outpost, a frontier town. To people from the coast it must seem not quite like China. Nor is it, if by Chinese is meant the majority race they call Han. For by tradition, Lanzhou is an enclave of Chinese Islam. This is easy to see, if you look down from White Pagoda Hill: here for a start, standing behind a curve of the Yellow River, is a mosque to illustrate the point. And as you descend the slopes, all the way down you will look past doors into the courtyards of Muslim homes, with bamboo trays of what these people call Fragrant Bean (and what the Chinese, for their part, call Bitter Bean) left out to dry. This is the herb the Muslims use to spice their bread, crushed and mixed with a little oil.

I tasted some when I came down the hill. I was loitering in front of a house against whose wall a trestle table was placed, with many rounds of unleavened bread propped up on it, when a woman came out and invited me in. She turned out to be the baker, and the room into which she ushered me doubled as her kitchen and living quarters. Takia and I bought two rounds of bread from her—these were large, hard things, about a foot in diameter—and she brought out a plate of beef and cucumber for us to eat these with. As we ate, she busied herself in a corner making more bread, assisted by her children. There was an old man silently smoking in an alcove in the opposite corner, who might have been her husband, or father. He had a solemn priestly look, as he sat cross-legged upon a platform; this, judging from the blankets laid across it, was his bed. He hardly noticed us at all; and the baker, as if to explain this, remarked to us that the old gentleman was ill.

Later, at the Yellow River Bridge, with the midday warmth rising around us, we came upon some stalls, and stopped at one manned by a handsome Muslim. There was something of a crowd round the stalls, but not really for custom—the Chinese are a nation of onlookers. The items the Muslim was selling, to list his entire stock, comprised a dozen copies of the Koran, half a dozen texts on Islam, a dictionary of religion in Chinese, a rosary and half a dozen nylon string bags hung from a cord, half a dozen packets of incense in a choice of rose, peony, and hygienic fragrances, and exactly three tins of tea.

Muslims are called Hui in China, a name perhaps etymologically related to Uighur, the Muslim minority that predominates in Chinese Turkestan. But the Huis are now thought to be ethnically distinct from the Uighurs, and are acknowledged to be one of the nation's five chief races—Han, Hui, Manchu, Tibetan, and Mongolian—by having assigned to them one of the five stars symbolizing that commonalty in the Chinese flag. Yet there was a time when no Muslim was allowed to live inside the walls of an administrative seat in China. The Muslim's history in China has been a distinctly ruffled one, with persecution, separatism, and a series of very bloody rebellions. Lanzhou itself, being in a heavily Muslim area, was once overlooked by forts standing as a barricade between the city and the jihad. The explosions occurred in the late nineteenth century, when mounting tensions and Chinese political disintegration reached a dangerous climax, and Gansu was racked time after time with rebellion and destruction.

Though Muslim rancor is no longer there for the unleashing, Islam in China has proved astonishingly resilient, and after being tucked away for so long, is busily dusting itself off as it emerges from the pall of the Cultural Revolution. Outwardly, apart from the white skullcaps worn by the men, there is nothing obvious to distinguish the Muslims here from the Chinese, but in their religious and some of their social practices they are distinctly removed from the unbelievers. Of course the ultimate aim of the government's policy toward ethnic minorities, for all the apparent renewal of religious toleration, is complete sinicization, but for the moment mosques and imams thrive, and besides their canteens and restaurants, the Huis have their own abattoirs and cemeteries.

These establishments usually announce themselves by the designation *Qingzhen*—Pure and True Religion—inscribed on their signboards and over their doors. The term, which was apparently borrowed from Chinese Jews, in fact covers a mishmash of races and cultures, and though the Central Asian origin of their distinctness from Han Chinese remains common, Muslim communities in China are woven with many ethnic strands: Mongol, Uighur, Kirghiz, Kazakh, Han, and indeterminate mixtures of these. Intermarriage with Han Chinese has diluted the original strain, and in matters of orthodox observance, the Chinese Muslim's punctiliousness probably would not measure up to Middle Eastern standards. Though one or two veiled women could still be glimpsed in the streets of Lanzhou half a century ago, today the Muslim female seems quite the equal of the male. Similarly, alcohol is not obviously abjured. Perhaps what most distinguishes the Chinese Muslim today is the abhorrence of pork. It is difficult for the Chinese, whose favorite meat this is, to credit the Muslim antipathy to pork; and, given as they are to incivilities about other races, they have a stock of stories and sayings which puts a prejudiced slur upon its genuineness. "One Muslim traveling will grow fat, two on a journey will become thin," they would say, meaning that while a Muslim alone will eat pork, two together will not. With the exception of the Shanghainese, who are generally more westernized, the Chinese are not given to porcine profanities, preferring the dog and the turtle for this purpose on the whole; but when it comes to swearing at a Mohammedan, their range can be insultingly concentrated on this animal.

Actually there isn't the slightest cause for this kind of condescension. On the contrary, as earlier travelers have often remarked, the Muslims are superior to the Hans in many ways: in trade, for instance, they could outwit even the astute Chinese, so much so that they dominated the more adventurous occupations, and there were proportionately many more traders, muleteers, carters, soldiers, and innkeepers who were Muslims than Han Chinese. Eric Teichman wrote in 1921: "The superiority of the Muslims over the Chinese in regard to housing, food, personal cleanliness and general standard of living is marked, and their spotlessly clean and well-kept mosques are in striking contrast to the dirty and dilapidated temples of the Chinese." The judgment still serves, and I found that in Lanzhou few places of refreshment were more agreeable than the Hui teashop, with its dark blue canopy fringed in red, its scrubbed wooden tables and yellow stools, its white porcelain cups and swept earth floors. When we looked in at the mosque glimpsed from the top of White Pagoda Hill, we found that there was a sheen to it, the wooden floor immaculately varnished, the long felt carpets spotlessly white, the pale green pillars glossy with new paint.

But it would be wrong to suggest that all our encounters that day were Mohammedan. Our way down the hill in the morning had led us past the homes of Chinese inhabitants who, whatever they may think about the Huis, were friendly enough to us overseas Hans. When we descended the hill, taking a footpath to the west of where we had come, we found ourselves amid a cluster of white adobe houses standing in terraces in a cleft halfway up the slope. (The path is the route that most of the inhabitants take several times a day, going down to the river and up again, their shoulders arched forward under their loads of water.) As we were peering into the houses, a small sunburned man appeared at a doorway, and catching sight of us standing there outside his house, nodded to us and invited us in. His daughter was about to bring him his lunch, and this he proposed to share with us, an act of hospitality both magnificently generous and touching, for lunch when it appeared consisted only of a few bits of pork and cucumber.

He had only one room, though another was under construction next door to house the rest of his family; yet one could not say that it was crowded. Its main impression was oddly of space and austerity. Partly it was the cleanliness, and partly the dearth of material possessions. The furniture was standard in this part of China: a *kang*, one of those platforms which, warmed in winter by a fire lit in the flue underneath, pass for a bed in northern China; a table with stools; an enamel washbasin on a wooden stand; a chest whose style suggested Korea but was in fact of local manufacture. Of the inessentials in his possession there were two tasseled picture frames each displaying an abundance of photographs superimposed upon certificates and commendations for effort and high productivity; a cushion in a quilted cover with a frilly fringe; a radio; an ornamented looking glass on the wall, and a beautiful old clock that did not exactly tell the hour.

By the standards of Chinese neediness, I suppose he must be judged well-off. Yet in this room, the living and sleeping quarters of the entire family, it was not difficult to see how bare a subsistence life offered him, indisputably improving though it was, judging by the extra room they were building next door. He had seven children. The youngest, who sat on his lap as we talked, was a seven-year-old boy and was the most deeply indulged, all the preceding six being girls. He himself had lived in this room for forty years; it was where he came home to from his work in a machine tool factory, where he laid aside a little money perhaps, and where he will die happy in the thought that he left behind him a male child. The world from which we had come meant very little to him and he didn't ask us any questions about it.

But this is not to say that his was the only life he knew. For though he was incapable of comparing his society with the other societies in the world, he had a historical comparison at his disposal, and he could very well compare the past with the present, and tell us what the contrast was, at least as it affected him, between the days before the socialist revolution and after. When I questioned him about Lanzhou in the days when the city walls were still up, he said that the place was much better then; supplies were more plentiful and you didn't run short of things the way you do now.

When we left him the sky had cleared, and every slope and crevice was dryly distinct. Though there were some trees and occasionally a patch of green, the main impression was of a bare and yellow austerity. At every turn there were slopes of dry, friable earth, with saplings dying in it. It was then that I understood why half the people who boarded the plane with me in Canton were clutching cuttings and potted plants—souvenirs of a lusher south which they hopefully envisioned transplanting here. Probably everyone in Gansu has heard the clarion call for the "greening" of China, but it must sound positively utopian here, in this province where half the land is taken up by treeless steppe and the Gobi Desert, and much of the rest is locked in a constant struggle against drought.

Earlier on, at a widening of the path, we had met some people who said they were engaged in the city's afforestation program; only they were preparing a meal, though it was still early, in a mud hut with a thin goat grazing listlessly in front. They were a middle-aged woman and two young girls, who emerged shyly from the hut when they saw Takia pointing his camera. Seeing the dun hillsides all around, I must say their task seemed quite fruitless to me. Later we heard that the entire provincial afforestation department had had to be sacked for lack of results.

It is not hard to remember, even as you take a gentle afternoon stroll down Zhangye Road, one of the city's busiest thoroughfares, that this is the capital of an arid, impoverished province on what was until not so very long ago the very edge of the empire. Rainlessness and frontier: one senses these in a symbolic sort of way, strolling down the street past the shops whose facades are startlingly painted in blue—the blue of Persia and Arabia, of lands that dream of water. One senses them in the name of the street itself, for Zhangye is a town which stood along the old Silk Route on the frontier between China and the barbarian Huns, with the westernmost extension of the Great Wall above it and the desert reaches of Central Asia beyond. The name is said to have its source in the ancient imperial ambition of "breaking the Hun's arm and stretching China's armpits," for in Chinese *zhang* means "to stretch" and *ye* "to support by the armpits."

Tempered though it has been by the extension of irrigation, much of this part of Gansu remains blighted, as the harvest in some communes fails in nine years out of ten. In the earlier decades of the

century, when travelers made their way up the Gansu Corridor,
they fell as a matter of course into a lament about its hopeless misery.
Of the images of poverty offered the visitor, there was one which
never escaped—and that was of children who wore no trousers. It
was a sight which the American traveler, Harry Franck, for one,
saw on his journey up here in the early 1920s and captured in a
photograph. His caption says, "The boys and girls of China are
'toughened' by wearing nothing below the waist and only ragged
garments above it, even in midwinter." Evidently it did not occur
to him that had the children had trousers, they would have worn
them, but I think someone more skeptical would know that if there
was one image that stood for dearth in China, this was it.

It was one of the more unexpected experiences of Fan Changjiang,
a Chinese traveler to the Gansu Corridor in the mid-1930s. From
a distance he had seen Zhangye reposing beautifully upon its river,
but when he had taken a closer look, he found it to be full of trou-
serless children. Some of the inhabitants he saw were inadequately
wrapped around with sacking; others, mature women, made do
with dirty loincloths or ragged squares of fabric hung from a string
around the waist.

I would have liked to believe that such indigence was a thing of
the past. I did not travel up the Gansu Corridor, and can only report
my experiences in the vicinity of Lanzhou, but if one present-day
observer is to be believed, the bad old days are not over yet. The
observer was Wei Jingsheng, and I remember that of the reports
about China that I and other Chinese living abroad had read, his
had most affected us with regret, for like all overseas Chinese, we
wish the country well, and when we hear unfavorable things about
it, few can be as disappointed as we. Wei Jingsheng is a young dissident in Peking who gained public attention for proposing to the
leadership that they consider democracy for a Fifth Modernization
that would make possible the other four. He has since been indicted
for passing military secrets about China's invasion of Vietnam to
a foreign journalist, and is at the moment serving a fifteen-year
sentence for treason.

In the article, published in a periodical in Hong Kong in 1980,

he describes the scene which greeted him when his train unexpect-
edly stopped at a small station in the Gansu Corridor. The beggars
who swarmed beneath the window of his compartment were
perhaps what he might have expected; that there was a girl among
them, her face smudged with coal ash and her long hair sprawling
loose and disheveled over her shoulders, was also something he
might have foreseen. But when he leaned out of the window to toss
them his bread, what astonished and outraged him was the discovery
that the girl, now that he could see her better, did not have a stitch
on under her hair. She was perhaps seventeen or eighteen, and
though she was not alone in her nakedness—few of the beggars
crowding around her had clothes—she must have seemed the more
shocking for being an almost fully grown woman.

Was Wei exaggerating? Was it an untypical experience? Maybe;
but all the same it was odd that, coming into the Gansu Corridor,
he should come first of all upon that classic Gansu image. It was
so much of a piece with what had been said of the place—as though
he were following the precedent of earlier visitors, or as though
such destitution were truly the permanent condition of the place.

As for beggars, the largest number I was approached by in one
day in Lanzhou was six. You come across them in restaurants, an
obvious strategic place. They are not abject though, like the beggars
you see in other countries of Asia, who sit on the pavement with
a tin can waiting dumbly for alms. Nor do they jostle or fall upon
you: they merely wander into the restaurant and, while you are
at your food, stand in a corner and wait until you are quite finished.
Then, almost apologetically, and often only if you beckon, they
will come and finish off your leftovers for you. Occasionally you
may come across one with hand held out for alms, but at the same
time you may find your offer of coins firmly rejected, for what
your beggar is after is not money at all, but grain ration coupons.
This usually means that the person is an unregistered town dweller,
for such coupons are issued only against proof of residence.

The rationing system is an inescapable fact of life in China. Quite
apart from conserving food, it is a very effective method for controlling mobility. Suppose a man decides one day to move out of

town to another. He will go to the local police station, if he is really determined, and he will find himself subjected to a protracted and thorough examination by the cadres there—to discover if he has incurred any debts, and if his employer approves of his request—any phase of which can end in failure, but none of which will be explained to him. If, against heavy odds, his request receives the approval of everyone, a move certificate will then be applied for from a police headquarters on a higher level. He must be in possession of this document before he can be considered for residence registration in the new place. If, with luck, he knows some people in the right quarter, this would of course greatly expedite the proceedings.

Once he is in his new domicile, he must see to it straightaway that he is in possession of an urban permanent residence card, for without it he will not be entitled to work, housing, education, a host of services, a marriage certificate, and, above all, grain ration coupons. And without these coupons, it is very hard to survive in the cities.

How hard we found out for ourselves one evening. We were at a dumpling shop near the main intersection in downtown Lanzhou. We had wandered in in search of dinner, for it was already after seven, and way past the hour when food can be easily procured in Lanzhou. But the woman cashier with whom I placed my order was of that special disobliging breed that you meet almost everywhere in China, her face blank, her manner stiff, her whole being frozen in a studiously unheeding pose. I was obviously beaten from the start, for I didn't even order the dumplings as I should have done —in terms of the requisite number of catties. No grain coupons? No dumplings then. I said I was a visitor from abroad, and would pay the extra charge in lieu of coupons that is normally levied in such circumstances. But my words fell on the barren soil of her stone-hard determination to give me a hard time.

I had quite given up and was about to walk away, when an old ragged man behind me touched my elbow and held out some coupons with the suggestion that I should take them. Wispily bearded, shabbily dressed, he looked too threadbare himself to be able to afford such generosity, and I immediately offered money in exchange. But he looked quite embarrassed at this, and raised his palm to wag it at me in refusal.

It is true that grain rationing is liberal in China, and city dwellers receive more than they can eat, but even so, the man's spontaneous, taciturn kindness touched me, and left me curiously conciliated by the country. As I was to learn, China is like that: the good is inextricable from the bad, and makes itself felt just when some impression or ordeal threatens to demolish all your sympathetic opinion of it, a touch of goodness rushing in to fill the hollows gouged out by the inhumanities of just a moment before.

Several times in Lanzhou we ate at a dining hall down the road from our hotel. No restaurant in the capitalist world would stay in business a week with the sort of service and atmosphere you get in public eating places in China. Except in restaurants reserved for the foreign tourist, I am sad to say that Chinese cuisine no longer entices—its texture coarsened, its gourmets long since proletarianized or driven to California and Hong Kong, its flavors reduced to one or two (soy sauce and salt). The restaurants themselves are places of hideous gloom and squalor—the floors harboring bones, scraps of chewed up meat, and gobs of spittle; the attendants rushed and surly. The kitchen quarters, sometimes visible from the counter, do not bear looking into; and half the dishes posted up on the menu board will be unavailable.

At lunchtime the Lanzhou Dining Hall is usually noisy and crowded. Groups of young men, straddling their chairs rather than sitting on them, are swigging beer, playing a Chinese drinking game and loudly exchanging the cries that accompany this diversion. Distracted women attendants in their stained white overalls waddle in and out of the kitchen. It is mid-June, too early for fresh vegetables other than leeks and cucumber. I order these and a baked omelette. There is a wait of half an hour, then the first two dishes are plunked down before us. Later, when we have quite finished, the omelette arrives. Through the window I see the beggars watchfully awaiting their turn outside. Two or three will come through the door in a moment, and down the long dining room these scavengers will shamble, with silent discretion and averted eyes, to lift the abandoned plates from the tables, and tip the contents into their plastic bags. At my table I have an old grizzled tramp, hung with canvas satchels and clutching a grubby plastic bag. I give him my chopsticks, my rice, and my scarcely touched omelette; and I hear, rather than see, the old man scraping everything into his bag—a scratch when he scoops up the egg, a rustle when he opens the bag, a plop when the omelette falls in. When he has finished he returns the bowls and the chopsticks, and I am reassured to observe that though all the gleanings of the day have been heaped into the one bag, so far as he can he has been careful not to mix all the dishes up.

As eating establishments go, I prefer the snack bar to the restaurant. Perhaps these places, called "Cold Drinks," seem the more welcoming for being ice-cream parlors as well; for though Lanzhou's summer temperatures are tempered by altitude, hours spent in the dusty streets can make you pretty hot. These places are a world away from their counterparts in the West, where in the best tradition of excessive consumer demand Dutch chocolate, pistachio, pecan, blueberry, and coffee are only some of the selections on offer.

One place we found on Nanchang Road had a long table piled high with cold noodles blanketed with a plastic sheet, with a lineup of uncovered oil, sauces, and chilis beside it. A curtain was hung across the entrance to keep out the dust. At one end, through a hatch, ice cream in small cups was being dispensed; and through the opening you could also see what you seldom find in China, a machine for making it. Behind, in the kitchen, a waitress was chopping blobs of buckwheat jelly into strips, then serving these with sauces the way one would with noodles. Besides Takia and me, there were only three other customers, one of them a plump middle-aged officer of the People's Liberation Army who sat down to his rapidly melting ice cream in between swatting flies with a fly whisk. In the languor of the afternoon, the flies, the few that I could see, were unprotesting, and as the minutes ticked by they one by one ended their lives on the walls and the tables, to be flicked with a light, sharp movement off the surfaces of these onto the floor. The officer, for his part, seemed quite devoted to the task, and looked to me as though he had been doing it all afternoon.

It was surprising, in that place, with that desultory officer and those unappetizing noodles, and the sluggish air, to find myself drinking Coca-Cola, or at least the Chinese version of it, with all its fizz and suggestion of the soda fountain. But it happened that the place offered Laoshan Cola, a dark drink whose taste and thirst-quenching properties closely approximate its American progenitor. Laoshan is the name of a mountain in Shandong Province; and for the same reason, I suppose, that its water makes Qingdao (Tsingtao) beer the best in China, it makes this cola the preeminent pop.

These cold-drink places have, at any rate, what restaurants have not—a cross-section of the citizenry. Restaurants are places of more masculine gathering, workingmen's places; in the snack bar you tend to have the diversifying custom of women, children, and single-sex groups of what in a Western country would be boys and girls on the make. In the restaurant people are merely at their food; in the snack bar they are more relaxed, less single-minded, and to me they exhibit a wider range of social behavior.

Sitting in one with my fizzy orange one late afternoon, I could almost imagine myself in a café, watching the world go by. Across the room four young girls in light-colored shirts sat attentively sipping their drinks, for all the world as if they were oblivious of the three boys ogling them from the next table. In front, a young man lovingly fed ice cream to his baby girl while his own melted untouched in its bowl. At the table behind me, three middle-aged women were gossiping away. But it was when I got up to go that the most interesting sidelight, sociologically speaking, was thrown on these people. When I had almost reached the door, I was stopped by the attendant at the counter and reminded of the twenty-cent deposit I had put down on my bottle, and which I could reclaim by bringing the empty bottle back to her. But when I turned round to fetch it from the table, I found that it was gone. The moment my back was turned, quick as a flash one of the three women at the next table had whisked it away to claim it slyly as her own. At first it did not dawn on me that this was what had happened, and for a moment I stood there, wondering where my bottle could be. But then I caught the attendant glaring across the bar at the guilty woman, and suddenly I had the strong impression that Deviance Control was subtly at work. Throughout all this not a word was spoken, but seconds later the bottle was back on my table.

On Sunday we did what the natives do: we went for a stroll in a park. The morning had got underway with a healthy breakfast of bean-curd "brain," a coagulated soybean milk served either sweet or spicy depending on the sauce, at an open-air place run by Muslims and strongly suggestive of the bazaar. A bus took us to the Hill of Five Springs, a lump of yellow loess to the south of the city. The approach opens out into a square animated by what in an earlier age would have been a temple fair but here seemed just the Sunday turnout, with a line of side stalls soliciting petty trade. There were sellers of popsicles, spiced beans, goldfish, potted plants, Qingzhen (Muslim beef noodles), and even some unripe apricots—the first fruit I had seen since my arrival in the northwest. Hard by the noodle stalls a man had set up shop selling rat poison, the effectiveness of which was illustrated by four dried-up dead rats arranged on a cloth in front of him. There were the standard offerings of the fun fair: shooting galleries, "electronic chest expanders," and weighing machines at two cents a go. There was, as part of a school campaign, an attempt to inculcate notions of public hygiene, with worms and unidentifiable organs pickled in bottles, a microscope for people to peer into, and back cloths illustrating the disadvantages of unhygienic behavior in a series of pictures, on the comic-strip principle.

The park is mostly flights of stairs, widening here and there to accommodate resting places with stools and balustrades and tapering at the top to a terrace encompassing a Buddhist shrine. For a park the vegetation seemed thin, but was no doubt the best they could do hereabouts. I looked into the shrine, where I found that the gilded Reclining Buddha had not been hacked from its pedestal by Red Guards, those over-excited iconoclasts of the Cultural Revolution. I noticed, when I managed to press through the crowd, that judging by the incense and the food offerings there was not a little worshiping here. In front of the gold and red folds of the Buddha's robe, there stood bunches of joss sticks and a number of buns. Holy pictures of the Buddha and Guanyin, the Goddess of Mercy and the bringer of children, were propped up on the plinth, and immediately below the altar stood two bronze braziers, stuck with white candles which an old lady was devoutly lighting. It was not these, though, that most powerfully conveyed the devotion that people still show this holy figure; it was the three or four pairs of bootees placed at the foot of the Buddha, so beautifully appliquéd in gold and black, in cream and brown, that they could only have been made by seamstresses who deeply cared. They smudged the line between religion and superstition, and suggested that there were devotees in whose minds, even now, the Buddha was someone you could enlist in the cause of your happiness.

Buddhist superstition holds its own among the older peasant women of China. But this is not to say that socialist atheism has been unsuccessful in its attempts to divert the followers from their faith, or change their attitude toward its trappings. One evening, waiting for a bus into town at a stop beside the Lanzhou petrochemical industrial complex in the western outskirts of the city, I was joined by a group of women just knocking off work. They expressed their attitude well when, staring at the thin gold chain I have always worn round my neck, they turned to each other and scornfully said, "Fancy being so superstitious"—evidently supposing the chain to be an amulet.

Even here, at the shrine, the statue drew more sightseers than worshipers, and for many a Chinese in the park the temple was no more than a background for their holiday snapshots. Cameras clicked away all over the terrace and the rest of the park. The Chinese are in a familiar, if anachronistic stage of leisure consumption. Cameras, transistor radios, TV sets, and tape recorders are still thin on the ground but all over China there are signs that people can now afford to acquire goods not just for their material welfare, for satisfying the need for food, clothing, and shelter, but also for psychic consumption and welfare.

At the Yellow River Bridge, you could scarcely get away from the portrait photographers sitting by the stands displaying specimens of their work. Propped up like so much theatrical scenery, a range of painted screens were offered as backgrounds: from a sedan, with its prestigious make, "Shanghai," painted prominently across it in English, to a two-seater airplane in green and grey. Standard photographic props, which in bigger cities may be supplemented by cardboard screens of leaping horses or headless bodies in flowing imperial robes. At one of the booths by the river you could even have your finished print tricked out with the frame of a television screen.

In China the photographer is a fabulist, his booth an instant dream factory. His camera is the device by which the subject becomes endowed with that which is unavailable to him in real life and that to which his fantasy lays claim. And in this surrogate possession, the honoring of capitalist material values is there for all to see. Take the make of the cardboard sedan. Like many another consumer the Chinese grades names by the desirability of the goods they mark; by most reckoning "Shanghai" comes at the top, and spelling it in a foreign language, another status signifier, gives it even greater cachet. Disconcertingly, you may even find the dream mistaken for the reality. On another occasion, in another city, I would read, on one of those propaganda boards you find in every town, of a case of accidental death involving a camera. A man, imagining himself a cowboy perhaps, or at any rate a man of power, was posing with a gun in front of the camera when, his sense of reality suddenly overtaken by fantasy, he pulled the trigger and killed the photographer. I found it a frightful story, both innocent and chilling, and I wondered if I was right in sensing behind the acted-out fantasy the all-too-real substance of humdrum, threadbare reality.

In the park, in multiple posturings on the steps and before the balustrades, the dream was in progress. You encounter the ritual often in China, the careful posing—the Chinese being at that early stage of camera culture and visual taste where a photograph is still intended to memorialize and idealize. The Chinese photographer has yet to find an old crinkled face or tumbled building beautiful, and to him a good photograph is still an image of something seen in its Sunday best.

Apart from taking pictures there was nothing much to do in Five Springs Park. There was a line of distorting mirrors for the children. There was a terrace where you could hire deck chairs and buy tea; this was almost entirely given up to men smoking or playing a finger-guessing game.

Every fair-sized Chinese town has at least one public park—a place to sit, to take your children, to run through your daily shadow-boxing routines, a place where you can repair to on your day off. In layout and design they stand in the line of the traditional Chinese garden, with its paths, grottoes, pavilions, and with its disdain of the herbaceous borders and flowerbeds beloved of an English park. But they are also the counterparts, I feel, of the Soviet "parks of rest and culture"; only, instead of the statues of Lenin, there sometimes looms ahead one of your plaster socialist-realist tableaux of Worker, Peasant, and Soldier with the usual look of distant purpose in their eyes.

In Five Springs there were no statues, but you need not dig deep for the inspiriting socialist image. Here were the slogans enlisting you to the cause of the Five Stresses (on decorum, manners, hygiene, discipline, and morals) and the Four Points of Beauty (the beauty of mind, language, behavior, and environment) that the Party in speech after speech had said must accompany the progress of socialist modernization. It is by campaigns such as this, as Premier Zhao Ziyang, for one, has suggested, that the people may "resist and overcome the corrosive influence of exploiting class ideologies and ideologies running counter to the socialist system." By the "corrosive influence of exploiting class ideologies" he means, of course, the wilted fervor, indifference, and sneer with which many Chinese now look upon their society and its leaders. It is true that in some other cities, the campaign has visibly improved manners and public cleanliness, but here, when I stopped to ask a passerby what the Five Stresses and Four Beauties were, and a young crowd immediately clustered around me in curiosity, I found that not one person could correctly remember them all. Indifference prevailed, and indeed seemed to be the only reasonable response to that overkill of mottoes by which the Party seeks to govern people's lives.

People must have something outside their narrow workaday world to live for, whether it is the belief in the inevitable triumph of the communist revolution or just that someday someone will come and sweep them off their feet. Here they are no longer much interested in the lives of self-abnegation, of "service to the people," or of selfless productive labor as hoped for by Mao. In place of submission to the patriotic call to sublimate, romantic love rides again. Or so it seemed, at any rate, from the group of young people I came upon in a pavilion in the park.

They were perhaps an office outing, seated there on the benches while a young man, most likely the office jester, entertained them with an act. An amateur performance was in progress, and when I sat down to listen I realized that it was *xiangsheng,* or "crosstalk," that very popular form of theatre in which a comic talks to his stooge in a clever, rapidly skipping tongue. I had arrived too late to hear anything much before the enthusiastic applause, but I happened to catch the exchange that followed it. At first it did not strike me as particularly telling, but I came to detect in it some of the attitudes which Chinese have about love and the sexes, and I began to eavesdrop more attentively.

He would begin a story, the performer said, with two possible endings, and of these the audience must try to guess the right one. He spoke with some verve, and not a few dramatic circumlocutions. But the story in summary was this: There was once a princess who had many suitors, but of these she loved only one, a commoner. Upon discovery of this her father, the king, was most displeased, and had the young man thrown into a dungeon in the palace. From this dungeon two doors opened, one to the lair of a hungry tiger, the other to a beautiful maiden the prisoner would be obliged to wed. The imprisoned commoner did not know what lay behind those doors, but the princess did, and secretly she sent word to him to let himself out by the right door. "Now," asked the storyteller, "to which of his two fates do you suppose this exit led—to death by the tiger or to salvation in the arms of a beautiful girl?"

A self-possessed girl, who had all this while maintained a flow of background chatter, every interspersed titter of which was a flaunting of herself, spoke up. To the tiger, she said, because the princess would rather see her lover die than fall into the arms of another woman. With a grunt someone mumbled his disagreement. Then a silence fell as everyone pondered the question—not in mock seriousness, I was slightly disconcerted to find, or for the sake of playing a game, but with the earnestness of those for whom the question mattered personally.

Into this silence the storyteller eventually spoke, and what he said seemed to give his audience further pause. "It was the door to her rival that the princess told her suitor to open"; for, as he went on to explain, love transcended everything. Amid the hubbub that followed he proceeded to tell his audience about a European novel he'd just read, to give his conclusion added credence. In it a man who has had many love affairs emerges from his eighteenth amour with the realization that the essence of the feminine heart is maternal. "If it weren't so," the storyteller asked, "why does a woman, even after she has been scorned or betrayed by her lover, look upon him kindly when she meets up with him some years later, however much she may have hated him at one time?"

The group took this gravely, some nodding, others trying hard to test this revelation against their own experience. All seemed to think it desperately important, these men and women who had long arrived at adulthood but yet remained in a state of boyish and girlish innocence, maintained there by aspirations not yet turned to doubt, by naiveté not hardened into knowingness. It was somehow appalling: as their Western peers think in their very earliest teens, so these Chinese were thinking in their twenties. When they spoke, giving themselves away each time they opened their mouths, one could only think: how immature they are, as immature as their Western peers are seasoned.

It is true, they are squares when it comes to romantic matters. Copulation comes late to the Chinese youngster, in consequence of the Party's strictures on early marriage and premarital sex. In the meantime he or she remains in a sort of quivering innocence.

Visitors to China have often remarked upon the prudery of the Chinese, or their apparent asexuality. Of course things cannot be what they seem; who does not know about the baby boom and the billion-figure population? We can imagine what goes on under these surfaces of passionlessness; nowadays the papers make no bones about the rapes and prostitution and the cases of illicit sex. But still there are these surfaces. Certainly there is not much in the way of environmental stimuli to prod the libido—not at all like the billboard-infested West, where if the art director's concept behind the advertisement is sometimes hard to grasp, the sexual overtones are all too obvious.

If the Chinese are square, they are also soppy. On top of the sentimentality they have inherited from the traditional Chinese view of love, there is that overindulgence in the romantic which is often produced when socialism, humdrum reality, and plain naiveté come together. Takia and I once saw a film which disastrously combined the simplism and sentimentalism of this attitude. It was called *Du Shiniang,* after the heroine, a courtesan who bought herself out from her bordello keeper to marry her scholarly lover, only to find in the course of their journey home together that he, in anticipation of his parents taking exception to her lowly origins, had contracted to sell her to another admirer. At this she threw herself and her jewel box into the river. There is nothing whatever wrong with the story, which is a well-known one handed down across the centuries. But I had not seen a more excruciating rendering. The director, perhaps because of the Chinese reluctance to leave well enough alone, had succumbed to that terrible overkill of schmaltz whereby every expression of thought or sentiment, no matter how banal or straightforward, is given a facial and gestural aura of immense emotional weight. In a way you cannot blame him: he is merely pandering to a convention of feeling. If he lays things on too thick, so does every book and newspaper in this country. In the scene in which the courtesan, in her wedding night bower of love, kneels beside the bed on which lies athwart and blind drunk her adored and faithless groom, and whispers to him, "My husband!" the breathlessness which throngs to your attention through the gauzy soft focus is indistinguishable, as far as I can tell, from that with which, in a time of Maoist cultism now past, people uttered the name of the Chairman or the Party.

It was all more than Takia could bear, and he left before the end, saying, "Oh dear, just think; the expectations of a whole generation of Chinese womanhood will be affected by this."

At dinner that evening, I asked our waitress, a lovely girl, if she had seen the film and what she thought of it. She had, and thought it good—"realistic," as she approvingly put it. When I pressed her to say more, she was a little at a loss, but in the end, eyebrows knitting, she came up with an opinion. It was as if she'd only just remembered it when she gave it, and although I was quite sure she thought nothing of the sort really, what she said was: "It's a tragedy, a social tragedy . . . a lower-class girl caught in a cage, whose bid for freedom failed because while she herself was elevated, society was base." The judgment, falling so gravely from her lips, was almost word for word an echo of what had been set out in the newspapers a few days before.

I find it telling that the film and the stories I chanced to hear in the park both saw woman as a high-minded and tender being. This is wishful thinking—specifically male, curiously tenacious down the ages, and demonstrably false. I talked about this to Takia, who, if he ever held such a view, has certainly been disabused of it. Chinese women don't play fair, I thought, because the odds were stacked against them from the start. It might have been different with fairer opportunity, when women would have asserted themselves the same way as men, and less would have had to be won by scheming and duplicity, or any of the underhand methods calculated to turn their handicaps into their strength.

There are more women than men in China, and in the months to come I would hear and read (in the national dailies, no less), again and again, how appallingly grasping young women are when it comes to laying down their conditions for agreeing to marry—the pieces of furniture they must have, the washing machine, the TV set. Here in Gansu, some girls even demand that the groom's family include a pair of coffins for her parents in the "bride price";

this because the locally available poplar, being white, is unsuitable, and dark wood would have to be brought down from the mountains, at a cost that is ten times the average monthly salary.

It has sometimes been pointed out that of the hundred and more words written with the root element "woman" in the Chinese language, a significantly large number are pejorative; take, for example, the words for jealous, reckless, traitorous, to obstruct, to toady. A male university student I met on my journeys once summarized for me the qualities of Chinese womanhood. "Chinese women," he said, "are seldom harmless." For want of a better alternative, I would have added.

Liujia Gorge

Liujia Gorge, the site of a hydroelectric power scheme on the Yellow River, can be reached by a coach leaving at three in the afternoon from Lanzhou's West Station, the one with the clock tower that is featured in at least one postcard of the city. We had set out for the station early enough, but when we were two-thirds of the way there, our bus all of a sudden came to a halt, and I saw with sinking heart the driver alighting and disappearing into the afternoon bustle. Presently he returned with a bucket of water, and though he had decided to become impervious to human communication by way of defending himself against what would very soon become a busload of excited passengers, I gathered that the vehicle had broken down and there was no knowing how long it would take to repair it.

Takia and I clambered down. Quite ridiculously, such being the state of my desperation, I tried to thumb a lift from a passing car, a practice quite unheard of hereabouts. The minutes raced by until, with only ten minutes to go before the coach's departure, a bus hurtled past us and rumbled to a stop just in front. We made a dash for it at once, though we had no idea where it was headed. It set off in the right direction though, and while it was so overcrowded I could barely see out of the window, the clock tower did in the end come into view. At a breathless speed we tore across the station hall and, as luck would have it, were at the platform at exactly three.

I climbed in and stood for a moment looking into the coach. Internally it seemed to carry about twice the number of passengers you would have judged from its external proportions. Under the circumstances I was thankful that we had reserved seats the day before, as otherwise we would have had to ride on the floor crushed between pairs of dustily shod feet. We found our seats in the front row and two men sitting in them. On seeing us appear they got up and went to the back, where it already looked too crammed to accommodate them. A young man, who appeared to be either the driver's friend or the conductor, or perhaps both, edged forward and peered back through the door, evidently to check that everyone was in who was supposed to be. By my watch it was now five or six minutes past three. We all sat, the driver looking out with detached interest, the passengers who could move, shifting their positions. Wondering if something was wrong, I tentatively addressed the driver: "Why aren't we off?" I said, "What are we waiting for?"

The driver made no reply, leaving it to time to produce my answer. It came, in the form of the clock in the tower striking three. At this awaited sign the driver switched on his engine and put the gear lever in second, and, glancing back in my direction, he said, mock seriousness tempering his smile, "That's the way it is, you see, under the peerless leadership of our Communist Party."

We found ourselves making for the suburbs, but this turned out to be a detour to the door of the driver's own house, where he had to drop off his little boy. This again was the way things are under the leadership of the Communist Party—you don't stint on state time or state property as you might if your employer were Mitsubishi or IBM. By the time the fringes of the city had yielded to the country, the bus had stopped three more times; but this was to pick up some more passengers, of whom, with two women already sitting on the steps, I would have thought the bus had already more than enough. How the extra capacity was achieved was quite simply demonstrated to me when a hefty country woman lowered her bulk half onto my knees and half onto the baggage lying beside my seat. She then proceeded to favor us with a song, and revealed herself both by her thumping extroversion and the unfamiliarity (to me) of her language to be a member of a non-Chinese minority. She was quite oblivious of my suffering, and when I tried to shift position under her weight, only leaned back and crushed me the more.

To the mechanically minded it must be hard to submit to the experience of being driven in China, because you can't help noticing the ruthless way in which mileage is forced out of the car. Cars in China are worked far into old age and senility; and even in a big city, you don't have to be told by your hotel that there is a wait of thirty minutes for a taxi to realize that they and their drivers don't come in capitalist profusion in this country. Riding a Chinese bus, one's impression is of valves, transmission, cylinders, bolts, and springs so worn that the whole seems tensed on the brink of flying apart. But until it finally gives out, the driver pushes his vehicle implacably on, honking with gusto and approaching each rise in gradient like an enemy, stepping on the accelerator as if crushing a beetle underfoot. In our case, about an hour and a half after we had set off, the fuel pump packed up.

We had found ourselves, as we ascended into the hills, in the burnt-out, terracotta-colored terrain of Gansu country. Here one is easily reminded that to the Chinese this is the "bitterest" of provinces, with "wild Muslims and no rice to speak of"; and also that vast tracts of the earth's surface are, if not entirely uninhabitable, quite unattractive to inhabit. Yet, a few miles back, we had seen through the window that, however much the landscape recalled Mexico or Arizona, this great sterile country was China: the most absolute distinguishing feature was the dot-sized splashes of green that materialized in the perspective of our passage with the suddenness of an oasis. Vegetable plots whose moisture could only have come from water laboriously borne by their tillers, day after day, bucket after bucket, up from faraway streams—by such archaic human exertions was color, the vibrant grass-green of closely cultivated vegetables, brought back to this parched and stony land.

But where we stopped there was nothing but a deep cut between slopes that might have been an ancient riverbed. Squatting by the side of the road while the driver and conductor got out their pliers, I saw straight ahead of me a barren hill of a dun color, with no trees or vegetation. At the bottom, where the terrain flattened out and where a stream should have trickled, there were only millennial stratifications of shale.

We were perhaps an hour there. To repair the damaged fuel pump the driver took a spare one apart—it was also damaged but in another way—and used some of the components. Meanwhile I reposed in the oblivious trust of the mechanically illiterate, conceding to the Chinese not so much the mechanician's touch as an ingenuity with makeshifts that I was confident would get us back on the road. As the afternoon wore on it became considerably cooler, and out of the stillness a strong wind suddenly rose, flapping my plastic windcheater and burdening the air with dust. We all piled into the bus, closing the windows against the sandstorm's unpleasant rasp; and presently the driver climbed in too, followed by his assistant. A start, a splutter, a halt and a lurch; and at a quarter to seven, only an hour and three-quarters behind schedule, we were in.

We had hoped to find some indication at the bus terminus of where we might find a room. But no, there was no sign; if it came to that there was nothing that could properly be called a terminus, only a stretch of street where by common agreement the bus regularly stops. I approached a girl whose scrubbed look and flushed cheeks spoke of the country to me, and asked if she knew of a hotel nearby. The girl, tipping her head slightly, said there was the Hydropower Station Guesthouse just up the road, offering at the same time to take us there. She had a quiet, unfussy manner, and when she insisted on taking my duffel bag from me, saying how unthinkable it was that I should carry such a weight when she carried none, I recognized in her a true child of the Maoist ethic, inculcated with a sincere dedication to "serving the people" that took Girl-Scout exemplariness as a matter of course: a true innocent. She dropped us off at the guesthouse and retreated before we could even thank her.

It is necessary at this point to say a few words about guesthouses like the one in which we now found ourselves. They can be found in most towns, however small, and make me think of those official hotels of old, the municipally owned *gongguan* reserved for mandarins on tour. For their guests are mostly cadres on business trips, though certain visitors not fitting this category (like us) are accommodated too.

The rooms are tidy and rather bleak, and the rule is that the best ones have a pair of armchairs and a rug. The bedclothes, printed flowery sheets and cotton-filled quilts, have been slept in by preceding occupants but are odorless; the small towel laid on them is not for washing but for resting your head on, serving the pillow rather as antimacassars do the backs of chairs. There is no bathroom or toilet attached; instead there are communal lavatories and taps, and enamel washbasins in the rooms. The meals, taken in a large unbeguiling room, are over in a minute and once past the hour, food can be had in exceptional cases only with the utmost difficulty and usually not at all. The run of the meals is rice, as much steamed bread as you can eat, and moderate portions of fried meat and vegetables.

In most respects these establishments are the same, but the Liujia Gorge Hydropower Station Guesthouse was distinct from all the others we had stayed at in segregating the rooms by sex, even to the extent of accommodating married couples separately. Extraordinarily, though the Chinese we met could not countenance the fact that Takia and I were not married—for otherwise how could we be traveling together?—they easily accepted the fact that he and I lived a whole continent apart. This seemed to me to be a comment on their own condition, their acquiescence to the not uncommon fate in China of being assigned to jobs in faraway provinces or cities unaccompanied by their spouses and children.

I was to share a room with a high-ranking woman cadre engaged in the fishery business in the east, who was here on a mission to look into the aquatic resources of the station's reservoir. I met her in the dining hall, and faced her like an enemy, for I am a little prejudiced against high-ranking woman cadres. Many of them strike me as bossy and unattractive; and rightly or wrongly, I suppose them to be, in their effort to achieve upward mobility in a society as unamenable to feminine progress as China's, more susceptible than men to the abuse of privilege and the corruption of power. My roommate was small, but compact with toughness, and when we turned in that night, she took off her trousers (she had another pair on underneath) hunched up in bed under cover of her bedclothes—not, as far as I could tell, from cold or habit, but more from a sense of prim propriety.

At dusk, after dinner, we found a promenade with benches beside the Yellow River, a sky plunging toward faint gold, and the sunset playing upon the frothing discharge of the spillways downriver from the dam. Of the people out strolling, there were as many young men and women as old people, for the day's work was done, and what remained was a gentle domestic intimacy—a baby in the arms, a child held by the hand, father and mother, and even granny too.

There was a group of visiting water conservancy technicians from a distant province staying at the guesthouse, and when they were given a tour of the dam the next morning, we decided to tag along. In the course of our travel we would come across many official delegations, for whose members such "business trips" are part of the enviable perks of their positions. We congregated, seated in rows facing the door, in a reception room in the guesthouse, and after a silence broken by those shuffling, throat-clearing, and scraping noises reminiscent of thinly attended lectures in cold English church halls, we suddenly found ourselves addressed by a portable cassette tape recorder reposing on a bench beside the door.

Of the facts that poured forth from this machine, I gleaned the following. That the Liujia Gorge hydroelectric power station, until recently the biggest in China, was completed on February 5, 1975, the first generator having begun operation in 1969, and the last one in December 1974. That the generation equipment was designed and built in China. That behind its forty-four-foot-high dam was a powerhouse producing an annual 5.7 billion kilowatt hours, an output greater than that of the entire country before the communists took over. From here power is transmitted to Lanzhou and Tian-shui; the valley around the confluence of the Yellow River and the Wei in Shaanxi Province; and to Xi'ning, the capital of Qinghai Province further upstream. Apart from generating power, the build-ing of the barrage meant that the flow of the Yellow's water could be confined and regulated in the interests of irrigation, flood control, and human consumption.

To the powerhouse we made our way after the introductory lecture by the tape recorder. A pleasant, if taciturn, young man drove us there in a van. The tour led underground, where the five power generators of the station stood like mounds in orderly solidity, Chinese-built and painted a pea green. There were not many people about, and the sound of the place, as I heard it, was a hum rather than a rumble. As we were leaving, two unauthorized visitors slip-ped in, urchins with time on their hands perhaps, stealing in here just for a lark. But though our guide showed some consternation as they flitted past us, and shouted at them to stop, no one bothered to intercept these interlopers or give chase, and the two boys tore up a ladder at the far end of the powerhouse to disappear into the installations above. This was the most remarkable surprise of Liujia Gorge; bristling as it was with dynamos and high-tension wires, the place had all the substance of great public works but not, fundamentally, the feel. The feel was homely, and my companions on the inspection tour, every one of them a hydraulic technician, reminded me of nothing so much as alumni visiting their old school after a long absence. For as one of the women in the group told me, they had all worked here at one time or another; from this project they had transferred to another, and as I think is also the way in the Soviet Union, they will get passed on from one new hydropower scheme to the next, constructing dams as they go.

The Soviets, with their ardor for spacious concrete and capital construction, had in the days of Chinese-Russian friendship selected this site for one of the forty-six they had envisaged for the Yellow River. They saw these cutting across the main flow down its length, a "staircase" of hydroelectric power stations that would produce colossal kilowattage on the upper reaches and radically transform irrigation and flood regulation downstream. When the grand "multipurpose" plan for controlling the river was unveiled in the mid-1950s, neither the Chinese nor the Russians could have known that the staircase would never materialize in the imagery of the river. It is true that within a few years of announcing the plan, work on four of the five key dams—at Liujia Gorge, at Qingtong Gorge, at Sanmengong, and at the Three-Gate Gorge—was zealously begun. It may even be true that, propelled by the Great Leap Forward, progress was accelerated by people working round the clock. In the case of Liujia Gorge, it is even claimed that, so that their work might progress throughout the year uninterrupted, the toiling workers went so far as to dig a conduit to lead floodwaters away from the riverbed, thereby defying the suspension of work forced upon them by the high-water season. But a vision which seemed the ultimate in socialist construction in the 1950s, the fruit of the brotherhood of the Chinese and Russian peoples, is in the 1980s a considerably scaled-down reality, humbler certainly, yet in substance and manner largely Chinese.

The hallmarks of Sovietism do remain of course. They remain at Three-Gate Gorge (Sanmen Gorge), the site of a grand "multipurpose" project for water conservancy in the middle reaches. This mighty project, of whose component works the key ones were completed in December 1974, was not a prodigious success. The dam structure was completed as early as 1960, the year Chinese-Soviet ties were severed, but very soon afterward the river's silt clogged up the reservoir, and the Chinese engineers found that they had to rebuild the dam and overhaul their plans for the auxiliary works. The power plant's kilowattage was reduced from a million to a measly two hundred thousand; and though the reservoir's storage capacity runs to billions of cubic feet, there is no way that all of it can ever be used. So what was to be the showpiece and fulcrum of Yellow River control now stands as a monument to hasty miscalculation and adventure.

But the 1950s, when this sensational project was conceived, were boom years of capital-intensive construction for the Yellow River, and the works at Three-Gate Gorge remain witness to the faith and boldness of that age. The official, face-saving version of the story, the one we heard at Liujia Gorge, goes that when the Russians departed they took all their blueprints with them, leaving the Chinese no alternative but to blow up the dam and raise another from scratch to an altogether Chinese design. The truth of the matter is that the Chinese planners were too sanguine to be seriously bothered about the silt problem when the project was still at its earliest stage, and had plunged into its construction heedless of the suggestion that silt-discharge gates be built at the base of the dam, or that the sediment be collected at one or more dams upstream before they started on the one at Three-Gate Gorge.

Such was the boldness of the conception that, of the six designs submitted for the main dam, the one selected was the most expensive. As so often happens, the work came to cost more and entail greater population relocation than was originally estimated. The initial investment had to be doubled and two and a half times the number of inhabitants moved than anticipated. It was an expensive business from the start, for most of the equipment—the heavy earth-moving machinery, the turbines, and the like—had to be bought from the Soviet Union, the Bloc countries, and Japan. Yet in the end this expensive marvel had to be whittled down to size, and when all the dust had settled, and the project put into operation at last, its effectiveness was no more than that of the cheapest of the six designs considered.

They had reckoned without their host. The Yellow River's famous sludge and its potential for havoc had yet to be grasped. They had thought that not for another fifty years would the reservoir's capacity be significantly reduced by silt, but within five years of the dam's completion, not only the reservoir but the valley all the way up to Xi'an was threatened. The reconstruction then began in earnest—tunnels were dug; pipes were pressed into service as silt-evacuation conduits; dynamos resistant to silt abrasion were installed; and the silt, as it entered the reservoir, was sluiced out of the dam through eight openings originally intended for water diversion during the actual construction.

In fact the Russians and Chinese had known all along that Three-

Gate Gorge was an ill-omened location for a large-scale water conservancy project. During the war with Japan, the Japanese East Asia Research Institute had conceived the idea of building a dam here, but more for the hydroelectric power that it would harvest than for any disinterested benefit. The American engineers who were consulted after the war had pointed out that such a project, if undertaken, would flood far too large an area of arable land—"It is not feasible to de-silt the Three-Gate reservoir and its useful life would be short" was their conclusion. Three of the American engineers of the Yellow River Consulting Board said that a dam here should never be contemplated, while the fourth thought it feasible only after the heavy silt load had been satisfactorily dealt with. They themselves proposed a dam some thirty miles down-river, and were in any case more interested in flood prevention than in hydropower generation.

But to the Chinese and Russian engineers, the site was too invit-ing in other respects to be ignored. Set against the geological fact that this was the only stretch of river in the vicinity not susceptible to earthquakes, the disadvantages seemed not quite so overwhelm-ing; set against the hydrographical fact that more than ninety percent of the basin's drainage area and most of the main tributaries lie upstream from this point, making it a veritable fulcrum of flood control, the disadvantages seemed hardly worth considering.

The Soviets were the last representatives of a long line of foreign consultants on the regulation of the Yellow River. Before the com-munist revolution there had been American hydraulic advisers as well as British ones, and highly eminent ones at that. Yet, for all the foreignness of China's modern hydraulic technology, these Western engineers were in many ways building on native founda-tions. The Yellow River is an ancient foe, and hydraulics an ancient science in China. The empire is hardly imaginable without its magnificent capital and court, without the grain shipments from the rich rice-growing areas which supported these, and without the man-made Grand Canal linking the river systems to bear the country's riches to the capital. If the Chinese are stirred by the socialist symbolism, romance even, of gigantic barrages, reservoirs, and levees, then in erecting them up and down the country they are also continuing an old tradition, for great works of water control are quite as much an enterprise of imperial rule as of socialist construction. If the site had been engineered to resemble Bratsk, far to the north in the depths of Siberia, it was also a successor to the native Grand Canal and other great waterworks of China's imperial past.

We had expected to be taken to the main dam as part of the tour and were surprised and disappointed when, the inspection of the water turbines over, we were told to wait at the exit for the van to take us back down. I had the feeling we were being herded to the guesthouse and to inactivity by the imperatives of clock watching, the sacred hour of lunch being no more than forty-five minutes away. Yet when I asked our guide why we couldn't have gone up to the main dam, the excuse she improvised was that there was no transport.

"What about this van?" I asked.

"The driver has other duties," she quickly replied, at the same time turning to look out of the window to clinch shut any discussion of alternatives I might offer.

I had learnt to recognize such excuses for what they were—a veil for laziness and for not wanting to bother. That morning, finding the door of the toilet on my floor locked, I had enquired at the desk and been told it was because the water closet was broken. I was not taken in, and believed it was only because, the staff having cleaned it in the morning, the guesthouse wanted it unpatronized for as long as possible, a suspicion borne out when I caught the receptionist unlocking it in the afternoon, to disclose a toilet in perfect working order.

Later, strolling down the street which leads away from the guesthouse, I spotted the van pulled up on the side of the road and the driver inside. When he looked out I asked, "Do you really have other duties?"

"No," he said, and with the rueful look worn by Chinese when they want to suggest the ironies they live with, he tilted his head and added, "Hop in."

We did, and he ran us up to the dam and past the sentries. But what made him such a boon was that he did not leave it at that. After Takia had photographed the masonry from every possible angle, and those surges of water tossing jets and curtains of spray, the driver descended to the reservoir to see if we could be included in whatever action was afoot. Following him, I found a launch tied up alongside what looked like a structure for evacuating silt. The driver poked his head in and asked the captain seated there if he'd take us out to the reservoir that afternoon. There were some deck-hands about, two of them napping and a third sprawled across a bench in a haze of cigarette smoke and after-hours indolence. I was apprehensive of the captain's caution, which might make him demur at such an impromptu suggestion; but he received the proposal well, and said it was all right by him as long as the German party to which the boat had been hired out agreed.

The Germans were here for the day from Lanzhou—a coachload of them, as I could see when the driver ran us back down the drive-way by which we had approached the dam. They were stopping for pictures, and some of them must have been wondering why, as there was nothing in particular to see—no abutment, or sluice gate, or misery laced with the picturesque. The tour leader was pointed out to me, an ash-colored German in a pair of blue jeans that, by pinching cruelly, emphasized his girth. Addressing him in English, I stated my request.

"How large is the boat?" he demanded to know.

"Quite large enough for us all," I said.

"I said how large is the boat," he repeated, "how many meters?"

I must say that that stumped me rather, not sharing the predilection which this German and his kind have for compelling all slurred things into numerical precision.

"I don't know how many meters exactly," I had to admit, "but the captain said we could go into the wheelhouse if necessary. You won't even see us."

The German pulled his lips against his teeth, so that his mouth appeared as a slash. "If the captain says so . . ." he stiffly conceded.

"But I want you to know that I don't like it. I don't want to see you, and I don't want you in our bus."

In other parts of the world the disagreeableness of this man would have gone unremarked; here it struck a jarring note, as the repugnant aloofness of the white man. I felt sorry for his Chinese counterpart, a girl in pigtails provided by the China Travel Service, whose fluster and uncertainty about schedules in the teeth of his efforts to coerce her into correctness must have made his dislike of us Chinese the more conclusive.

Instead of June, had the month been September or October, when the water level rises high enough, or had our craft been a flat-bottomed vessel, the trip upriver would have had as its climax the sighting of Bingling Monastery, where Buddhist caves and niches speckle the cliff faces above the water. Cut in the sixth century, their walls brilliantly embellished in the Song (960–1279) and Ming (1368–1644) dynasties, these caves were alternately a goal of Buddhist pilgrimage and a faded, forgotten relic. The mood of the place is set by the Big Buddha, a giant seated statue carved in the Tang dynasty (618–907), and to see it coming into sight above the river, surrounded by cliffs full of holes and overseeing your boat's advance in silence, must be one of the most memorable moments of travel. The rediscovery of the site is of relatively recent date, and it was not until 1952, after they had been ignored for a century, that the caves became the object of archaeological study. But centuries of wind had already blotched the chiseled features of some of the bodhisattvas, leaving only a hint of their past splendor.

We were in neither the right month nor the right boat. All the same there was much that was worth our attention, as we chugged our way through the reservoir's fifty square miles. The hills were quite high here, and their slopes lay wrinkled and dry around us, reddish and yellow, like the folds of velvet. The reservoir extends from the point where it is entered by the Tao, a tributary of the Yellow River, so that sailing into it is like emerging from a neck and finding yourself upon the waters of a huge lake. In the distance one or two men were fishing, and though it hardly seemed possible amidst that desolation, potatoes were said to grow behind the shores.

The captain, older than the deckhands but otherwise indistinguishable from them, stood at the wheel with his cigarettes lying on a ledge in front of him. He was a man of few words, but hospitable, and he offered me some sips of hot water from what seemed to be the communal mug, tea being a luxury not available just then. Takia made for the bows to take his pictures, and presently I followed him outside as far as the deck. There were two Chinese boys out there, and one of them observed, gesturing at Takia's cameras, "You people from outside take pictures of scenery; we take pictures only of ourselves."

He was a tall, handsome boy, with a wide dimpled smile that suddenly lit up his face. When I asked him why it was that Chinese took pictures only of each other he said, quite simply, "Poverty."

"Can't you see," he continued, "how poor we are? Here in Gansu especially. Look around you; isn't this aridity the very image of poverty?"

"But the reservoir irrigates thousands of acres, not just here but all the way up to Inner Mongolia," I ventured.

"So they say, so they say. It makes no difference though; truly it does nothing to narrow the gap between our living standards and yours." He said this without any bitterness, some strain of dark humor lighting up his eyes.

After a while he told me about himself, dramatizing nothing, and about the place where, as a member of "those awaiting employment" (the official Chinese euphemism for the unemployed), he'd been taken on as an apprentice of sorts. Today he was obviously playing truant, but he said that no one would bother to tell on him and "anyway, there is nothing whatever to do at work." He was only sixteen, but in his canniness looked ready to take on all comers.

The other boy, more frailly built and older, had some time before this joined us. He was from Xi'an, downriver to the east, and he was here with his supervisor to carry out some hydrological work. He gave, in talking, some clues to idealisms that I had assumed to have expired in China—as when he described, with obvious admiration, his supervisor's dedication and humility, or when he said, "He should be the object of every worker's emulation," I could see that the quiet conviction with which he expressed himself was too genuine for anyone to challenge it, and when he said, again of his supervisor, "He works hours at a stretch, sometimes all day long, just to accomplish a task," you felt he was talking of a perfection rare in the real world, but you took serious note of his idealism in a way you would no one else's.

He was a proper counterpoise to the sixteen-year-old, who stood on my other side idly smoking his cigarette. He was bothered by things the younger boy easily dismissed. When he said, "You know, you could save a lot of money not smoking," the other boy just grinned. "Never mind," he said, "I'll tell my grandchildren it's all the fault of the Gang of Four."

Just then a German woman, wandering up here alone, squeezed past us to head for the bows. "The two roads," the sixteen-year-old instantly responded out of his stock of Maoist phrases; and looking over his shoulder at her, he made a face.

I shook my head at him to indicate incomprehension, and with a wink of complicity he explained, "You know about class conflict, don't you—the struggle between the 'two roads' of socialism and capitalism?" Then, when I nodded: "You have heard, haven't you, of the *fuzaxing* (the complex nature) of class conflict?" And when I nodded again: "Did you not see her face, the tangle of 'roads' the years have left on its skin, their complex nature?"

I laughed at that, but at the same time the conspiratorial look crossing his face, for all its smiling charm, represented to me a potential for mockery that was not all kind. He was sarcastic all right. But then, when you come right down to it, he was disenchanted. If he thought the world a squalid place, he had a right to such skepticism, for while the sight of those bare yellow cliffs was imposing to me and to other tourists, it was grim enough for him, for whom it signified an unchangeable condition of life.

The excursion took three hours, and it was four-thirty before we got back to our point of embarkation. The Germans, met by their coach, drove off back to Lanzhou, while Takia and I, and the hydrological surveyor from Xi'an, made our way back to the guesthouse on foot. It transpired that the surveyor was staying at the same place, but on the ground floor, among the underling rank and file. At dinner we found ourselves at the same table, and I gathered from the look he cast me that the elderly man beside him was the supervisor he so admired. But as so often happens, the man didn't look cut out for hero worship at all, what with his slight build, ragged appearance, and subdued manner. Yet China is full of veterans of Five Year Plans who look as though they clean drains or mend shoes for a living.

At nightfall, Takia and I began the aimless wandering that would come to characterize our evenings in small Chinese towns. There was nothing much to see, except for a dusty building site where the men were packing up to go home. I learned they were erecting a child-care center there, working twelve hours a day, starting at six-thirty in the morning, to complete the two-storied building in three months. How was it possible, with what they had in the way of machinery, which was medieval?

A quarter of an hour out of the center, past sections of barrack-style housing, I came upon a handwritten notice pasted on a telegraph pole. It advertised a foolproof method for curing body odor, a forty-minute treatment that would root the affliction out once and for all. As in Lanzhou, where I came across two notices, one at each end of the main street, providing telephone numbers and contact addresses and promising permanent cures for premature ejaculation, I realized I was confronted with that rare thing—a glimpse into Chinese sexual anxieties.

Early the next morning we were headed west for Xi'ning, the capital of the neighboring province of Qinghai. We were to catch a connection at Hekou South, a station at the confluence of the Yellow River and the Huangshui, the tributary on whose southern banks Xi'ning lies. For some reason our train was an hour late arriving at Liujia Gorge, an unusual occurrence in this country, where, cancellation of service apart, the trains generally run according to schedule. But perhaps we had a right to expect punctuality only of trunk lines, and not of these little feeders into the main network.

The railroad from here follows the valley of the Yellow River on its way to Hekou South, involving two crossings of the main stream and passing two more hydropower dam sites (Yanguo and Bapan), both downstream of Liujia Gorge. Through the window of our carriage I sometimes saw this great grave river, flowing silently by. There were fields bright yellow with rape flowers; spring wheat, big-eared, had a month to go before the harvest. I was staring at this, and at a section of the river being drawn past my window, when a man on the seat beside me started a conversation.

In China such conversations tend to take this form:

"Where do you come from?"

To this I sometimes reply "London" and other times "Hong Kong"—the latter inducing the greater interest, as the consumer paradise whence come the most coveted makes of cassette-tape decks and the proscribed but rampant strains of China's favorite songstress, Deng Lijun, Taiwan's answer to Petula Clark.

If I say "London," my interlocutor will observe, drawing probably from the translated works of Charles Dickens and Conan Doyle, that it is very foggy there. (The Chinese insistence on London's fogginess, incidentally, was something Margaret Thatcher had to contend with during her visit to Peking in 1982, on top of their claim to the sovereignty of Hong Kong.) Mercifully he will not follow this with an attempt to practice his English on me as he would on a real Britisher.

"How old are you?" I am then asked. By an assumption based only on the presence of a male traveling companion, my status, which might have been the subject of the next question, is taken to be "married."

How much of my income is spent on rent and food is then ascertained. He will then tell me how little rent *he* pays, so fragile is his sense of getting a fair deal from life, and so great is his need to reassure himself that not everything is better in that modern money-laden world beyond the borders from which the tourists come.

If I claim to be from Hong Kong, my interlocutor will ask, almost conspiratorially, if women going out on their own at night do get raped in every corner, as is the image of the place trumped up by the Chinese media. Although he will listen with apparent interest to what I say about the true state of Hong Kong's public order, seldom will he really understand my meaning. Except to the very few, the mechanics of life outside their country are a closed book to the Chinese, and one which they ultimately do not wish to open, for fear that it will confirm all the doubts that they have about their own.

In this case, while the exchange of civilities did follow the usual pattern, it turned out to be preliminary to a proposition, in undertone, for an exchange of quite another kind. I learnt that my interlocutor was really after my foreign currency certificates, the scrip coupons issued to tourists against foreign cash and traveler's checks. These coupons were something the Chinese copied from the Soviet Union as a way of thwarting the black marketeering engendered by the diversion of foreign currency. They are highly prized by the Chinese, who are not supposed to use them but do, for they provide access to merchandise not normally available to the resident, sold by shops open only to the privileged in China and the visitor from abroad. When the man asked to buy mine I reluctantly obliged. He alighted happy at the next stop, the distance between him and a Japanese cassette player reposing in hard-to-get splendor on a shelf in some Canton, Shanghai, or Peking emporium considerably reduced.

The transaction narrowly missed being witnessed by the conductress and the railway police, who now came into our carriage and sat down sociably to talk to us. These conductresses in their blue suits and caps are a great asset to the People's Railway, possessed as they are of a commendable thoroughness when it comes to sweeping and mopping the prodigiously littered floors of the carriages. They are a basic ingredient of travel in China, as basic as the hot water that they endlessly dispense for your tea from their oversized kettles, as the overwrought dining-car attendants, the vendors at junction platforms selling things to eat, the pungent emissions from the lavatories, the jets of spittle shot through the carriage window at frequent intervals.

To us they were a godsend that day; for, arriving at Hekou South only seconds before the departure of our train for Xi'ning, we would never have caught the connection if they hadn't raced across the platform with our luggage, pressed us forward up couplings, down over the tracks, and brought us to the very door of our train.

If we could, we would have leaned back in our seats in relief and security. But traveling "hard" class, our seats had ramrod backs and were as unyielding as their class label suggests. As in that other class-ridden socialist society, the Soviet Union, first-class (which seats the Party nobility, the officers of the People's Liberation Army, and the rich foreigners) and second-class (for the rest of the Chinese millions) are called "soft" and "hard" in China, the terms applying equally to seats as to berths. Linen-covered headboards, upholstered seats, frilly pillowcases, flowery satin quilts, potted plants, curtains, por-celain teacups with lids, reading lights—these are the familiars of soft class. Three-tier berths in open-plan, uncovered wooden seats, overhead racks crammed with luggage, a furnace fueled with coal at one end of the compartment and a repellent lavatory at the other, rods laid above windows from which hang the passengers' face flannels—these are what you will find in the hard class.

In Chinese trains, Soviet practices are uncannily preserved, in, for example, the unremitting way in which conductresses appear in your carriage to give the floors a thorough going over with their long-handled mops. As in the Soviet Union, China still loiters in the railway age: it is not only the hiss of steam and the muffling of coal dust; the ritual of the uniformed station masters and mistresses standing rigidly at attention on the platform as the train pulls out— it is the feeling that for millions of people and thousands of miles, the railway still stands in the very center of life. In China the annual turnover of passengers is a staggering 922 million.

The border between Gansu and Qinghai had been crossed some-time ago, and now, at midday, we were nearing Xi'ning. Sitting where I did, squashed in between two seasoned railway travelers in a carload of dozens like them, it was not easy to imagine arrival at this place in the days before the railroad reached it. But in one half of my mind certain details came to me, from an account of just such a journey by the great traveler Peter Fleming, who covered the distance between Lanzhou and Xi'ning by mule in 1935, undertaking to do it in five days instead of six. Because, I suppose, his traveling companion was a woman from Geneva, he kept up his spirits during the journey by singing the Swiss national anthem to the tune of "Rule Britannia." They crossed the Yellow River in a flat-bottomed boat, and entered the gorges of the tributary he knew as the Xi'ning River (and which we now call the Huangshui) at about the point, I think, where we had just now changed trains. On the waters, he tells us, huge rafts of inflated oxhides were gathered, poled with their wool and skins through the rapids; and men at the water's edge, squatting, panned for the specks of gold which he on the shore could see glittering at his feet. Instead of rolling stock there were camel caravans, mules, carts, and Tibetan ponies. And when they came in sight of Xi'ning eventually, it was not sidings or platforms or signal boxes that they first saw, but the gates and bastions and armed sentries of the city walls. Thereafter, there would be some similarity between my experiences and Peter Fleming's. One, in particular, made me feel I was back within the pages of his book; this was when, the question of our accommodation settled, we found ourselves in a friendly Muslim eating place, and, like Fleming, "stuffed ourselves with delicious and contrasting dishes of chopped meat and vegetables."

Since Peter Fleming's time, some forty thousand miles of railway have been thrown down throughout the country, most of the new lines in this western slab of territory. In many of the world's largest countries railways are the clips that fasten district to district and foster a sense of nation: Soviet Russia would be ungraspable in its immensity without the Trans-Siberian; Canada would not have been a confederation without the Canadian Pacific. Yet, though the construction of these two railroads depended on Chinese coolie labor (as did, for that matter, the Southern Pacific, the Union Pacific, and even the railways of British Malaya), China did not truly become a unity bound by a rail network until the middle of this century. It was only in 1960 that the railroad on which we were traveling, the Lanzhou-Qinghai line, was opened to traffic. Once open, it mitigated the remoteness of Qinghai, and turned it from a place that was Chinese in theory, but lumped with Turkestan and

Tibet as the unknown western regions in feeling, into an unequivocal part of China. Industrial development was the primary impulse, I suppose, for there are rich mineral resources to be tapped in Qinghai, and railways are a necessary component of what is called the infrastructure in development terminology.

The Chinese like to say that their country is nowadays crossed by a "web of steel." Considering the difficulties besetting the builders when they came here after the revolution—the emptiness of uncharted desert land, the high altitude—the accomplishment is undeniably impressive. The more so when set against the state of railways before the communists took over: only 13,750 miles constructed in the seventy-three years following the laying of the first line by the British, most of them crossing the settled southeast, and half of them rendered unusable by war.

"The People's Railway, for the People," goes the stirring slogan of Chinese rail; and with the way the passengers take over a locomotive when they board it, spreading their snacks and face flannels all around, these trains do seem wholly domesticated. Yet when railways were first introduced to the country, in 1876, the natives vastly distrusted the idea. It was not entirely because of conservatism and superstition—the fear that the rumble would startle the grazing cattle, the sparks would ignite the farmhouses, the smoke would poison the air, and the general disturbance stop the hens from laying. Apart from the fact that they violated the rules of Chinese geomancy and barged into the tombs of the country folk, the railroad tracks were laid without the consent of the Chinese government, on land bought under another pretext. The people responsible were British merchants, among them those famous Far Eastern traders Jardine, Matheson and Company. The line, only ten miles long, linked Shanghai with Wusong, a town beside the Yangtze River. Service began in May, but a melee beside the track, involving the shooting of a Chinese bystander by an Englishman riding past on horseback, so aroused Chinese ire that the Chinese authorities bought it back in September and had it destroyed the year after.

Despite this inauspicious start, China became a lively arena of European rivalry for railway concessions, with the Trans-

Manchurian signed over to the Russians, Shandong to the Germans, the connection from Indochina to the French, the Long-hai (linking Lanzhou with the coast) to the Belgians, the Hankou-Canton to the Americans, and so on. By the outbreak of the war with Japan, something like ninety percent of Chinese railways was controlled by Britain, France, Japan, Russia, the United States, and other powers.

It did not stick though, the foreign domination. How overwhelmingly Chinese the railways have become I could easily see and hear as the train pulled into Xi'ning Station that afternoon, with the mammoth crowd stirring, the conductors and conductresses putting on impassive faces, the plastic and canvas bags (emblazoned with the names of familiar Chinese cities) tumbling from the racks, and the high-pitched female voice over the loudspeakers intoning in Peking dialect, or rather in that inexplicably nasalized form that is the lingua franca of Chinese railways on all but the Cantonese lines: "We shall soon be arriving at Xi'ning Railway Station. Will all those passengers alighting at Xi'ning Railway Station please make ready to alight. We shall soon be arriving at Xi'ning Railway Station. . . ."

The Blue Sea

For several days, we travelled through what seemed the excava-
tions of a great cemetery. Human bones, and the carcasses of
animals presenting themselves at every step, seemed to warn us
that, in this fatal region, amidst this savage nature, the caravans
which preceded us, had preceded us in death.

　　　　　　　　　　　　　　　—— Evariste Régis Huc
　　　　　　　　　　　　　　　　　in Qinghai, 1845

Qinghai, which is Chinese for "blue sea," is named for the inland
salt lake, the largest in China, that lies in the province's eastern
corner, and which is better known to the West by its Mongolian
name of Koko Nor. The province shares with Tibet, to its south, the
world's largest and highest tableland, the Qinghai-Tibet plateau
that some call "The Roof of the World." This is a conglomera-
tion of mountains, a stupendous mass which has the Kunlun massif
to the north running away into the Pamirs in the west, and the
Himalayas to the south arching in a string of peaks down into
Nepal. It is from here that several of Asia's greatest rivers start to
flow: the Yellow River, the Yangtze, the Mekong, the Salween,
the Brahmaputra, and the Indus (the first three arising in Qinghai
Province, and the last three in Tibet proper).

The portion drained by the Yellow River reaches northward
into the Tsaidam Basin, once the bed of a huge body of water, where
one lake alone, among the thousands that dot it, is said to be deposited with enough salt to supply the whole of China's population

for eight thousand years. Beyond the salt marshes lies the desert, where the Chinese empire petered out into inner Asia.

Until fairly recent times all this was another world from China, barbaric and culturally distinct. Qinghai itself was Amdo, part of the Tibetan world which, before the Manchu empire established complete paramountcy. fell under the sway of the Dalai Lama, with his seat in the Potala Palace in Lhasa. In earlier days it must have been very like the Northwest Frontier in India—an arena of constant warfare, and one to whose chilling exaction of lives, so often the corollary of militaristic ambitions, many famous Chinese poets have memorably responded. Here, for instance, catching the tragedies of loss, of distance and separation "as the barbarian hordes probe at the Blue Sea," are six lines by that greatest of eighth-century poets, Li Bo:

> It is known that from the battlefield
> Few ever live to return.
> Men at garrison look on the border scene,
> Home thoughts deepen sorrow on their faces.
> In the towered chambers tonight,
> Ceaseless are the women's sighs.
>
> (translated by Joseph J. Lee)

And writing against war, too, his contemporary, Du Fu, summons up the image of Koko Nor (which he calls the Black Lake) to suggest the horror and the waste:

> But have you not seen
> On the Black Lake's shore
> The white bones there of old no one has gathered,
> Where new ghosts cry aloud, old ghosts are bitter.
> Rain drenching from dark clouds their ghostly chatter?
>
> (translated by Arthur Cooper)

In this setting, against this backdrop, the Yellow River starts its 3,395-mile journey down to the sea. It starts as a stream, called the

Kar, in Kusikuyag, a mountain in the Bayankara range. From this headstream it seeps eastward through a scoop in the highlands the Tibetans call the Sea of Stars—a wide marshy expanse enclosed by mountains and studded with springs, where the combination of height and water achieves a glimmering quality, and the spectator fancies he is looking at a galaxy. The river then crosses Gyaring Nor and Ngoring Nor, twin lakes separated by a strip of land about 8 miles wide. Before it leaves Qinghai, the river swings right down to the edges of Sichuan Province, before winding up in a twisted S, to plunge across the Qinghai uplands and out of the province in a rush of waters.

Xi'ning

The landscapes of Qinghai are among the most beautiful I know, but if any place could have persuaded me that Qinghai was magnificent, it was not Xi'ning, its capital.

When we arrived, the China Travel Service had been open for business for only a month, and those assigned to work in tourism here, as yet having only Chinese émigrés as clients, were still finding their feet. This being the case, the hotel where we were staying was without a working boiler and running hot water, and thus my first introduction to the city was through the public baths. Of course it was June, and of course there was unheated water, just as there was a bathroom attached to our room. But whereas it was summer nearly everywhere else, Xi'ning, on account of its altitude, was cool and its tap water icy.

I found the People's Bathhouse, just down the road from the hotel, to be an uninviting place. When I'd bought my ticket, I looked for a door into the shower room by following round the discolored walls of a poky corridor. A woman attendant seated in a corner took my ticket and pointed to a door on my right. When I pushed it open, such was the smell that hit me that for a moment I wondered if I could have made a mistake and stumbled upon a lavatory. In I went all the same, and found a room with a broken-down bed along one wall, where, I presumed, you put your clothes, for there were no hooks or shelves that I could see. As the only shaft of light came from a small high window, the place was in semi-darkness and very gloomy.

Now and then I heard a drip of water, and overhead you could make out four nozzles from which this might have come. But I could find no tap or any mechanism for turning on the water, and so I went out of the room to ask the attendant. She was busily playing with a child, most probably her own, but she found time to look up and tell me, with undisguised contempt for my stupidity, that all you had to do was to stand beneath the shower and the water would come on. I daresay such mechanical wizardry is not unknown in many places, but somehow I found it difficult to believe that Xi'ning was one of them. But the attendant had dismissed me, by preoccupying herself with her child once more, before I could question her further; and there was nothing for it but to position myself beneath one of the douches and hope for the best. I now observed, when I had had a closer look, that on the floor beneath each shower there was placed a small square wooden board, and when I stepped on one uncertainly, a dribble did issue from the nozzle overhead. It did not exactly douse you, but in time you could get more or less wet all over.

By now my eyes were used to the darkness, and presently, when I could see quite well, the door opened to admit two girls to the room. Of those who have wondered what Chinese girls wear underneath their baggy blue trousers and jackets, few could have had as mesmerizing an inspection as mine. Their shyness, their breathlessness from having hurried, slowed down the stages by which these girls undressed; and as they emerged, layer after layer, from their blue encasement, I discovered what I always knew but had not fully grasped—that the colors of Chinese underwear are not just bright or gaudy, but psychedelic. Filtering milkily down through the air, the shaft of light from the window picked out here a large peony on a small bodice, there a frond on a pair of bell-shaped drawers. Speaking in hisses, the girls tried to conceal their bodies from me, but at the same time revealed them, standing as they did on the platforms facing the other way, so that their backs and legs were fully disclosed. How stocky they looked, as stocky as most southern Chinese girls seem slender. They were perhaps eighteen or nineteen, but already there was a heaviness to them that suggested the coarsening of middle age, but which was, I suppose, the result of peasant roots and constant physical work.

I never went back to the People's Bathhouse for a repeat performance, and how to wash myself became a nagging preoccupation during those first few days in Xi'ning. In the end, what rescued me from this uncomfortable condition was a six inch by six inch plastic ice-cream container I'd brought along more or less on impulse, just in case there was leaky food to be carried during my travels. It was a chilly operation, but I found that if I used this box like a dipper I could very well have a shower on very little hot water. Standing in the bathtub, I would fill the box with cold water from the tap, lace it with a dash of hot drinking water from the thermos flask (that staple of Chinese hotels), then sparingly and methodically pour the contents all over myself, soaping the while. In this way did I have a bath every night in Xi'ning; and I can remember the proprietorial pleasure with which, after I had got the ratio of hot water to cold to a T, I imparted the technique to Takia; he, to my chagrin, never did adopt it, immune as he was to the middle-class obsession with hygiene.

Fu Tsong, the pianist, once said, prompted by what he had seen of musicians' homes in China, "In China, even cleanliness is a luxury." Certainly dirt is inescapable in China; soot and sulphur dioxide lie thick upon the Chinese city (in Peking the density of pollutants in the air is six times the level considered safe), and the horrors of a Chinese public lavatory are enough to make any Westerner shudder. A typical women's toilet consists of a row of holes in the ground with a raised surface for a foot on each side and a line of women companionably defecating. Only in the largest cities have I found this elaborated by a contraption that sends water flowing along a groove connecting the separate holes; in most other cases, until it ends up in some field as night soil, the excrement just lies there, accumulating in promiscuous heaps.

I well realize that dirt, like beauty, lies in the eye of the beholder, and that differences in notions of purity have to do with class distinctions and so on. Even so, to anyone with an urban squeamishness, it is difficult not to link the fecal stench that frequently greets you in China with uncleanliness, although nothing in the behavior of the Chinese themselves acknowledges it—not the relaxed way they go about the business in hand, or the casualness with which they use the same mop to clean the living room floor as has mopped up the overflow of the lavatory. Indeed, the Chinese perception of dirt seems altogether unrelated to any notion of hygiene, arising as it may well do from some deeper level, of primitive ritual perhaps, or defilement beliefs. On crowded trains, for example, I noticed that the passengers would vigorously wipe their faces and hands at the washbasin (an inviolate ritual), and then hang the wet face flannels up smack in front of the window, where, if anywhere, they would catch the most dust. Another Chinese abhorrence is the floor, which is considered unclean willy-nilly, and a Chinese could no more think of going to bed without washing his feet—that part of the body most likely to have been in touch with the ground—than of starting the day without thoroughly clearing his throat.

It was something constantly brought home to me in China, that like so much else, dirt is often a subjective matter. That was one reason I was so disconcerted by it, for I never learnt to accept it in their terms. I hope this does not make me sound like those early European visitors to the country, whose dirt consciousness was only another facet of their race consciousness. In the travelogue written by the American I mentioned earlier, Harry Franck, you will find a good deal of contempt for the standards of hygiene in China; and when I read again and again the adjectives he uses for the people— soiled, begrimed, filthy, unlaundered, unwashed, unsoaped—I am Chinese enough to find them jarring. All the same I must confess that the scruffiness you encounter in China is often very distasteful to experience.

Yet it would be wrong to suggest that dirt avoidance was anything more than only a tiny fraction of the many daily distractions of my stay in Xi'ning. Though the place is undeniably a backwater, its interests, if not its charms, are quite the equal of many cities in China. Xi'ning became the provincial capital when Qinghai was established as an independent province in 1928, but it had been important much earlier, as a strategic point on the western frontier of the Chinese empire and on the main trade route between China and Tibet. Its violent history is still remembered in its name, which translates as "Peace in the West," and was conferred on it by the Song dynasty in 1104, when it was recovered from the Tibetans, who had overrun it three centuries before. You would expect to find much diversity in Xi'ning, where the Tibetan strain is strong, and where the old Muslim quarter in the eastern suburbs can still evoke visions of fierce Mohammedan rebellions, as did indeed occur here in the nineteenth century.

One Friday afternoon I went with a group of Hong Kong visitors to the mosque at a place the locals call Eastern Pass. The buildings, wrecked during the Cultural Revolution and recently renovated, are in the traditional Chinese style. In the reception room of one of these, red hangings on walls bore legends reproducing the slogans of the national commitment to the Four Modernizations and commemorating the longed-for reopening of the mosque. At first sight it seemed all too Chinese, all too like the rest of China. But then amidst the commemorative hangings I noticed two bravely inscribed in Arabic, and learnt that they were the words not of the Party but of the Prophet. And presently, when we reemerged into the courtyard, the Islamic influence upon Xi'ning was suddenly revealed in the devotees hastening to their prayers. There was apparently no more room in the mosque, whose interior I could not see but which gave the impression of being thronged, and the late arrivals were spreading their towels (these passed for prayer mats) here out in the courtyard. All of a sudden I realized that my Hong Kong companions and I were the only women there. This, when you came to think of it, smacked of the purdah. At the entrance to the courtyard I found two old women and some children lurking in a corner, and when I asked them, "Don't you pray?" they said, "Yes, but only at home."

On top of being a military garrison, Xi'ning has been a trading center since the sixteenth century, living off the rich Koko Nor commerce in furs, deer horns, gold, musk, and especially wool. Wool still partly sustains the city's economic life, as I learnt when I went to the Number Two Carpet Factory. We were given a tour of this factory, where, on floor after floor, we saw workers at the loom, on the floor, weaving and trimming the beautiful rugs that were stored in a room at the top. The wool had a strange smell, not raw like the smell of animals but mellower, less stale than an attic but musty, a cured smell that still had the hills and valleys in it. The weaving took two years to learn, we were told; and the girls—for they were mostly girls who worked here—earned between sixty and seventy yuan (U.S. $30–35) a month, more than they would make if they were anywhere other than in Xi'ning, which is recognized as a hardship post by those who set the salary scale.

Some of the girls held electric scissors and, going over the rugs for imperfections invisible to me, trimmed around the outlines of the figures of decoration embedded there. The largest of these carpets go for three thousand yuan (about U.S. $1,500) a piece, but the factory's marketing agent in Tianjin marks that up by two hundred percent before selling them abroad. Tianjin, whose own carpets are famous, has been the place to which all Xi'ning's wool once went, and could not be circumvented even now, though Xi'ning is manufacturing carpets itself, and might have achieved a measure of autonomy. The factory had been going for two years, we were told, and just about broke even; but though the management was only too anxious to make a profit, now that no one, not even the most thoroughgoing socialist snob, turns up his nose at the word, Xi'ning is too far away and too new to the game to have made the best of the winds of economic change.

I sometimes thought Xi'ning impervious to the rhythm of modern activity. But then again there was the young professional photographer, who said he handled over a hundred clients a day—the figure rising to three hundred at times. We had called at his studio one afternoon while wandering about the streets of the city, and the longer I stood there, watching him work, the more I marveled at his efficiency. As we talked mothers were plumping their babies down in front of his camera. He handled these women briskly, but allowed them time for a last tweak of the collar, a final tug at the trousers. Observing through his lens a puddle suddenly appearing around the legs of one little boy, he reached for a cloth, walked across to the puddle, mopped it up, and without finding it necessary to interrupt what he was saying to us, proceeded to light up and place on record the flushed look of his squirming if subdued subject, aged two.

I think his style of work was unusual though, and what we found at the bank, where we went to change our money, was altogether more typical of the kind of service you get in China, where it is said that for every three people who work, two others sit and watch. The bank was actually closed, it being the day for "Study," an activity often indistinguishable from "Rest." But knowing how susceptible the Chinese are to inveiglement, I tapped on the window, and caught the attention of a bank officer. In the ordinary course of events he would have sent me on my way, but in this case we were invited to step in. At first I thought he was going to attend to us, for all his colleagues were lounging about their desks drinking tea and reading newspapers from Hong Kong. But not so; he summoned a man from another room—clearly an underling from his youthfulness and air of obsequiousness—and told him to take out the exchange forms, while he himself returned his attention to his paper. The transaction took a long time, for the poor boy was patently inexperienced, and we complicated matters by wanting half the amount in exchange certificates and the other half in local currency. The complication was not beyond him, but he was understandably hamstrung by the paperwork, which seemed to me to be overabundant.

So many chits and receipts, in so many copies: procedures are as elaborate in China as in any people's democracy. As often as not they are a hedge against future criticism or attack, a sort of alibi. I remember something a Chinese taxi driver once said to me, when I told him not to bother to write me out a receipt. "Look," he protested, "you don't want to get me into trouble, do you? What if they start another campaign, or another Cultural Revolution? I don't want to be clobbered, see?" So transactions are often protracted. Once, asking for some envelopes and some notepaper at a Xi'ning department store, Takia was nonplussed to be told by the sales assistant that he could only buy the latter after he'd paid for the former, and that two separate bills would have to be made out for his purchase.

If becoming acquainted with working styles is one way of getting to know a place, seeing what people do for leisure is another. There was, as always, the People's Park. When we went there we saw children extraordinarily got up in rainbow colors, young men swimming in their socks, couples boating, magicians and other fairground familiars such as performing animals and stunt motorcycling, a profusion of litter on the paths with spat-out melon-seed husks predominating.

There was also opera. Taking a walk after dinner one evening, we came across a shabby grey building bearing a plaque which proclaimed it to be the home of a Qin opera company. Curious, we wandered in, and seeing a man emerge from the inner premises, I asked him if there was a rehearsal in progress. The man was unmistakably an opera singer, with a refinement of feature and manner unusual in this part of China. He said that as a matter of fact there was, and leading us through some narrow passages and up some dark staircases, he admitted us to another world.

We had come upon a climactic moment in a rehearsal of an opera about Li Shimin, the young man who became the greatest emperor of China. There were two carpets on the floor, and a shaft of summer evening light from windows set so high up they might have been skylights. Though the general aura surrounding the performers gathered there was less than vivid, there was a suggestion of intensity to the details. An actress in costume, practicing hand movements in a corner, was wheeling around in a flurry of sleeves. The director, sitting at his desk with the script and score in front of him, was clicking his tongue to the rhythm of a nonexistent orchestra, now reproducing the whine of the *huqin* fiddle, now the sound of the date-wood clapper. An actor, with an appositely stagy air, was pacing up and down with determined movement and accelerating the rhythm of his aria. Qin opera is a popular form of music and drama originating several centuries ago in Shaanxi Province to the east, and to see its traditions so vigorously pursued here, in a town that in so many ways lies outside the frame of things, was to feel all the excitement of an unexpected discovery.

The more popular form of entertainment is easily the cinema though, despite its preoccupation with precepts rather than amusement. *Xi'an Incident,* the film we saw in Xi'ning, was no exception. This is a reconstruction of a historical event involving Chiang Kai-shek, Mao Zedong, the patriotic warlord Zhang Xueliang, and the late Chinese premier Zhou Enlai. The incident in the title refers, of course, to the kidnapping of Chiang Kai-shek in December 1936, in a mutiny engineered by, among others, a battalion of Zhang Xueliang's personal guard. In return for his release, Chiang was to promise an end to his anticommunist campaigns and a grand alliance of Nationalist and communist forces in the fight against Japan. It was crisis and high drama, and we hear of Madame Chiang courageously taking a plane to be by her husband's side. But in the end he was rescued by a most unexpected savior: emerging from behind the mountains, Zhou Enlai, representing the very enemy Chiang had set out to destroy, arrived in Xi'an to persuade Chiang's captors to make him an ally and spare him his life. Released, Chiang returned to the capital a national hero, and promptly gave orders for Zhang Xueliang, who had offered himself up for punishment, to be put under house arrest for the rest of his life.

Though I could hardly hear for the hawking and shuffling of the audience, and though I could hardly see, being squeezed into a corner seat behind a pillar at the back (all the best seats having been taken up by the ushers and their friends), I managed not to miss the point of the movie, which is that, for all his patriotism, Zhang Xueliang was unfitted by his capitalist class background to the challenge of revolution.

Though the casting was done with an eye to the physical resemblance the actors bore to the historical figures they portrayed, only the man who played Mao Zedong was a true look-alike, with thick black hair worn very long, a high-bridged nose, and searching eyes.

But the chief interest of the portrayals was not how they reproduced the physical attributes of the originals, but how they represented them temperamentally. You could scarcely miss the jolliness of Mao Zedong, it was laid on so thick. Breezy, laid-back, earthy of tongue and rough and ready of habit, short on niceties, rich in hearty good humor—this was the image the actor conveyed. There was none of the effeminacy that writers like Robert Payne and Agnes Smedley had noticed when they first met him, or the spiritual isolation that made him seem sinister. As for Chiang Kai-shek, the man was scarcely to be recognized in the buffoon he was made to appear in the film. Madame Chiang, for her part, seemed the incarnation of disagreeable Westernization, addressing her husband as *da-ling* ("darling"), entertaining Europeans, and even speaking a couple of lines in English. Considering how lewd dancing is considered in China, it is not surprising that at her party couples are seen to be waltzing. Few Chinese film makers can bear to let slip an opportunity for introducing a dance scene, so enticing is it an occasion to give their fancy free play, under the safe pretext that they are only representing history. But such scenes can pitifully show up their ignorance of the outside world, for it is when they try for some approximation of foreign manners that the Chinese are at their most provincial.

The most obsessive of the nation's concerns is still with eating. Xi'ning does not do well in the way of food; certainly it felt very barren in June, starved of fruit, or greens, or any fresh vegetable. Nevertheless the citizens take much pleasure in their roadside food stalls. The pavements in the neighborhood of the Southern Pass fill with charcoal braziers as the dark comes down, and on the night that we were there, the place was thronged with people eating. Skewered lamb—more like the Malay *satay* than the shish kebab— was being cooked over the embers, and its smell intermingled with that of the men bunched together on stools around the barbecue. The briskest business of all was done by a stand selling what I had not had since I was a child, the waffle we call Crabapple Cake, which a middle-aged man with practiced deftness was turning out from his irons, while winningly swamping his audience with many favorable mentions of his product. He spoke in Shanghainese, which happens to be my dialect as well, and at a guess I would say he'd been deposited here, far from the security of home, by that great migration following upon the First Five Year Plan. From fellow-native feeling I bought a cake from him, but when I bit into it, I found there nothing akin to my memory of it, only a skimpiness of flavoring that bespoke Xi'ning's scarcities.

They seemed to go in for drinking too. Across the street there were bulletin boards setting out the risks alcohol exposed one to, just as there were billboards along the highway forbidding you to drive after drinking. Returning from the long-distance coach station the previous day, I had seen a sozzled man slumped on the pavement surrounded by a pool of his own vomit. But public drunkenness and other signs of social disintegration are on the whole rare in China, though the one commodity Chinese towns are never short of is drink; at a late hour it is more easily available than food.

Another way I found to catch a sense of life here was simply to strike up acquaintances. Sun, as I will call him, was a driver, and when we met him he was sitting by himself at a table in a Muslim canteen in the neighborhood of the Eastern Pass. He was a strapping, open-faced, affable man, who did not hesitate to start up a conversation with us and to tell us what he thought of the Four Modernizations: "Nothing but codswallop and talking big." We didn't have time to take up his invitation to visit him at home, but I imagine he lived quite well, for he said he earned 110 yuan a month (about U.S. $55), which is a very good wage in China.

As a driver he'd been everywhere, he said. At this, the cook, who had come to sit with us, remarked, "Ah, but not Taiwan."

"Of course not," said Sun. "If I had I wouldn't be here now, would I? I'd have stayed." He rattled on volubly, and at one point observed, "It's per capita income that counts, let me tell you. Taiwan can't be a bad place, can it, if its per capita income is so much higher than China's? I've always maintained the proof of the pudding is in the eating."

Months later, Takia would receive a letter from him saying that he had been framed and imprisoned. He had lost his job, he added;

and seeing he had eight mouths to feed—himself, his wife, his four children, and two parents—would we please send him some money?

We were treated very kindly by Fang Zhinan, a painter to whom we were given an introduction by someone we had met on the train from Liujia Gorge. His house was hard to find, being in an old part of town where life is lived behind mud-wall enclosures shutting out the dusty lanes. Fang was napping when we arrived, for, as his wizened wife explained when she admitted us, he had had a heart attack and needed plenty of rest. They seemed to live in two rooms, he in one and she in the other. When he woke she led us into his room and then withdrew. He turned out to be a man of seventy, with a dignified and quiet manner, and a thin, sallow face that bore the marks of his recent illness. When he had settled into his chair his wife popped in with tea and toffee and cigarettes. They spoke to each other in a dialect I did not understand, in the half-heard voices of people who could afford to mumble because they could perfectly sense each other's thoughts.

He was still painting; you could see this from the brushes on his desk and the drawing pegged across the length of the wall above his bed. Recently sketched, this rough was to be a mural of the Qilian Range, the thickly forested mountains to Qinghai's east. I marveled that he could paint in that room, it was so cramped. He is a painter in the old style; one would not have cared to be in his shoes, I thought, during the Cultural Revolution. But he appeared to have no grievance, and never spoke of that traumatic time or, indeed, of the past at all, except to mention that he had gone to art school in Shanghai, and to point to an old framed photograph on the wall of himself when young and his very eminent mentor, Qi Baishi. Now he seemed to be active in the provincial art society, and spoke of an official attempt to reach out to the regions inhabited by the Tibetan minority where lie, in all their opulence of color, the artistic triumphs of lama Buddhism.

Presently Fang summoned his son to meet us. The younger Fang is a graphic artist with the Provincial Light Industrial Products Design Research Office. His wife is a librarian, and they and their children live in two rooms in a building next door, sharing a court-yard with the parents and several other households. That Sunday he most kindly invited us to lunch, which consisted of noodles he had cooked himself, his wife being on duty at the municipal library. (We visited her there one morning, and found the place as little like a library as it was possible for a building to be, with the ground floor suggesting a farmhouse and the upper floor a ghostly tunnel unenlivened by any hint of people or books. It was heart-rending, the dearth it reflected.)

Their old-world good manners obliging them to make a return visit, the younger Fang and his wife came to our hotel that evening. At the desk they were told we were out. This was a lie, the sort Chinese functionaries often tell when they want to isolate the foreign visitor from the native. The compatriotic feeling strikes most Chinese émigrés when they go to China, but it only takes an incident like that to make me feel the enormous gulf that still separates insider from outsider. There is no escaping it: anybody from across the border is necessarily a carrier of ideas or habits incompatible with the ideological health of the inhabitants. Before our stay in Xi'ning was over, Mr. Chen, who headed the newly instituted branch of the China Travel Service in the city, would pay the old painter a visit. (The China Travel Service, the Foreign Affairs Office, and the Public Security Bureau are the officialdom from which almost no visitor to China is free.) The visit was certainly not prompted by mere sociability, for the two had never met before, and when Chen turned up at Fang's doorstep his pretext was that he had come looking for me. We heard of it only later, and it disconcerted me to think how put out Fang must have been, for until recently people who associated with foreigners ran great risks of being denounced and attacked. Before our departure we made a point of calling on Fang to apologize for the trouble we had caused him. He with great tact brushed it aside, and said that it didn't matter. But actually it did matter, or at least it did to me, for it suggested that an outsider can never really evade official surveillance in China.

Chen himself was someone we saw much of in Xi'ning. Almost

as soon as we arrived we applied to him to travel to the county of Maduo, near the headwaters of the Yellow River. In his bid for tourism he seemed amenable at first, for we bribed him with the offer to let the Travel Service use Takia's photographs for postcards and publicity; but when it came to the point he did not deliver. He'd referred the matter to the Foreign Affairs Office and the Public Security Bureau, and they had said "No"; ours not to reason why.

For his part, he thought I'd never make it anyway: the journey was very arduous and I looked far too thin. There was no answer to that; all the books I'd read suggested it was a disagreeable area, and there was something in the desolations of Qinghai that put one or two authors in mind of death. One thing I must say for Chen, he never ceased to bathe us in his smiles. Even as he shook his head at us he beamed. Though he had seemed keen enough on the idea at the beginning to discuss with us the details of transport and costs, and even the possibility of a discount, the proposed journey was now spoken of as though it were a folly to which no seriousness could ever conceivably have been attached.

It was quite out of the question, he implied as he said, grinning, "I don't mind telling you—speaking strictly personally—you don't want to go up there, you'd never withstand the altitude sickness . . . the rarefied air up there . . . your heart palpitating like mad . . . at least five days to recover—and we've no oxygen masks."

That was not all. There had been—we must have heard about it— a frightful snowstorm up in the Qinghai grasslands in April, with millions of sheep stranded and miles of road blocked. The government had had to pump millions of yuan in relief funds to the stricken areas, but the poor livestock had died in the hundreds of thousands.

Chen was of ineffable good humor, but in between the flashes of bonhomie he gave us to understand that his patience was not inexhaustible. Although I expostulated, and bargained, it was clear that there was nothing more to be said, and that he wished us away. When I got up to go his round face looked up at me, creased for a good-humored chuckle. When I left his office I could feel him putting us out of his mind with a dismissing mental grin.

Kumbum

The bus, which only left when it was full, left Xi'ning at 11:15 a.m. By 12:20 we were in Huangzhong, having driven in a southwesterly direction, passing pink hills tinged with the green of what was possibly barley. Huangzhong itself is nothing much, but the terminus where the bus stops is the start of the incline which takes you up to where the Yellow Sect of lamas was born.

According to legend, what happened is this. One day, drawing water from a stream, a shepherd's wife fell into a swoon upon a large stone. She awoke to a feeling of pain in her side. Nine months later, in 1357, she gave birth to a son, who from the time he was born was adult in appearance and demeanor, possessing a white beard, and speaking as though he had an awareness of man's destiny.

When, at the age of three, Tsong-Khapa (as the child was called) decided to renounce the world for the religious life, his mother shaved off his hair. From where she had thrown his flowing tresses, there instantly grew a scented tree, on every leaf of which a character of Tibet's sacred language was inscribed. He himself retreated to the mountains, approaching eternal mysteries through prayer, vegetarianism, abstemiousness, meditation, and, above all, through taking instructions from a wise stranger who appeared from a remote place in the west. Later Tsong-Khapa's wanderings would take him to Lhasa, and there, in the loneliest corner of town, he began to teach the doctrine that would turn the old forms of Tibetan Buddhism upside down. His disciples, who came to be called Yellow Cap lamas after the headgear they wore, greatly multiplied, spreading not only in what is now modern Tibet, but also in Tsong-Khapa's native Qinghai, or Amdo as it was called then.

Pilgrims came to worship at the mountain at whose foot Tsong-Khapa was born, and lamas of many regions gathered here from afar. In this way the lamasery of Kumbum was born. The Chinese nowadays call it Taersi, but it is better known to the outside world as Kumbum, which is Tibetan for Ten Thousand Images, a reference to the leaves of the tree which grew from Tsong-Khapa's hair.

It has long been a destination for travelers. Father Huc, the intrepid French Lazarist who set off for Lhasa with the aim of converting the Dalai Lama to Roman Catholicism and turning him into a sort of branch-Pope, came here over one hundred and thirty years ago. He thought Yellow Cap lamaism uncannily suggestive of Catholic inspiration, and identified well over a dozen things the two religions had in common: " . . . the cross, the miter, the dalmatic, the cape, which the grand lamas wear on their journeys, or when they are performing some ceremony out of the temple; the service with double choirs, the psalmody, the exorcisms, the censer, suspended from five chains, and which you can open or close at pleasure; the benedictions given by the lamas by extending the right hand over the heads of the faithful, the chaplet, ecclesiastical celibacy, spiritual retirement, the worship of the saints, the fasts, the processions, the litanies, the holy water . . . " He was quick to propose the Catholic origin of these features, and went on to suggest that, since Tsong-Khapa's lifespan coincided exactly with the introduction of Christianity into Central Asia, the stranger from the west under whom he studied could have been a European missionary!

Yet to Peter Fleming, who came here in 1935, Kumbum was anything but familiar. "I had been, as every traveler has, in many kinds of temples," he writes, but "never before in one where I had that tight, chill, tingling feeling which I suppose is something between spiritual awe and physical fear."

All the same, whatever one may think of Father Huc's theory, one does find in Kumbum, beyond that certain sameness one detects in all holy places, a quality—of barbarity and splendor, intensity and fright—that suggests the Spanish Church, say, in Mexico. At any rate, Mexico was what came to mind when I wandered about the purlieus of the lamasery, and I could only put it down to the effect produced when you have people living high up on a plateau. It also came to me, seeing a Tibetan lady in a homburg hat, that translating her into a South American Indian would not meet resistance at too many points.

Kumbum is unmistakably a Tibetan stronghold. Yet, for all that the Tibetans in Qinghai are descended from the sanguine Tanguts, the so-called Western Barbarians who used to rampage about Qinghai, I could not help feeling that the true go-getters of the place remained the Huis, or Muslims. It was Muslims who manned the shops and stalls lining the approach to the lamasery. And not only were they offering tea, popsicles, and the tasty Muslim dish of noodles spiced with crushed chilies, black pepper, and garlic, but, being astute businessmen, they were also selling religious souvenirs of a distinctly lamaist cast. The effect of this was not unlike that of coming upon a Chinese immigrant running a kosher takeaway outside a synagogue, say, in New York.

These vendors stand in the true line of the Mohammedan trader, I thought, the line of the Tartary caravan, the rich merchant dealing in fur. The races are not really equal in China, the Han Chinese being all too dominant everywhere, but as Takia observed, "Even among the minority communities you see a pecking order, with the Muslims exploiting the Tibetans." Just as, say, the immigrant Indians of the Caribbean maintained the upper hand in retail trade over the native islanders, while they themselves were lorded over by the British, so Muslims are pursuing their advantages over Tibetans under the overall control of the Chinese here.

As well as Huis and Tibetans, there were other minorities about Kumbum. I saw not a few Tu women, in black waistcoats and blue tunics, the collars high and attractively trimmed with embroidery. Their tribe, which numbers some one hundred twenty thousand, lives clustered about the northern banks of the Huangshui, the Yellow River tributary, especially in the settlement called Huzhu. The Tus consider themselves related to the Mongols, tracing their ancestry to a general once stationed here by Genghis Khan. Certainly, though they borrow many religious terms from Tibetan, the language they speak is of the Mongolian-Altaic family. Yellow Sect lamaism is very much part of the grain of Tu life; and it used to be that, because so many of their boys went off to become monks, girls when they reached the age of fifteen were, by a ceremony marked by dressing the hair in a different style, rendered fit for casual couplings, the fruit of which was deemed the responsibility solely of the girl's family.

I am told that such mores no longer prevail, and I suppose that in the end this is the fate that will overtake the whole tribe—to go through the ordained stages of sinicization until it has lost its distinctive customs and become Chinese. And I see this happening even as, under the government's more liberal minority policy, the non-Chinese races are regaining their native identity. For I cannot see how the Chinese policy toward minorities, or for that matter the policy of any dominant race toward a minority, can be aimed at anything other than assimilation, however gentle the Chinese way may seem compared to, say, that of the white settlers where American Indians or Australian aborigines were concerned.

Ultimately the tribal communities will have to accept the Chinese socialist way of life. For the moment they live side by side with the Chinese, rather than together, in the administrative units—the autonomous region on one level, the autonomous prefecture and county on another—that are set apart for them. In theory the minorities have a hand in running their own affairs: in areas that are racially mixed or predominantly occupied by minorities, representation in the local organs of political power is supposed to reflect the ethnic composition of the population. And at the National People's Congress, the minorities are vouchsafed one hundred fifty votes, more than twice the number they would have got on a proportional basis. Yet in the last resort it is not these organs, but the Communist Party, which calls the tune, and in that quarter it is the Chinese who have the upper hand. There is no question at all of who is boss.

The issue is big, but the scale is small. While by official count there are fifty-five minority peoples in China, they make up only six percent of the population. Nevertheless, they inhabit over half of the land area of China, and though much of this comprises some of the most inhospitable places on earth, forests and mineral resources are bountiful there, and when you think of the uncongenial neighbors these places adjoin—the U.S.S.R., for instance, or Vietnam—you can understand why the Chinese cannot just let the minorities be.

Besides, one can never really know which, for the minorities, is the better deal: to be left alone, and therefore to have the cultural gap widen into material economic ones; or to opt for Chineseness, and thereby to have at least the potential for competing with the Chinese on an equal footing. Is it better for them to learn the Chinese language (at the expense, necessarily, of their own), or is it better to remain unacquainted with the wider world because of their ignorance of Chinese, the language into which foreign literatures and scientific works are translated? Is it better for the Tus to be left grazing their sheep over the hills above the valleys of the Huangshui, or is it better to persuade them to irrigate and make their land fit for profitable farming? It is impossible to answer such questions for others.

The questions got short shrift in 1966, when the Red Guards set out to destroy every old custom, however cherished or religiously significant. It surprised me to find Kumbum whole, when all but the greatest monuments in Tibet, I am told, were destroyed. It was because, my informants told me, the power of the community proved stronger than the power of the Red Guards. Whatever the explanation, Tibetan Buddhism did seem to hold its own here. I hear that in the world's largest lamasery, the Drepung Monastery in Tibet, the number of monks has shrunk from ten thousand to a mere two hundred forty. Nobody could give me comparable figures in Kumbum, but it felt to me intensely religious still; and when I stepped into the grounds of the monastery, and caught sight of my first worshiper, I could see for myself how inviolate was the inner force of the faith.

It was a most peculiar spectacle. What an image of far-gone veneration, I thought as I watched. The setting is a sandy triangular space, along one side of which some Muslim hawkers are gathered. Towering across the other side of it, two and a half times the height of man, is a row of eight stone stupas (*chorten*) raised to commemorate martyred lamas. Surveying all, the buildings of the lamasery rise up in tiers of shimmering roofs. Here, at the apex of the triangle, a Tibetan woman is measuring out with her body the holy distance to the lamasery. She is covered all over with sand; her hair is knotted and long; she is at one with some mysterious force, possessed by

some arcane ecstasy. First she stands at attention facing the lamasery; then she bends her trunk and, placing her hands on the ground
and straightening her legs, falls to her face and lies full length with
her forehead on the ground. A moment later she lifts herself up,
almost like someone doing push-ups, straightens up, faces the monastery again, and repeats the whole exercise from start to finish. She
will go on doing this all day, flopping at one step, standing up at
the next, until she has crawled the length of the sacred grounds on
her belly, leaving off only when darkness falls, and returning to
complete the circuit at dawn.

It is easy to see why Tibetan Buddhism has habitually repelled
unbelievers. Picturesque though it undeniably is, to many observers
the beauty wears an evil aspect, like the magic and witchcraft of
the Indian Tantrism by which it is said to have been debased. "De-
monology" and "degeneracy" are the terms which observers have
often used of it; and the element which they see standing, above
all, as a focal illustration of this is the lama priesthood. Headed by
the Dalai Lama, the reincarnation, so Tibetans believe, of all his
predecessors, these monks seem the very negation of saintliness—
"perverted," some have said of them, "moralless panderers," others
have thought. "No priestly caste in the history of religion," wrote
Percival Lander, the *Times* correspondent who accompanied a
British military expedition to Tibet in 1904, "has ever preyed upon
the terror and ignorance of its flock with the systematic brigandage
of the lamas."

Such was the range of his role and power that the lama was not
only religious officiant and truth expounder, but predator, landown-
er, and despotic regulator of the lives of his stupefied congregations.
There used to be thousands of them, their ranks ceaselessly renewed
not only by the decree that every first son become a monk, but by
the practice, prompted as much by devotion as by indigence, of
offering up children to the monasteries. This made for a disproportion between the marriageable members of the sexes, for the lamas
are celibate in theory, if not always so in practice; and this is perhaps
why, as among the Tus, illegitimacy is not looked upon as a disgrace.

The immediate impression the lamas of Kumbum gave me, though, was of robustness and charm, and not the qualities one expects of an order supposedly sunk in degeneracy, or from reading accounts of Tibet, where all is squalor, it seems, and raggedness. These lamas didn't look at all worn-out: tall, smoothly shaven, their shoulders handsomely slung about with the folds of their brick-red robes, their skins the mahogany glow which living in the mountains gives to the complexion. Here was a group, gathered on the steps of a lesser temple, companionably cleaning and polishing a stack of brass butter lamps, and engaged in animated conversation. It was a vivid spectacle, so vivid that it suggested a tableau, as the sun bounced off the lamps and the shaven heads, and picked out the temple cornices' filigree.

To get up to where the monks were we had climbed a bumpy path, with the distant cirque enclosing our view and the drizzle suddenly clearing just as Takia was mentally putting away his cameras. It wasn't a particularly busy track; here and there we met boy novices in their early teens, carrying pails of water up to the monastery. They passed us silently, smelling of butter. Their black skirts gave them the sexual ambiguity of priests. At one point a Tibetan woman appeared around a corner, a beautiful creature, with her hair braided in many slender plaits, the ends of which, hanging below the waist, were bound by cloths of different colors. She smiled at us as we passed—a flash of white teeth brilliantly set off by the gleaming copper of her skin.

At the top we found ourselves amidst a complex of buildings and symbols: temples, halls of meditation, stupas, pillars of Buddhist inscription, prayer wheels, the monks' quarters. The exteriors were a jumble of colors—emerald, red, yellow, blue, and golden—the interiors more so. In one shrine we saw a glorious array of Buddhist idols carved out of gaudily tinted yak butter. In another we saw the bronze statue of Tsong-Khapa, in a motley of brocade, tassels, gems, and gold. In the Hall of Meditation, the figures of Buddha paneling the wall, the tankas (Tibetan paintings on cloth), the carpets, the silk-swathed pillars and the canopies were a claustrophobic riot of color. As we wandered about these places, the sensations followed each other so thick and fast that the memory of them is a blur of scarcely separable images.

Outside the hall, the entire porch was taken up by prostrating pilgrims, many of them women. Some stood with their arms raised before flopping forward on their bellies; others, their absorption not quite total, looked out of the corners of their eyes at us looking at them. Once they were on the floor, they did a scraping and sliding routine, heaving themselves up and down the porch while their hands, resting on pads, moved back and forth along grooves which countless pilgrims had gouged and rubbed smooth in the wooden floorboards.

The passages between the temples disclosed rows of large prayer wheels, rainbow-colored barrels which, at a flick of the hand by a pilgrim, twirled about a vertical axis, symbolically releasing prayers. When we came upon them two pilgrims had set them all spinning. Takia fell into conversation with the older of the two, a large swarthy Tibetan whose station was proclaimed not only in his adoption of Chinese costume—the blue, baggy, high-buttoned suit—but in the quality of its cloth. It transpired that he was a big shot in the Autonomous Prefecture of Gande, a vice chairman of the Standing Committee of the People's Congress (the younger man was his son-in-law). Moved by sociability, he lent us the benefit of his position, and offered to take us into the inner reaches of the monastery.

We entered another set of buildings, one that stood higher on the hillside, above and behind. There was a floor of apartments, approached by a steep and dusty staircase. The place was dark and, as far as I could see, unfurnished. As I reached the landing, followed by my guides and an old monk who had attached himself to the party, there was a slight creaking noise from the recesses of an upstairs room. I peered into the dark to see who it was. A moment later and he appeared from around the door, a little novice in a burgundy cloak, very bashful and sweet. Seeing Takia point his camera, he darted back into the room. The old monk, wishing to oblige Takia, almost overdid the thing by dragging the boy out into the sunshine

and, his eyes smiling impishly, telling him exactly where and how
to pose. I noticed that the boy held something in his hand; it was
the scriptures he was studying when we came upon him—an old
book in Tibetan, with movable leaves which, not being bound or
sewn together, lay between two thin wooden sheaves fastened together by string. It was perhaps a hundred years old.

The vice-chairman led us on at a spanking pace. We went through
a backyard or two, round and about some buildings undergoing
repairs, in and out of shrines, until we arrived at an opening into a
courtyard. In the course of our tour we met many more monks,
but as we had no language in common, they were profitless if pleasant encounters, with much shaking of hands and nodding of heads.
At the courtyard we were left to our own devices. We entered, and
found ourselves looking into a Tibetan surgery.

It was a small, wooden building, with two physicians seeing patients in one room and a pharmacist dispensing herbal medicine in
another. The doctors took not the slightest notice of me, and so I
strolled over to watch them at their art, not from the door as might
have been proper, but right by the desks at which they were sitting. Each had a book (it may have been the eighth-century medical
classic *The Four Tantras*) by his elbow open at a page with a diagram
of human anatomy, and each flittered his bony fingers across it. I
was struck again by that fine Tibetan skin that seems like polished
wood. Their patients were three Tu women, one of them young and
full-skirted, and charged with a sort of gypsy smolder. Old and
confident in their heritage, the doctors worked with regal ease. I
watched one of them place three of his fingers on his patient's wrist,
to feel her pulse. Was it the throb of the arteries he was feeling, the
pulse Tibetan medicine terms "black," to distinguish it from the
imperceptible "white" turbulences of the nervous system?

Diagnosing by pulse may have been a Chinese graft, transplanted
with the two Han princesses, who when they came to marry their
Tibetan kings in the seventh century, and thereby to forge the first
links between the two cultures, were accompanied by an entourage
of medical practitioners and books. But there was also the native
know-how, centuries old, accumulated through experience and

through the opportunity for first-hand anatomical and pathological study afforded by the peculiarly Tibetan way of disposing of the dead—by cutting up the corpse and feeding the pieces to vultures. There is said to be great truth to Tibetan embryology, for all its seeming implausibility. It was in advance of other ancient medical systems in positing the embryo as a union of paternal semen and maternal blood, and in seeing its growth as a progression of forms—from fish, to turtle, to pig—that mirrors the stages of the evolution of mankind, rather as modern theory supposes fetal development to do.

Like any healer worth his salt the Tibetan physician can read the signs that point to a patient's malady from the tongue and the urine (specifically its color, smell, sedimentation at different hours, and the sound it makes when jiggled). A Tibetan physician knows 440 maladies in all—no more, no less—and for each he has a remedy. At the same time as he administers to the age-old beliefs in charms and spells, in the excrement of the Dalai Lama and the efficacy, for restoring faltering virility, of swallowing a young man's piss, he can name just such combinations of vegetable, mineral, and animal ingredients, from the thousand and more listed in his pharmaco-poeia, as would restore his patient to health.

The Qinghai-Tibetan plateau supplies most of the ingredients named in the pharmacopoeia, gentian and hawk gizzard being two of the commonest. Father Huc tells us how, returning from its "botanico-medical expeditions" to the mountains, Kumbum's medical faculty used to prepare these drugs for consumption: drying them over a fire, grinding them into powder, dividing them into smaller doses, and packaging them for sale in red paper, every one appropriately labeled. Because water boils on the plateau at a lower temperature than at normal altitudes, it never gets hot enough for making the medicinal broths common in Chinese folk medicine; and, pills apart, the drugs come pre-soaked in alcohol as liquors, ointments, and pastes. What impresses me most about these drugs is that they can be encapsulations of thirty or eighty different in-gredients, as for example the margarita pill, a treatment used both in China and abroad for paralysis and the after-effects of cerebro-vascular diseases.

We saw some of these medicines for ourselves in the dispensary next door. The pharmacist was an elderly man in sun-faded blue who gave us the run of the place but disdained to talk to us. The interior, while threadbare, was clean and neat. The drugs in their containers looked arcane to me, but did not suggest quackery. Apparently Tibetan medicine is of proven efficacy in the treatment of certain ailments to which mountain dwellers are particularly prone: ulcers, high blood pressure, an excess of red blood corpuscles, rheumatoid arthritis, and epilepsy.

Time sped for us that afternoon. In the declining sunlight we left Kumbum for Xi'ning. We shared the bus with a mass of humanity and one resplendently robed Mongolian, a giant of a young man who moved cumbrously in his boots and dress. His dress, fleece-lined, was bordered with otter skin and faced with jade-green satin brocade.

The bus completed the journey safely and we arrived in Xi'ning in the early evening and smack into a cloud of dust. A sandstorm had sprung up, and threatened to wipe out the remaining light as effectively as night. I put on my glasses, partly because I sometimes think I see better with them on, and partly to screen my eyes from the dust. I trudged to the hotel going through in memory and anticipation my routine with the thermos flask and ice-cream container.

Koko Nor

All through the drive from Xi'ning to the vast blue scoop the Mongols call Koko Nor, we were chased by jagged snowy ridges and signs of pasturage in the foothills. The day had begun overcast, but in the afternoon the sky cleared, and the distances became purplish. A flash of blue signaled the approach to the lake, an iridescence below the horizon, whose hazy reaches were duplicated by a blur at the base of the sky. So few people had seen these waters that to Peter Fleming, sighting them in 1935, they gave a feeling, as he put it, "of forgotten magnificence, of beauty wasted." To his Swiss companion Ella Maillart, the lake "symbolized an almost unrealizable ambition." To us, seeing it for the first time that cold afternoon in June, the impact was nothing short of stupendous.

In that setting, with the mountains marching away behind, and the colors shifting one against the next with the movement of our car, seeing the immensity of the lake unfold was like the curtains drawing apart for Cinemascope. It defies the wide-angle lens, having no visible culmination or limit, you cannot tell where the water ends and the sky begins, the blue of the one melting into the azure of the other. And as your car moves along the shore, it is hard to know whether the bands of aquamarine, Prussian blue, or lapis lazuli streaking across your view come of the depth or the light. In all China there can't be a more vividly blue place than this.

It is partly the scale, running far beyond ordinary bounds, that makes you think there isn't always that sameness to your lakes after all—the same backcloth of mountains, the same luminous sky. But it is also the feeling of utter solitude to the place, the feeling that, once stumbled upon, these deserted shores should remain a jealously guarded secret, so remote are they, so romantically isolated in sensation.

About a million years ago the lake was formed by a fault in the earth's strata. For a time it was the source of the Huangshui, the Yellow River tributary which runs through Xi'ning. But as the climate grew drier and the surrounding country higher, so the Huangshui was cut off from the mass of water.

Legend has it that the lake was filled with the waters of a vast reservoir once covering the site on which the Tibetan capital of Lhasa now stands. In those days, so the story goes, there lived a Tibetan king who, each time he raised a temple at a certain spot, saw it crumbling to pieces before it could be finished. Anxious to know why, he sent a lama to the east, to seek the counsel of a saint who, it was rumored, possessed the secret answer to this riddle.

The lama set off; but though he looked everywhere, he could

The furrowed face of immemorial China: an old-timer in Qinghai Province.

One of the many women workers in the Victory Oilfields, Shandong Province; this one mans diesel engines.

◀ (left) *Popsicle hawkers and commercial advertising in Daguanyuan Bazaar in Ji'nan, Shandong Province; the hoarding used to carry political messages.*

◀ (right) *Fruit and vegetables on sale in an alley in Ji'nan, Shandong Province.*

◀ (bottom) *The Chinese instant dream factory: a portrait photographer snaps two women behind a cardboard car beside the Yellow River Bridge in Lanzhou, Gansu Province.*

(top) *A lama polishes a brass butter lamp in a courtyard in Kumbum, birthplace of the Yellow Sect of lamas in Qinghai Province.*

(bottom) *Chinese Muslim worshipers gather for prayers in the courtyard of a mosque in Xi'ning, Qinghai Province.*

(top) *The First Yellow River Bridge stands to the southwest of Maduo, close to the source of the river.*
(bottom) *Fishermen encamped on the shore of Ngoring Nor, a lake near the source of the Yellow River, twelve hundred feet above sea level, in Qinghai Province.*

(top) *Men and donkeys pull earth-moving carts along the Garden Entrance embankment, Henan Province.*
(bottom) *The Yellow River waters an oasis in the Tengger Desert, near the Shapotou Sand Control Station.*

Crossing the Yellow River by ferry near Zhongwei, to the north of which lies a remnant of the Great Wall.

Industry and agriculture go hand in hand in the Victory Oilfields, Shandong Province: an oil extractor, oil drums, workers' housing, and grain farming.

◀ *The Yellow River is held back by a dam across Liujia Gorge.*

High dykes and piles of rock stand in readiness at Luokou, Shandong Province, for the summer spate of the Yellow River, a mere stream in November.

turn up nothing. One day, as he was setting back home across the steppes separating Tibet from China, the girth of his saddle snapped, and he was tumbled from his horse. It was near a pond, with a tattered tent pitched to one side. The lama entered, and finding a blind old man huddled at prayer inside, asked if he could have something for mending his strap. The old man offered the lama one of his own straps, and, believing his visitor to be a fellow Mongol, spoke disdainfully of the Tibetan efforts (which he had heard tell) to build a temple equal in splendor to the Mongol ones. They would never succeed, he added, for unknown to them they lived above an underground sea, the waters of which sapped whatever foundations they drove into it. "I only impart this secret," the old man continued, "because you are a Mongol lama; but if ever it gets out to a Tibetan the waters of that sea will march from his kingdom to ours, and we shall all be buried under the waves."

The lama revealed his identity then, and, urging the old man to flee at once, he leapt onto his horse and disappeared into the desert. When the old man's son returned to the tent he found his father in great dismay. A foreign lama had stolen a strap from him, the old man said, and unless the thief was killed they shall all be inundated. The son thought the old man was probably raving; so, when he did catch up with the Tibetan lama, he took only the strap and not his life. When he returned he handed this to his father, whereupon the old man shuddered all over. The son had been outwitted, he realized, for in Mongolian the word for "strap" was the same as the one for "secret."

And so the deluge came, a great rumbling and heaving, the earth opening with convulsions, and the underground torrents spilling forth and spreading. Like an immense sea it rolled, over the plains, the animals, the people. To the east the waters rushed; to the west, the waters having evacuated it, the Tibetans were able to raise an incomparable temple. And as the years passed and the population grew, there accreted to the temple a great city, to which the citizens gave the name of Lhasa.

Thus Koko Nor, the sight we were after that morning. I made the trip in the company of several nurses and students from Hong

Kong; for nowadays even forgotten corners have to pay their way, and Koko Nor, long out of bounds, is open to visitors provided they are of Chinese origin. The nurses were bound for the Gobi Desert, but thought they would make a detour while they were at it. This was all to the good, because it meant Takia and I could split the cost of the minibus with them. We set off just before nine, taking the road which the People's Liberation Army built in the 1950s to link Xi'ning with Lhasa.

Our guide was a young, fraiily built, bespectacled man, a graduate of Chungking University, where he said he'd studied French. At first his distant manner had about it the character of someone nervous at finding himself in charge. Later on, though, he noticeably relaxed, and even accepted my offer of a windcheater to put over his blue cotton suit when the temperature suddenly dropped. Still later, catching sight of his too big shoes trampling on the prairie, and of the holes in his socks peeping above their heels, I quite surrendered to the pathos of his appearance.

We left Xi'ning behind us, passed under poplars, erect as chimneys, and found ourselves running close to the Huangshui, the rivulet which held within it a green shimmer that was the wooded banks reflected. I never thought Qinghai could be so lush, my preconceptions having led me to expect the wastes of the encircling Tsaidam Basin. If it weren't for those solitary figures in straw hats glimpsed crouching amid the wheat ears, I could quite easily have believed myself in Switzerland.

At Huangyuan, a staging post, we turned abruptly southwest, and presently arrived at Daotanghe. The name means Backward Trickling River, and is a reminder that a stream once emptied into Koko Nor here. As we lunched off some bread in the minibus, I could feel the pastures climbing and the air thinning and getting sharper. We were soon in lovely alpine country, with the panorama of snow peaks stretching to the left and right of my horizon. Just after two o'clock a high wind rose, and suddenly we found ourselves buffeted on all sides by snow. The driver said we'd never make it to our destination, for in this weather the last stretch, an unpaved path, would be impassable with mud. He pursed his lips, shook his head over the prospects, and I formed the opinion that he was secretly delighted because, as he'd said at one point, he didn't much care for driving. But we were to be in luck, for the snow stopped as abruptly as it had started; long before we reached the turning at Heimahe (or Black Horse River), the town where we were to abandon the road for the dirt track, the sky had cleared. A little later the skylit lake broke upon my vision in crystalline immensity, and all pessimism went from me.

We were following the southern route, the one that put the shore on our right. To our left, on grassy slopes, there would sometimes appear grazing yaks and sometimes solitary tents. At my first sight of these black, shaggy-haired animals, I had thought them perfectly hideous—neither ox nor hog, the hair on their bellies trailing on the ground. But later I thought them just right for the landscape—well architectured, with their short, strong limbs, for the rugged slopes. Their meat is said to be excellent, their milk even more so. When we stopped at a Tibetan tent I saw a girl churning the milk into butter with a thick round wooden stick which came up to her eyes. The Tibetans eat it melted into tea, with the parched barley meal they call tsampa.

Tibetan tents were the only human habitation in sight. The one we looked into, out of simple curiosity, had a few sheepskins strewn on the earthen floor, a collection of ash-smeared pots in a corner, and a small stove fueled by dung patties in the center. Here was all a Tibetan wanted of civilization; few people could be much nearer Stone Age man. In front of the stove was huddled an old man such as you always seem to find in a Tibetan tent, gazing silently ahead of him. I was sure he could not see; but it was not this which made him take not the slightest notice of us, it was his utter self-absorption. There were two women, one young and exquisite, the other—her mother?—wizened and too ugly to be true: amongst these dwellers in thin air one never seems to encounter any transitional age between bloom and decay. The girl was dressed in the Tibetan style in a skirt of cord and an oversized sheepskin robe worn with the wool inside and the top half slipped back from the shoulders and held up by a bright pink sash wound several times round her pelvis.

The most spectacular part of a Tibetan woman's toilette, I think, is her hair. I had occasion to study this closely the next day, when we stopped at a tent where a religious ceremony was in progress, and I found myself standing behind a seated row of women at worship. Artfully braided, their hair was a tallowed glory, ornately patterned, stuck with shells and silver ornaments of a heaviness surely to precipitate balding, the multiple ends threaded into the cloth of a rose-colored, two-ply band. I thought to myself: once dressed, it must never be loosened, so lavish is the time and labor it costs. And I wondered if there was a connection between the elaborateness of their toilette and the rudeness of their living conditions.

The women, with lolling children in their laps, were sitting on the far edge of the tent. Not an eye strayed from the lama, conducting the ceremony at the other end. The place was thronged to suffocation, and the air smelled of Tibetan religion, from the lamps of yak butter on the altar. Outside, the wind lashed whiplike, flapping the tent sleeves and giving its prayer flags wings; these were red, and streamed from the roof. Sheep and horses, the nomad's wealth, grazed nearby. The pasturage was rich, the first grass having emerged in April and waited out the more than usually vengeful snows of that month. We would see sheep often in our journey to Koko Nor, and horses occasionally—a sudden charging herd across the grasslands, all arching backs and flaring nostrils against the empty sky. Like a cloud they would pass, chased by sun-browned Tibetans on horseback, the hoofs stamping the earth.

From the bus I watched them wonderingly, struck by the contrast between the nomadic existence of the mountains and the settled life of the valleys. What is it that gives the life of the saddle and the tent its envied quality, even as cold grips it in winter and rinderpest scourges it in spring? The horizons unrolling in continuum (because in any one encampment the land is poor)? The lungs expanding in fullness (because in any one inhalation the air is thin)? Where has that life led the nomad, but to the most inhospitable habitats on earth? So inhospitable that he has to move his herds six to seven times before the last move to the winter encampment, in every kind of weather, and at upwards of fourteen thousand feet.

It is an exacting life—yet how untrammeled is it by meanness—of scale and freedom. As well as their religion, the sapping effects on virility of horseback riding has been advanced as an explanation for the Tibetan nomads' low birthrate, for compared with the Chinese the Tibetans reproduce themselves thriftily. Yet set against his brother the sedentary Tibetan farmer, the nomad on horseback is acknowledged to be superior—healthier and more manly; to almost all Tibetans, whether of the steppe or the valley, nomadism is unquestionably the higher form of life. These nomads have shown that you can go short of telephones and live.

Yet I must confess that, much as I admire the Tibetan way of life, I was quite glad we were not sleeping in one of their black, sloping tents that night. From the few that I had seen, I knew them for what they were, uncomfortable and inadequate shelters; and I could easily imagine the clamminess of sleeping on damp earth, and the snow gusts blowing through.

There was, in fact, some uncertainty as to where exactly we were going to be put up. We were assured that arrangements had been made, but our guide seemed unaccountably reluctant to disclose the name of the place, and each time I brought the matter up, he clumsily changed the subject. When the time came we did all have a bed for the night, but to this day I am unable to locate the place on the map. When we arrived it was eight o'clock and the deferred dusk of June was settling in. I could see that it was a guesthouse of sorts, standing squat and barracklike in a yard. When Takia set off down to explore he found the lake to be within walking distance, but the approach to the shore was barred by a fence. The man in charge made us very welcome there, and rushed up and down the corridor to try and rustle up the right number of beds. A place to rest was all that had been promised; and sure enough, it was rustic. Except for the arctic room temperature we did not mind in the least, and anyhow, we successfully overcame that difficulty by sleeping two to a bed.

Before turning in I was visited by three children, two girls and a boy. I had found them peeping into my window, and I had invited them in. They were curious about everything I had with me, and inspected my plastic soapdish and Bic pen with especial awe. One of the girls, the taller of the two, looked long and hard at the dish, an expression of great admiration crossing her face; and then, in a tone of hushed respect, said to herself, "How perfectly lovely . . ." I had the sensation of being confronted with someone living in a pre-plastic age.

The girls told me they were twelve, the boy a little younger, but all of them looked small for their age. I asked them where they came from, and when I used the word "commune" they corrected me, saying it was not a commune, but a state farm (this is a large organization where, instead of work points, the workers receive cash wages). They lived nearby, which was how they had heard we were coming. Scarcely thinking that I would discomfort them, I then questioned them about their parents. Mother worked on the farm, the taller girl said. And what about father, said I? To my surprise she went quite shy, and hanging her head and looking down at her toes, gave me to understand that she did not wish to answer. For a moment I thought I had been tactless, that perhaps the girl didn't have a father; but Takia, from having noticed the security measures by the lake, grasped the point at once.

We had been struck by the beauty of the lake, and had not seen it in strategic terms. Now all was clearer—the guide's reticence about where we were staying, no less than this girl's uneasiness. The guesthouse, I realized, had something to do with the Chinese navy; and next morning an informant I had shamelessly cultivated confirmed what I already now suspected—that the lake was where warships were tested and crews trained in tactics. I thought it impressive that the girl was so well schooled in discretion she could not bring herself to tell me her father was in the navy. She quite put me to shame, and makes me feel like some craven blabbermouth even as I write this.

I wonder how the Tibetans feel about the presence of a submarine in their holy waters. For to them Koko Nor was decidedly holy, so much so that navigation upon its waters was forbidden, and to reach its islands they could only think of crossing it in winter, when the surface of the lake is iced over. Earlier travel accounts speak tantalizingly of a lamaist retreat, of golden temples and mystic monks, on an island hidden somewhere in the heart of the lake. The Russians had apparently reached it at the beginning of the century, and wandering missionaries had gazed upon it from the shore. But it was Sven Hedin, the greatest Central Asia explorer of all, who most stirred the imagination of later travelers with his descriptions. Later it turned out (if the explorer Leonard Clark is to be believed) that the golden temples were really caves. The island was a treeless hump, upon which, so Clark claimed, there could be detected an obo, that votive cairn of stones by which one recognizes the cult places of Tibetan shamanism. There were hermits who lived there; Clark heard of an old woman who had been a recluse on the island for fifteen years. Because of the difficulty of getting food supplies to her, her life must have been a sort of slow suicide, or, as I can't help thinking, a kind of debauchery in reverse.

Though monasteries are enjoying a revival of sorts in China, the days of holy retreats are long past, and today the hermit community no longer exists. What the lake offers, naval testing ground apart, is a remarkable colony of birds. Though only the most up-to-date maps will show it, there is a place in the northwest quarter of the lake which flourishes as a home for resident and migratory birds, and is for that reason named Bird Island.

Since 1977, the island and the bays around, an area 232 square miles in extent, have been declared a nature reserve. We were to drive across some of it, but before doing so our guide had to stop at the conservation office and obtain passes for us. While waiting for him my attention was drawn to a notice: in Chinese and English it prohibited the despoliation of the reserve, the collecting of eggs, the hunting of birds, and the taking of photographs; offenders were liable, it said, "to punishment, education, or a fine" by the Politics and Law Department. Another thing which stood out were the long rows of fish hung up to dry: the *huangyu,* a bright yellow scaleless fish with which Koko Nor abounds (two of these, each eighteen inches long, would end up as our supper that night).

After a few minutes we were on our way again. The reserve seemed wild, and the outcrops of rock made our progress bumpy.

Soon it became impossible to advance any further by car, and we all got out to walk the last stretch to the shore, with the sweep of a promontory within our sight. Nearing the water the land plunged, and as I dropped down the rocky cliff I saw in front of me a great white pitted rock, poking straight out of the lake like a giant finger, or a fang. It was a grotesque and disturbing sight, for all around the rim of its summit, which was coated with seasons of their droppings, were perched a brooding huddle of the blackest birds. They were not buzzards, but they had a raptorial feeling to them. I waited to see if one might leave the perch to dive for a fish, but there was not a stir of feather, or a beating of wing; there was only this mass of blackness up there against the sky.

But the sight of this perch, dramatic though it was, proved only a preliminary to the climax of the trip, which was the moment we came upon the main ornithological refuge at some distance from this spot. The narrow strip of water separating the island from the mainland having receded, Bird Island is strictly speaking a peninsula, and you can reach it quite easily on foot. One of the reserve's wardens came to show us the way. As I bounded down the island a fierce wind blew. The place seemed empty. But presently, reaching a hump that opened my view to the water, I saw the bird population thick upon the curve of the shore.

There were perhaps one hundred thousand of them: seagulls, cormorants, wild geese, the rare white swan. I did not move, and stood well away from them. But some of the people in the party, unable to overcome their curiosity, edged closer. There was a screech and a rustle and the flapping of wings, and then a sudden swarm of birds swooped all together toward the lake above our heads with an overarching spread of wings. One day the impact of this very dramatic place will be weakened by photography, for though it was not allowed, at this point half a dozen cameras clicked. I was sorry then that we were there, for if Bird Island is to remain a wildlife sanctuary, a place where birds will come every spring (as they have done for many generations), to lay their eggs and hatch their young, then trippers like us should never be allowed to come. Though we had come a month after hatching time, there were still some eggs about—blue for cormorant, speckled for seagulls—and even as I watched, I saw two baby wild geese writhe out of their shells.

The species seen here are only a fraction of the varieties to be found in Qinghai, for the plateau remains one of the wildest places in the country, home to more than six hundred varieties of water-fowl, or half the number native to China, as well as a range of exotic fauna, from wild camels to gazelles. One hears of snow leopards, musk deer, wild asses, lynx, foxes, antelope, and the "dragon-bred" wild horses of Qinghai lore. There were once some elks about, but the Chinese prize their horns as medicine, which no doubt reduced their numbers somewhat. Marmots have been spotted in these parts, and also alpine weasels. Qinghai even boasts of a blue sheep, a species known only to China, which grazes at sixteen thousand feet, and is said to be twice the size of the domestic sheep. Qinghai still offers wildlife without busloads of tourists, scientists, and hunters, and yet I couldn't help thinking, as I made my way back to our van, that we ourselves were the beginnings of that invasion—a fact I found unspeakably sad.

When we left the reserve a man and a woman emerged from a wooden cabin at the exit to inspect our van and make sure we hadn't taken any birds' eggs with us. We returned to Xi'ning by way of Mount Sun and Moon, a green, windswept height named for a moment in history. It was in the seventh century, when a Chinese princess, traveling with her retinue to the kingdom of Tibet, where a politically inspired marriage with a chieftain awaited her, ascended these heights and, seeing the highland harshness around, succumbed to a pang of homesickness. The contrast with her native Chang'an, that most glorious of capitals, must have been cruel. We are told—and here history is elaborated by legend—that at this point she took out a mirror, hoping to see in it an image of loved ones left behind, and all at once there came a flash, and bathed the place in a shining aureola.

Climbing to the summit of the mountain, I came upon a stone bearing the name Mount Sun and Moon. It was at this spot, perhaps, that the princess looked back upon the empire for the last time, for here China ended and foreign savagery began. The guide, telling us the story, told us also, raising his voice above the wind, that the mountain's other name was The Gateway to the Steppes.

Longyang Gorge

For fear of escorts and assistance, Takia and I did not tell the China Travel Service that we were going to Longyang (Dragon Sheep) Gorge, site of what will be, when completed, the biggest hydro-power project on the Yellow River, as well as the one furthest upstream. Allowing for stops the construction site is between five to six hours away from Xi'ning by car, and may be reached by a regular bus service (a 4-yuan or U.S. 2-dollar ride) by way of Mount Sun and Moon.

We arrived at the station early, and found it to be a place of unspeakable squalor. The waiting room had all the gloom of a cavern, with a smell that suggested a congested outhouse. There were huddled figures against every wall, gazing vacantly as they squatted there, their faces set in an expression of dazed resignation. There were Tibetans and Mongolians lying tumbled in dirty heaps, surrounded by bags of possessions. In that setting, where lines of motorbuses awaited instead of horses, these people looked sad, pinched, out of their depth, and in the last analysis degraded. It was impossible to contemplate them without thinking, they shouldn't be here, they should be upon the wild open steppe. This is not because they live in less poverty there, but because they seemed such sad misfits here, away from their open prairies, where the clouds run like herds of gazelles, and each spring brings forth, behind the line of retreating snow, carpets of blue gentian amid the green meadows.

The bus left on time, at 8 a.m. About half an hour later an inspector got on to carry out a check. This was evidently unexpected, and one passenger was caught without a ticket. When brought to book the offender could not have been more contrite, offering at once to pay. But the inspector, who was obliged to see the matter in terms of discipline and punishment, ordered the offender to get off the bus. This the man protested, and before we knew it the two were embroiled in a private row. The driver interceded, and though it may seem surprising that he chose to plead the passenger's cause against the inspector's, this was what he did and is something, I am quite sure, which happens often in China. The rest of the passengers sat through this with the attentiveness the Chinese usually accord public disagreements; I was surprised that more people didn't pitch in with opinions. As far as the discharge of his duties was concerned, the inspector seemed to me to be adequate in all but intransigence, and, invited by the driver to let the matter be, decided with a helpless shrug to get off the bus himself. But as we drove off I could still hear him shouting "Get off! Get off!" at the passenger.

For all that China is supposed to be a police state, a remarkable part of life escapes being squeezed by regimentation: sometimes there is no insuperable difficulty about circumventing a rule. And very often bystanders can be counted on to rally and smooth things over when a person is found out and brought to account. It so happened that in front of me sat a handsome Hui with his small son; just before our departure the conductor, coming upon the pair, told the father that the child should have a ticket as he looked well over a meter tall. Something less than a sound came from the father as the conductor yanked the boy from his seat with the growl, "Let's get him back to the station to be measured." But the boy wriggled out of his clutch and refused outright to be maneuvered out of his seat.

The conductor continued to tug at the boy, but even before the father could gather himself to protest, I could hear the bus stirring and the passengers murmuring objections. As the conductor went on tugging and the little boy went on ducking, the murmur grew louder, and there was no doubt that the conductor was making himself more and more unpopular. You could see that he did not want to give in too easily, but then he did not want to seem mulish either. Eventually, however, he felt compelled to let the matter drop, and walked back to his seat somewhat deflated. The father had put forth no defense, admitted no guilt; but it was everybody's opinion that in the case of a child not wishing to be parted from his father, even if it were for a few minutes only, any insistence on it must be considered churlish and pettifogging. In the tissue of Chinese life, sometimes strict, and often reached by too many functionaries and tensed by too much government, there does seem to run a streak of what Takia, witnessing all this, termed a "rigidly regulated anarchy." For the rest of the journey the conductor confined himself to what has always seemed to me to be the main function of the Chinese bus conductor, which is to light cigarettes for the driver. This ours did with expert aplomb, puffing at them two at a time.

Some time later we came in sight of an adobe hut. At this the driver stopped the bus, climbed down and disappeared into the hut. It was ten thirty—time for the driver's lunch. National behavior patterns will need a lot of modification before schedules cease to be at the mercy of the stomach. Most of us got out and just stood about, wishing there was something to drink. The air was very dry and dusty, and dull with a backwater torpor. It felt like the middle of nowhere.

The bus was slow to depart, but once it got going we did the rest of the journey in an unbroken lap. The road led us upward, into the terrain of Mount Sun and Moon. At a certain height the colors faded, the scrub vegetation giving way to patches of sandy desert. Then we were suddenly descending, and at a curve of the winding road I could see the wide valley below, the land turning greener as you watched, until you began to believe that this was a country with water in it after all. Far away, below the mountain's edge, lay the settlement that had sprung up around Longyang Gorge— like a town seen from an airplane, hazed by distance and the rushing chute of thickening air. It took some time to get there, the bus bounding down and round the hillsides toward the plain.

Then we were entering the station, and people were clambering onto the roof of the bus to retrieve their luggage from the rack. Blankets, crates, and parcels were unloaded, and mishap developed into confusion as a three-tiered bamboo basket, a yard in diameter and held together with string, tipped over as it was being lowered and a pale yellow fuzz of baby chicks tumbled out.

A fellow passenger pointed to the road we should take to reach the guesthouse of the power station. It wound upward, and on either side I saw that the houses, though recently thrown up, were made of mud and walled in the old Chinese way. But when the main street came into view, it was noticeable for being different: instead of the low adobe houses of the approach, it was lined with two- to three-story concrete blocks.

Arriving unannounced at the guesthouse, we were guilty of a breach of custom: the correct thing would have been to arrange it all beforehand through the China Travel Service. Nevertheless, we were made welcome, and the head, when summoned, personally guided us to our room and urged us to *xiuxi*. *Xiuxi,* meaning rest, is a convention in China but was in this case a not to be evaded confinement to one's room while the guesthouse put a call through to the authorities in Xi'ning to get the lowdown on us.

The authorities evidently attested to our *bona fides,* for the head returned to ask if we would like some lunch. He had expected unreasonably to find the cook still about. Of course the man had gone off duty already, it was 2 p.m., or nap time. So Shen, as I will call the head, took us to an eating place down a back street. We were served bowls of ravioli by two robust middle-aged ladies, the wives of dam workers, Shen explained, for whom the shop was a means of supplementing the family income.

I asked him about his own family, and he said that his wife and children were all living in Peking. He had a father in Hong Kong, but he wasn't attacked for that during the Cultural Revolution, when having overseas connections made you deeply suspect, because he'd been in the People's Liberation Army and fought in the war. He seemed to like talking, but underneath his sociable manner I could feel a strain of deep melancholy.

I thought I knew why later, when he introduced us to his assistant Yu: he was suffering the insecurity of an older man about to be elbowed aside by a younger subordinate. Yu, in whose company we would spend all of the next day, was one of the ablest men I met on this trip. He was originally from Shanghai, and it showed, not in his speech, for he had a distinct preference for the northern tongue, as is perhaps natural for a man who has spent most of his life in these parts, but in his self-possession and lack of reserve. He seemed game for everything.

When the jeep arrived for us in the morning, a colleague of his showed up too, a small, chipper lady in her late thirties, whom I shall call Mrs. Liu. We were not told what her job was, but I figured it had something to do with public relations. When Yu romped up the construction site and rammed us through the scaffolding, she would always make sure I hadn't slipped or fallen off the cliff before pushing on herself. Later, when we were alone, she asked me if it was true that women sold their sexual favors for money in Hong Kong.

Yu turned out to be a camera buff, and took us all over the construction site, up and down the gorge, to point out where Takia could get the best shots. He was so eager that I was suddenly very touched, and wanted to agree with everything he suggested.

The gorge was about twenty-five miles long and only 164 feet across, and when the project is finished, a 574-foot-high dam will stand across it. The giant engineering hum gave me a strange sensation, as though I was standing in the bows of a ship, listening to the sea divide as the vessel pushed forward. It was a spectacular tour: the giddying, plunging view from the air that made absolute dimensions difficult to grasp, the silvery flash of welding torches against the steep face of rock, the dredgers and the toiling masses. The sight of multitudes at work in China never fails to impress me, or to remind me of a Cecil B. DeMille extravaganza. The gorge was completely dry, as the Yellow River had been separated from its bed, but you could feel the river's held-back presence beyond it all, only waiting for that moment in 1985 when, the first spillways opened, it could bounce a titanic spray into the air.

When we descended, and found ourselves upon the riverbed, I saw that other visitors had arrived at the site. One was a photographer from *China Pictorial*, a large format magazine devoted to the colorful *mise en scène* of socialist construction—bumper harvests, land reclamation, national heritage, and the like. He was a tall man with the look of a seasoned avant-garde film maker about him, and though he was dressed as simply as the next man, he nevertheless gave me cause to wonder why photographers are always trendy, regardless of country. Because he had come all the way from Peking he was attended by a detachment of the local press, all but one of them slung about with cameras (the makes, Nikon and Rollei, made Takia's eyebrows lift).

The woman without a camera turned out to be their chauffeur. As for the others, the little elderly woman, wearing glasses and a Nikon, was the head of the photographic section of the *Qinghai Daily,* while her companion, a younger woman in the olive green uniform of the Chinese army, was a reporter from the *Liberation Daily*. There was also a male reporter from the Xinhua News Agency. The two women strode back and forth, their cameras clicking. Not so the men, who merely gazed, when not roaming, at the work site, which men in their hundreds were embanking with hay, their bare feet trampling the stalks into the earth the way wine makers press grapes. The presence of an audience made their diligence faintly false, yet it was not the put-on spurt of workers on camera.

What interested me most was the fact that they were not using solider material for filling the bed. One expected heavy-duty cement and lavish concrete, not armfuls of kaoliang stalks, which were surely too flimsy for so massive an undertaking. Yet I'd read somewhere that these fascines are quite effective when it comes to closing up dyke breaches against heavily silt-laden water, for the stalks catch the sediment and allow the water to be filtered through. The Chinese have used them on a lavish scale for centuries—these and bamboo gabions and hemp.

The operation was altogether Chinese. Doubtless there was Japanese machinery somewhere, but the only foreign imports I saw were Perlini dump trucks from Italy. They all seemed to be driven by young girls; Mrs. Liu told me there were well over a hundred women truck drivers working on the site. When we were talking I suddenly remembered that the Chinese minister of water conservancy and power is a woman: Qian Zhengying, a civil engineer who became deputy minister when she was only twenty-nine, and whose favorite pastime is said to be swimming.

I saw something of the town after dinner, when I strolled through it in dimming light. I was told the population had grown from zero, in 1976, to thirty-two thousand, when large numbers were moved up here from Liujia Gorge and Three-Gate Gorge. As I walked I could hear the trucks hurtling down to the site; they worked round the clock here, in three eight-hour shifts. Some of those who had come off duty were working in their own backyards, raising mud walls or banking up the sides of the hollows in which their houses were niched. It seemed to me then as if the whole nation were engaged in dyking, that if there was one activity the Chinese will always be good at, it was this. I reached a playground, where I saw youngsters playing badminton and basketball, and oldsters selling vegetables and popsicles. None of them took any notice of the propaganda van, which drove up and down the street with loudspeakers blaring, enjoining full-hearted participation in the national census scheduled to begin next month. When I returned to the guesthouse the evening light had turned blue, as if filtered through water; and everything had become still and silent, except for the distant rumble of trucks down the street.

We flattered ourselves that Yu and Mrs. Liu enjoyed our visit; we were a change from routine. When they were driving us about in the jeep I asked them what other visitors they had had. They spoke then of someone I'd read about in a newspaper clipping a friend had sent me when he heard that I was planning to travel about the Yellow River. His was a remarkable story, and the more I saw of the Yellow River terrain the more I wondered at it. It's hard country, with desert and impassable ravines; yet Yang Liankang, as the man is called, succeeded in walking along the Yellow River from one end of its course to the other.

Yang is a geomorphologist, a graduate of Peking University. He was also a casualty of the Cultural Revolution, and only four years before his historic walk, had been paralyzed from the waist down. It had all started in 1964, when he asked to attend a national geology conference in which two of his papers were to be read. The head of his research team, who for some reason bore a grudge against him, turned down his request and sent somebody else instead. Had Yang swallowed the insult, all might have been well. But being more of a scientist than a politico, he protested against the injustice. The mid-1960s were the wrong time to be talking about injustice, however, and he promptly found himself charged with insubordination.

As the Cultural Revolution unfolded, the attacks against him grew more vicious, to culminate one day in arrest and incarceration. While awaiting trial he went on a hunger strike to protest his innocence; the muscles of his legs began to atrophy and he found he could no longer walk. He was given a ten-year sentence; for four of these he sat paralyzed in his cell, resisting every attempt by his jailers to extract a written confession from him. Instead he stealthily wrote for himself—page after page of notes on the Yellow River, scribbled with a pen he had fashioned from a weed.

For all this time the river, whose fascination had worked on him before, continued to exert its hold over him. From a fellow prisoner he learnt Tibetan, the language spoken around the upper reaches of the river. He was quite fixed in his purpose, engrossed in his studies, and perhaps deep down he never doubted that fulfillment was only a matter of time and persistence. When still a student at university, he had prepared for his career deliberately, going on periodic fasts to accustom his body to the pangs of hunger, and inuring himself against heat and cold by sweltering in a leather coat in summer and taking icy baths in winter.

In 1976 the Gang of Four were toppled from power and China began to take on a new character. Before Yang was released a very different kind of temper would attend scientific endeavor: the new leadership, looking ahead into the post-Mao era, saw national progress as a matter of modernizing the country's agriculture, industry, science and technology, and defense (the so-called Four Modernizations). In 1978 a national conference was convened to ponder ways of retrieving Chinese science from the disarray into which it had fallen during the years of the Cultural Revolution. In the new mood what Yang now did struck the right note: he addressed a letter to the central committee of the Chinese Communist Party asking for a study of the Yellow River to be considered by the conference. In his letter he also asked for his own case to be reviewed.

At the end of the year he was released. He spent the next twelve months recuperating in a sanatorium. He was honored by the scientific establishment; he presided at meetings; in the summer of 1981 he set out alone for the headwaters of the Yellow River. In his backpack he had a few changes of clothes, two atlases, some notebooks and envelopes, a mug, and textbooks of Tibetan and Mongolian. In the months to come he would be exposed to fearful hazard, numbing cold, and immense solitude. At times access was hardly possible, the river plunging through gorges that drop perpendicularly into the water. But one day, tracing the feeder streams which earlier expeditions had supposed to be the source of the river, he managed to walk to the furthest point from which the main flow of the river may be said to issue, and upon a stone at this point, the exact origin of the Yellow, he scratched the words "River Source Reached."

The walk took 317 days, from July 1981 to May 1982. The journey made Yang Liankang the first man to survey the Yellow River on foot. It had led him through thirty-five hundred miles of country, nine Chinese provinces, thirty precipitous gorges, and millennia of geological and cultural history. When, at last, exhausted but triumphant, he reached the mouth of the river, a boat took him out to the sea. There the river was a broad dark current, flowing turbidly until its brown was interrupted by the blue of the sea. Somewhere at the limit of view there was a span of horizon, but there could have been no boundary to his exultation at a hard and hazardous mission accomplished, and a lifelong ambition achieved.

Everything he set out to do, he had done. He had followed the river's ancient course, dug up rock and earth samples, lifted fossils from their geological pasts. He had, like Mao Zedong, the key and the power to success—the compulsion to follow a dream.

Desert and Steppe

The Yellow River brings a hundred sorrows, but there's prosperity in its bend.

—— A Chinese saying

If ever Chinese construct strong sluices in this country they will form of the Yellow River a Mesopotamia which will be able to feed many millions of their superfluous population.

—— D. V. Tafel, 1908

Of all the place names of my journey, none excited me more than Ordos, that name from which we get the word "horde." It is the name of the slab of country which lies within the great loop of the Yellow River, bounded to the north by the river's right bank, and limited to the south by the Great Wall. It was the land of the Tanguts, whose kingdom, the Western Xia, stretched from across Koko Nor. It was overrun by Genghis Khan, sweeping down with his horde. It conjures up steppes and dunes, nomads and flocks, white lambskin pelisses and the paleontological excursions of Pierre Teilhard de Chardin. It is shared administratively between the autonomous regions of Inner Mongolia and Ningxia. It is intensively irrigated, but wherever irrigation ceases there is desert.

Where the Yellow River Rivals the Yangtze

You do not simply decide to go to Ningxia. It is a region still closed to the foreign visitor, and you plead for a special visa, sometimes granted to Chinese émigrés, waiting three days for it to come through. I did this in Lanzhou, to which we now returned, and where I immediately sought out the office of the China Travel Service. I was lucky in Mr. Shen, the chief, who did what he could for me, even as he was badgered by an obvious American, a terrifyingly determined girl in a striped T-shirt, who could not see why she shouldn't be allowed to go to Xi'ning. A student at Peking University, she spoke Chinese, but with the intonation of one whose voice is better adapted to cope with words like "Hi, there," "Listen, man," "C'mon," and "asshole."

A telegram came from Yinchuan, the capital, on the third day to say that all was clear and I was very welcome in Ningxia. We left as soon as possible, on a Sunday. By train it was nine and a half hours to Yinchuan, and semi-desert nearly all the way. We skirted some remains of the Great Wall, and passed under the lee of the Alashan range.

It being a long journey, I looked for someone to talk to, and decided on a mid-thirtyish man reading a collection of American, English, and Japanese detective stories in Chinese translation. I asked him if he liked the book and he said it was OK; he liked Raymond Chandler and also enjoyed Graham Greene's *A Gun for Sale*. Takia offered him a cigarette from the carton of "555" he is never without in China—not because he smokes them but because they work like magic as bribes and fillips to conversation and camaraderie. The man took one, and dragged on it with obvious relish—proof that he was a sophisticate, an urbanite of at least five generations, since country men do not take to foreign cigarettes. " '555'—that's the brand those detectives in books smoke," he observed, somewhat inaccurately.

It is not surprising that people open up so much more on trains and buses: apart from having to pass the time somehow, they choose fellow passengers to talk to the way a man might more readily engage in a chance love affair, knowing that the encounter will be without emotional entanglement. I had wanted to talk, and in this man I got more than I bargained for; I had seldom met a person so little given to silence. On and on he rambled, treating me to many details of his life, one-third to one-half of which I judged to be untrue. The content was coherent, the Peking accent flawless, and the purpose a sort of ego trip.

Leaning toward me with heavy confidentiality, he told me he worked as a detective, earning 110 yuan a month (in other words, twice the average salary), as did his wife, who was a head nurse.

"Thefts," he said, "I handle a lot of thefts. Cracking a case is worth money to me. I get to keep half of what's recovered, you see. Take the case I cracked last week. A peasant was staying in a guesthouse, and thought it best to keep his money under his pillow. It got nicked, of course, all 300 yuan of it. It turned out a worker had taken it—you know these guys right away. I recovered all of the money; it was a piece of cake. I'd have kept 150 for myself if I hadn't felt sorry for the poor sod and returned two-thirds instead."

It appeared his father was a famous film director, and artists being a favorite target of persecution in the Cultural Revolution, the family had fared badly. He himself did time—nine years—in Qinghai and Turkestan, China's answer to Gulag. He informed me he was a Manchu, and hinted at aristocratic descent. "Being that," he explained, "I'm sure you'll understand why I can never go home to my parents or parents-in-law without a couple of thousand yuan in presents. That's why, after all these years, I only have about 600 yuan in savings."

He asked me if I regretted anything in my life.

"What?" I didn't think I'd heard right; he seemed to be giving me a chance to speak.

"I do," he said, not waiting for my answer. Shaking his head, and sighing, he contrived a wince. "I did something once which I shall regret all my life." He paused. "I broke a girl's heart. We were in love; we were to marry. But by socialist measure her class background was all wrong and she was not nearly proletarian enough. My fear of being further disadvantaged politically was so desperate it swept away all thought, all feeling, and I gave her up. She never married, and you know that's a terrible thing in China—not to marry." He married, but I suppose she pined for him for the rest of her life.

In the end he did want to know something of me: could I tell him how much a Conic 8080 tape recorder cost in Hong Kong (the place of its manufacture)? "You never bought one? How is that possible?" It is only living in an affluent society, soaked in consumerism, that renders people immune to the seductions of material possessions.

Sometimes I clammed up on trains, knowing that the conversations would be all too predictable, or feeling the distance between myself and these people too great to cross. At other times I thought I took too much for granted, for as soon as I had decided how alike all Chinese were, I was confronted by some startling differences. More than once I was surprised to find that a system so bent on leveling should allow so much individuality.

But individuality up to a point only, as a young man I once talked to on a train intimated. He was reading an article in a popular periodical, whose heading, which he showed me, was the question "Are the Chinese overdoing their openness of disposition?"

"We've been repressed for so long, you see," the young man explained to me, "that introversion comes more naturally to us. Anyhow, that's what this article wants you to believe. This openness, extroversion, is something new, an outbreak which may get out of hand. A person can't be his own man yet; it is too soon. In China you can scarcely begin to talk of individualism."

He himself was a little ambivalent. "Think of the peasant," he continued, "yoked to the wagon of crude survival. What, to him, is liberty of individual action? His needs are dictated by a life—no, not even that—an existence, more earthbound, more enclosed, simpler, which makes individualism no more than an abstraction. Not all that many years ago, I saw for myself some places in China where they'd never seen a watch, where they didn't know such things had even been invented."

"Of course," he went on, "who would not like to change? Yet for that change not to be shattering, it's got to be gradual: the majority of Chinese are so ignorant of the outside world that its sudden intrusion can violently shake their balance."

By means of these conversations I was able to pass profitably many hours of my journey. But when the detective started to be repetitious, I pointedly gave my attention to the scenery; he gave his to Graham Greene. It was now late afternoon, and we were within a few miles of Yinchuan. I had taken in the dunes, the river. At the station I took in the girl sent by the Foreign Affairs Office to meet me; she was a Miss Fu, pretty, about twenty-five, completely unguarded, inexperienced, a person for whom irony or skepticism did not exist.

Yinchuan, with its Drum Tower, its Temple to the Jade Emperor (the supreme deity of Taoism), its pagodas and its city gates, has as many of the familiars of Chinese cities as any I've seen. But of that considerable Tangut civilization of which it was, until Genghis Khan destroyed it in the thirteenth century, the center, I was able to see only some relics in a museum: bronze vessels and animal carvings, and some samples of its printing and writing. Genghis Khan died after his campaign against the Tanguts—mangled, so legend has it, by a Tangut princess. There are several versions of how it happened. One of these goes that when Genghis was out hunting one day he wounded a hare; seeing the animal stumble across the snow, he said to his entourage, "Find me a woman as white as this snow, with cheeks as red as this blood." They did so, and she turned out to be the wife of a Tangut prince, living in the capital city. His life threatened, the prince had no choice but to surrender the lady to Genghis; but when he came to claim her, she brought out a knife she had hidden in her clothes and castrated him. She then escaped, and drowned herself in the Yellow River, which the Mongols call Khatun Gol, or River of the Princess. Meanwhile Genghis fell into a sleep, and from that sleep he never woke.

Today, though, the strain that is most clearly reflected in Ningxia is neither Tangut nor Mongolian, but Mohammedan. Of Ningxia's 8-million population, the Hui minority constitutes a third, and wherever you go in this so-called autonomous region—*the* Hui region—you are never far from a mosque. One we saw, approach-

ing the sunset hour of the five appointed prayers of the day, had
cupolas and minarets that looked like something out of Herat.
The wall surrounding the mihrab, the niche used to show the direction of Mecca, was covered with unpatterned tiles, ivory and
beautiful. The effect was one of white upon white, with everything
else in celadon green—green pillars, green Arabic calligraphy. All
this I espied only from the door, but in what mood of expansiveness
or sex egalitarianism I shall never know, the imam invited me to
look in on the ablutions of devotees preparing themselves for prayer.
A rare treat indeed for a woman.

The great surprise of Yinchuan, though, remains the Roman
Catholic church I stumbled upon one afternoon. I had seen no
building in China more obviously loved. The interior, though dimly
lit, was kept in a glow of color and decoration. Above the lace-
covered altar hung a picture of Christ, attended by figures of angels.
Upon it stood candles and plastic flowers, overlooked by pictures
of the Madonna. In a niche stood the confessional, curtained in a
green and white floral print. There was a breath of scent, perhaps
of musk, in the air. It was like no other chapel I had seen: European,
and yet not European, Chinese, and yet not Chinese.

In this remote corner of China, long supposed to have expelled
Christianity, here was an ecclesiastic saying, yes, he knew a little
Latin, but he read his Bible in French; and yes, when Mass is said,
the place is filled to overflowing. He was sorry I couldn't see the
bishop; he was past eighty and a little unwell that day. Here, where
you would least expect it, was a living memorial to the Belgian
Church which, seventy years ago, established missions on lonely
steppes all around the western arm of the Yellow River.

The wisest of these missionaries believed that Christianity would
not triumph in China, but they had left their mark here all the same.
Not just in this church, but in the territory's irrigation system,
which, copying the Jesuits before them, they extended with many
a ditch and channel. In the end this proved damaging to the con-
version business, for the techniques made the peasants more independent of rain and heavenly succor. "Other people look to the
Father up there," they said, "but we look to the Yellow River."

Ningxia is irrigation country through and through, and if ever the river ceased to flow, or the canals to crisscross the valleys, Yinchuan would be no different from the wastes that lie to its east and west. If you climb to the top of the North Pagoda, on the far side of town, you will see that Yinchuan lies in an oasis of rice fields. To the west rises the majestic Alashan; behind and beyond these hills, you know stretches the vastness of the Tengger Desert; but under your feet, marvelously laved, lies a shining leek-green plain of rice seedlings in water. If the scene puts you in mind of the rice valleys of the south, this is the gift of the river; and there never was a place where irrigation more evidently redeemed landscape. This is where the Yellow River rivals the Yangtze, they say; and it is true that the valleys are uncharacteristically moist, and that the rice is just as good, if not better.

Takia and I were taken to see the structures that distribute this water. This covered an inspection of the Qingtong Gorge dam, a canal dating from the Tang dynasty, and another going as far back as the time of the first emperor of Qin (which would make it more than two thousand years old). It all seemed well-ordered and made to last. We were then shown an apple orchard and a commune that irrigation fecundated, near the town of Wuzhong. Talking to a peasant there, I also saw how economic policy, as well as water supply, could enrich a land. Under the so-called responsibility system, which allotted him a plot he could cultivate for himself, and sneaked a material incentive into his labor, productivity had leapt. This peasant had a fifth of an acre to himself, and he probably produced twice as much food on that private plot as he did on the communal fields. He said his annual income was two thousand yuan, which means he was three times as rich as the average wage earner.

On all these trips we were accompanied by Miss Fu, to whose conversation I became all but addicted. Having graduated in English from Hangzhou University, she liked to wish me a formal "good morning" everyday in that language, though we always otherwise spoke in Chinese. Here are some of the things she said. What is Roman Catholicism, she'd never heard of it? Oh no, thank you, she won't have a popsicle because she had ten at the cinema the other night, and they gave her insomnia. She is sorry she is too unwell to accompany us on our excursion to Shapotou: her stool was dry and hard that morning. Once she swam in the Yellow River, in emulation of Chairman Mao's feat of swimming the Yangtze. She actually asked to be assigned to work in Ningxia, this Utah of China, she had liked it so much when she was condemned to manual labor here during the Cultural Revolution. Sure it was hard, but oh, how fat you got, with all that food you had to eat just to be able to withstand the physical toil and hardship! (Here she shook with laughter, as if she couldn't remember having had more fun.)

She had said the popsicles had been bought for her by "Dad"; how was it possible, I wanted to know, that her father lived in Yinchuan, seeing she herself was transferred here?

"No, I didn't mean my own father; I meant my friend's father." She glanced at me, and was suddenly very coy. "Do you have this custom where you come from?"

"I think only after you're married." I did not need to ask who her "friend" was, that word had such a matrimonial ring in China.

She said they would marry soon. He was away in Shanghai right now, doing a three-month training course on electronic calculators—clearly a promising lad.

"You chose him yourself," I said.

Yes, she thought that was best, to choose one's marriage partner oneself. Of course there were marriage bureaus, but she never had to resort to one. (The Yinchuan Marriage Bureau, I later discovered, was housed in an enormous grey building in Zhongshan Park, sharing its premises with the Workers Club.) It was all just dandy; the two sides had met, her parents and his, and had given their approval. Between them "furniture and things" had been settled, as well as the form of the wedding—the banquet, the guest list, the honeymoon in Wuhan and Shaanxi, where bride and groom had a set of relatives each. The groom's family would fork out the money (1,000 yuan, roughly U.S. $500, for the travel, 2,000 yuan for the banquet), but contributions from the bride's family (600 yuan's worth of furniture) were welcome and even accepted as due. She had all that her heart could desire. One could not see how it could be otherwise, when girls aged between eighteen and twenty-five, she herself had informed me, aspired above all to a good job and a good husband; and both these things were well within Miss Fu's grasp.

Her place as guide, when she retired on finding she did not like the look of her stool, was taken by a Mr. Jing, who, if reticent about himself, was a good deal more informative about Ningxia. I liked him enormously. We traveled to Zhongwei together, and between gazing out of the train window at the terrain we were crossing, we talked about land reclamation here and in the rest of northern China. From what I learnt, certain items have stuck in my mind. These two claims for instance: nine-tenths of China's land area is desert, mountain, and steppes, and China brought more land under irrigation between 1957 and 1958 than in the whole of its history. But by itself irrigation is not enough; nothing short of a massive shelter belt of trees, covering the three main irrigation areas in northwest China—the Gansu Corridor, the Yellow River valleys in Inner Mongolia, and the Yellow River diversion area in Ningxia—is needed to keep desertification at bay. It is said that much of this has been planted, placing a third of the region's 2.5 million-acre farmland under protection; but what is planned is nothing less than a Great Green Wall of poplar and weeping willow, barricading north China against the corrosions of wind and sand, and, by controlling run-off, tempering the killing impact of erratic rainfall.

It was difficult to see how you begin to tackle such a mammoth task. "Well, there's been a campaign, calling upon everyone to do their share to 'turn China green'. In 1981 the National People's Congress passed a resolution, obliging every able-bodied man, woman, and child over the age of eleven to plant and maintain five trees a year. Then there is desert afforestation by sand stabilization, which you'll see for youself when we arrive at the Shapotou Sand Control Experimental Station." The station, whose reputation is said to be high among Saudi Arabians and international development agencies, is where they are trying to roll back the shifting sands of the Tengger Desert.

Past Zhongwei, for miles the railway cleaved the invading dunes of the desert. To my left and right, I could see the sand lying in varying degrees of light and shadow, bare and lonely. Something extraordinary, in this landscape bereft of human habitation, were the signs of human effort everywhere: the land was a quilt, mazed acre after acre, apparently by hand, with squares of wheat stalks each measuring three feet by three. Had I seen a picture of it, I would probably have said it was strange, and left it at that. But coming upon it in full context, I was startled into seeing its scale. Jing explained, referring to a scientific document he had brought along, that it was a mechanical method of checking sand drift, less effective than planting, but useful nevertheless. He gave me the document to read, but it was not the facts it furnished—that laying a grid of straw on the sand increased its surface roughness 220 times and lowered wind velocity by seventeen percent—that were remarkable. To me it was its being all done by hand that made it stunning.

I was now eager to call at the Shapotou Sand Control Station. We arrived shortly before sundown, and were greeted by the scientists there, middle-aged, genial men slightly crumpled in dress, who had about them the air of a frontier community. One of them gave a speech of welcome; another read a scientific report. They were reclaiming the desert with the waters of the Yellow River, I gathered, and they had been trying out various species of shrub to discover the best ones for holding the sand (the plants had Chinese and Latin names, which I have forgotten). The glummest of ecologists could scarcely pass this place without feeling cheered. When we took a walk about the purlieus, the sight of green trees springing out of the sand, and of sheep grazing in their shadow, lulled me into thinking the desert was not advancing. There were sounding sands behind the station, flowing like molten gold down a sheer slope and straight onto a lush and dappled grove. It would be weird, I thought, and quite wonderful, to have caught these sands at a time when they hummed.

The Yellow River is the waterer all right. You could see the sands rolling down to the very edge of it, with patches of green sandwiched between. The more you looked at these, the less likely they seemed. Seen from afar, these dabs of green stood out in the otherwise pallid undulations of the Tengger Desert unnaturally and abruptly, like exclamation marks.

Takia went off to photograph the oasis in the last shreds of sun. Jing and I waited in the car. It was dusk and shadows swept across the flaxen sands. When seven o'clock went by and Takia failed to return, I decided it was time to go in search of him. Avoiding the quicksands between the dunes proved impossible, and I found that the best way of negotiating a sandy desert was by running; otherwise one constantly wallowed over dunes. This I did for about an hour, sprinting up one slope and tumbling down the next. The shadows were quite deep now, and dune after dune lay in half-moons of black and gold, with the westering sun above and the desert stretching to some unknown distance ahead. Tiny insects with blue carapaces skittered across my path, but otherwise all was still and silent. When I caught up with Takia he was standing on the crest of a dune, and when I presently ascended the bluff, it opened the oasis to my view, and I saw the back of the Yellow River sweeping in a half circle below.

It was as fine a sight as I could ever hope to see, worth every minute of my journey. The lateness of the hour was the least of Takia's concerns, now that the light was just right. I didn't care either, though I knew it would be cause for silent reproach from the driver, who was being kept from his dinner.

It was nine before we got back to Zhongwei, so dinner was very late by Chinese standards. But the kitchen staff were understanding, and produced a river fish, meat, and the splendid Ningxia rice. Like Miss Fu, though with far less reason, I had developed an enormous appetite in Ningxia—here amply satisfied. I had expected a culinary aridity, in view of the deserts around. Instead I found, if scarcely three-star gastronomy, at least plenty of originality and experimentation. I remember very well that occasion when, sitting down to my first course in the hotel dining room in Yinchuan, I was served a large cake, the sort you produce for celebrations, covered with spines of icing in canary yellow, like the back of a porcupine. I was told, when I inquired, that it was because the cook was sitting his exam in European cuisine that day.

Of Zhongwei, I remember little. It is an old city, once enclosed by walls. In its modern form it is like any number of northern Chinese county towns. The plains around are rich and wide, a web of irrigated fields and poplar windbreaks. Close at hand lies a remnant of the Great Wall. I read somewhere that the city walls of Zhongwei had no north gate, because there was no more China to the north of it; beyond it moved the Tartar barbarians, galloping their horses across the steppes. As I thought of this, it seemed to me that the wall, the dykes, the windbreaks were all aspects of the same thing: points on which an empire, a shore, an area of cultivation could be protected, a frontier where the thrust of barbarians, or waves, or desolation could be distanced and arrested.

Inner Mongolia

It may be the land of the Golden Horde for all I know. But the historical fact of those rampaging Mongols lives only in the imagination. "Here!" you think, it was right here that they swept across the grasslands in the full pride of their triumph. There, out there beneath the sands, the remains of Genghis Khan lie buried. You try to find a trace of those energies which propelled the Mongols to found an empire stretching from the Yellow River to the Danube, and you fail.

In the Ordos the Mongols had long been ousted by the Chinese colonist—a case of pastoralism losing out to agriculture. In the process the Chinese spoiled the country, cutting down the few trees that grew, destroying the soil of the steppes, and generally speeding up the deadly erosion of the land and causing the desert to extend.

Nor were the people spared. As so often happens in the grafting of one culture on another, the bad habits of the colonizers transplanted faster than the good, and the Mongol became corrupted. It was all very sapping, the encroachment upon his pastures, the opium which he took to the way American Indians took to drink. And racially subject as he was, he couldn't help becoming more and more Chinese.

In Baotou and Hohhot you wonder: what has happened to the Mongol? Her appearance and manners sinicized, you can only distinguish a Mongol girl from Chinese by the fact of her wearing earrings—a concession to "ethnic" adornment. Evidently here, as elsewhere, the successfully assimilated win. The most successful seemed to be the city slickers, wearing the Chinese urban uniform of shirt and trousers, modish down to the bell-bottoms.

At first sight Baotou, where I now arrived from Zhongwei, seemed a mixture of Chinese and Soviet, rather than anything Mongolian, though the origin of the name is either the Mongolian word for "sacred" or "a place where deer roam." Baotou has mines and is importantly industrial, which is to say that it is grim and poisoned. Walking through the city, past dour citizens and block after numbing block of raw concrete buildings, I did not wonder that the best stocked shops appeared to be liquor stores. After only one day in this place, I was persuaded that it was not for me. To be fair we had arrived at an unsuitable hour—3 a.m.—a fact which perhaps ensures an unfocused frame of mind. But it demands a greater richness of spirit than I possess to take to a place which lists among its chief places of interest the Baotou Iron and Steel Company, third most important in China, built with the help of the U.S.S.R.

There was, moreover, that satiety and weariness which besets all travelers at a certain stage of their journey. The introduction to Inner Mongolia coincided with such a stage in me. It was here that I began to yearn for bright lights, ritzy hotels, shiny shop fronts, transcontinental telephone lines, chocolates, *Time* magazine, not having to think about when the water comes on or where to find food after seven o'clock, all the swing and razzle dazzle of the capitalist metropolis. The closest I got to all this was when I switched on the radio, and found myself listening to a burst of Russian, followed by a jazzy rendering of "The Girl from Ipanema."

The culmination of this glumness (which seems thoroughly reprehensible in retrospect) came with a trip to the Yellow River crossing, undertaken for no reason other than that going down to the river had become a ritual. The bus which took us there ran east from the new town to the old, and in the way the two are set miles apart from each other, you recognized the pattern of Lanzhou and Yinchuan, where a new town has arisen beyond what would have been the ramparts of the old. After more than enough of the unvarying scenery, Takia withdrew to the land of Nod, filling me with envy. The absolute invariability of the diurnal rhythm in China has your biological clock ticking to a timetable: hungry by eleven, soporific by twelve.

My first reaction to my destination was the question: why would anyone come here? Of course people come here to cross the river, but just then there was little activity. There were some huts, of a tone so neutral to the land that they seemed to grow from it. The impression of a hamlet abandoned was hardly altered by a rheumy old man who sat listlessly beside the track selling five or six glasses of boiled water, who kept so still he might have been sitting there forever. The only thing I found to stir my interest was the thought that, right up to the 1940s, as I'd read somewhere, murderers liked to bring their victims here in winter to push them through a hole in the ice, with the expectation that when the ice thawed in the spring the river would carry the corpses away.

What did me in once and for all was the toilet. There was no good way to get there, the water seller said, but the quickest was to climb to the top of the river levee, walk some distance along it, and then follow one of the footpaths cutting across the fields. I did so, for most of the distance not knowing where I was or what I should be looking for. Just dropping one's trousers was out because the fields were completely open. When a peasant woman waddled into view I made a beeline for her. "Follow me," she dourly said. We came to an enclosure walled in by mud. To enter this enclosure, which I found floored with excrement, I had to fight my way through a wall of coruscating, metallic looking flies. Once inside, these made a dead set for me, leaving the other woman alone.

The next day Takia and I took the first train out. In retrospect

I reproach myself for my haste—in retrospect one always reproaches oneself. When safe again at home one wonders at one's hysteria, and what was so awful about that place or this experience; after all, it wasn't as though one had to fight bandits or pick lice off oneself all day, which was the lot of travelers in Inner Mongolia as recently as forty years ago. The bad moments of travel, the fatigue, the surfeit, do not transmit themselves to one's memories; and I now tell myself, had I not given way to these in Baotou, I would have seen the lama Buddhist monastery the Chinese call Wudangzhao and the Mongols Batogar Süme. I had known of the place, but I had not foreseen that regret which should nag me whenever I recall what Owen Lattimore, that most traveled of writers on Mongolia, said of this temple: "Batogar is the most beautiful monastery that I know."

In the train, skirting the Ordos to Hohhot, I thought of something both Owen Lattimore and Teilhard de Chardin had been dazzled by on the steppes—the multitude of bird life. Where are they now, all those larks, cranes, swans, geese, ducks, spoonbills they saw? Most probably ensnared by the Chinese, who think of the natural world only as something to be eaten. Besides, when are times not desperate enough for the hunting of animals, of whatever species? Seeing the birds and ducks in English parks never fails to recall to me the words of a Chinese tourist I once overheard in London's Trafalgar Square. "All these pigeons," she observed to her companion, "there for the eating: you'd think they'd catch them, wouldn't you?"

Recalling this, there came to me an image of the Chinese masses swamping the animal kingdom, and as we neared Hohhot, capital of Inner Mongolia, this was merged with the idea that Mongol distinctness will all too soon be absorbed into a larger racial pattern.

Hohhot was founded by the last of the great Mongol conquerors in 1581, and was named Guihua, or Restored to Civilization, when the khan pledged submission to the Chinese emperor. All the insufferability of imperial China is contained in that name. But if the Chinese set the tone for Hohhot then, they are hardly less obtrusive today. Mongolness is muffled in Hohhot. And there was no more ominous foretoken of its fate, I found, than the posters for one-child families stuck on billboards all over the city. The norm of one-child families, imposed on all the country to try and limit China's monstrous population, does not in theory apply to Mongols or any ethnic minority, whose population has thinned while that of the Chinese has swelled. Yet everywhere I looked in Hohhot, there were these fur-hatted Mongolian parents looking out of giant posters, their eyes bright with the joyousness of abstaining from further procreation.

We were four days from July 1, the cutoff date of the census. Three months from now, the figures will be totted up to reveal a staggering total of 1.1 billion. All through this first of my three journeys, from Canton to Hohhot, the apparatus of propaganda for the census—posters, agitprop, newspaper articles—had greeted us in every town. All through the next, the talk would be of the government's decree for each couple to have no more than one, or at most, two children.

In this part of the country the over-populousness of China is not a graspable horror, for densities are not nearly as intolerable here as they are elsewhere; but the longer I traveled, the more I came to be appalled by it. I believe the leadership really mean business when they say they want to bring the birthrate down to 0.59 and to stabilize the population at 1,200 million by the end of the century, for the alternative is unimaginable. Let the birthrate continue as it did in the mid-1970s, and the Chinese population will increase to about the present population of the world in a hundred years' time—this to be fed from only seven percent of the world's arable land. It would never actually happen, of course, because mass starvation, mutual slaughter, and revolutionary convulsions knowing no bounds and no proportion, whose beginning and end alike are death, would have occurred first.

The too-muchness of humanity had yet to impress itself upon me, but I would come to feel it soon enough—the crushing dreariness of it, the far-reaching implications of it, the meanness and squalor it creates. Now the census was imminent, and opinions on family size

were heard more and more. And my own questions, whose elucida-
tion I sought in conversations and newspapers, were inextricable
from these. Questions and answers such as these: Is China congested?
Not uniformly, nine-tenths of the population live on one-sixth of
the land. What if they were to reclaim all the wasteland? Even if
feasible it is still doubtful whether the present level of per capita
cultivated land can be maintained. Suppose the target were met by
the end of the century, would that make everything all right? No,
according to the government's own estimate there will still be more
than 100 million surplus laborers in the countryside and tens of
millions of unemployed youths in the cities. Supposing the birthrate
were curbed, what do you do when, with the aging of the population, couples increasingly find themselves the sole supporter of two
sets of grandparents? What are the long-term effects of undoing the
Chinese kinship system at a stroke, depriving it of aunts and uncles
and cousins? There are no answers to these.

The leaders have all my sympathy; they can't be faced with a
more difficult task, or be more hamstrung. For this is a land with
the curse of changelessness, where, at the heart of many a village,
you will hear the echoes of Confucius and Mencius, and even if they
don't exactly say, "Of the three unfilial acts, the greatest is the leaving of no descendants," you can be sure that those words of Mencius
linger on the mind suggestively. This is a land where the men revel
in their women's childbearing. You can't expect them to accept with
good humor this curb on their procreation; or be surprised that
they beat the daylights out of their wives when they go and produce
daughters instead of sons. You can't even stop them when they
strangle their baby girls at birth, so that their wives may have
another try, and get the sex right the next time.

Watching the national obsession with procreation grow, as I
did in the course of my journey, you could only wonder at the
overwhelming odds—economic, cultural, and psychological—that
are stacked against the government's enterprise, and admit to a
certain sympathy for those who have to work in it. For no policy
is better calculated to court unpopularity. Everywhere I went in
the countryside, I heard of women hiding from the family-planning

worker when she comes round. The Chinese love having children, and indulge their babies to a sickly degree. Besides, they can think of no better way to give birth to the future. Even more will they cherish their children now, now that they are limited to one or two. And it is an alarming thought, what the future holds for China come next generation, when every one of its members is a spoilt child, every one a mother's darling.

"We made a mistake in the past," a family-planning worker said to me, "not appreciating the need for birth control." I observed that this was an understatement, thinking of the near doubling of the population since 1949. Close to half of the present population is young, born in the baby boom years of the 1950s and 1960s.

Who was to blame? "It was the improvement in health care and living conditions," she said, "and the consequent reduction in death rate."

"But don't you think it was Mao too? His blind wrongness in believing that the more people China had, the faster it would develop. Didn't he say, 'China's populousness is a good thing . . . on no account must we think we have too many people'? Didn't Mao sack Professor Ma Yinchu from his job as president of Peking University, and disgrace him, because, sensible economist that he was, Ma argued for birth control?"

The family-planning worker was a forgiving person, but not entirely uncritical, and she went as far as agreeing with me that Mao's misguidedness had left China with a terrible burden, though not so far as to agree that as wrongnesses went, it was the worst.

Neither she nor other people I talked to shared my sense of foreboding; they were not given to thinking in such stark terms as the ratio of resources to population, and did not quail as much as I did at the thought that arable land per capita, already farcically meager, had shrunk by half in the last thirty years. In Inner Mongolia, who can be surprised? There seems plenty of room. Those illimitable spaces, beyond which there always extend the steppes—vast, untenanted, pristine. When we were lurching across the edges of these one day, the driver of the minibus said to me, "Why, I'll take a Mongolian lass to wife. That way I'll have lots of kids, since exceptions are made for minority races." I believe he was only half-joking, and young as he was, in him all the old ideas—about having male children to carry on the family line and offer sacrifices to the ancestors—lived on.

When he told me this we were driving to Wulantuge, a commune about three hours from Hohhot, where we were to spend the night. There were a dozen of us, including a group of affable Chinese nurses, two Americans who spoke Chinese and held hands, and three Swedes who wore backpacks of German and American manufacture. Everyone was amiable, but the trip was a bore, and made me think of packaged safari holidays for rich business executives who put up with spartan living conditions and inedible food as the price for hunting wild beasts and adventure in darkest jungle. The grasslands were authentic enough, the camels were real, the lamb we had for dinner was genuinely local, even the yurts we slept in were doubtless made by true Mongolian hands; all the same the authenticity seemed staged. I was disappointed by the scenery, as I was bound to be, comparing it constantly to Qinghai's piercing beauty. And when we were taken to see a Mongolian woman, I thought that she, though her bearing was proud, was far too consciously and elaborately dressed in native costume.

When we arrived at the camp, Takia broke away from the party, and I, too, wandered off by myself. I walked for about an hour, through a changeless scene. Then I came upon a stream, and a flock of thin sheep grazing about its pebbly edges. A shepherd boy guarded them, who when I said hello stared at me mutely, as shepherd boys will the world over. Exploring the grasslands still further, I came to a dwelling, more hovel than homestead, in which sat a Chinese woman and a small child, waiting for the men to come home from herding. That shepherd boy and this herder's shed set me thinking: they seemed a hint that I had crossed the line between the sown and the steppe, between the farm and the herd. I had been thinking about the retreat of livestock before the plough, and so had expected to find cropland here; instead I found pasturage.

Perhaps, I reflected, the steppe will hold its own now. Mao's power over agricultural policy is gone, and with it, presumably,

the obsession with growing and storing grain, that *idée fixe* born of
the instinct of guerilla warfare, and imparted to a whole nation. It
was another one of Mao's fanaticisms, the opening up of land for
crops. If land reclamation by irrigation was one of his best legacies
to the country, clearing the land for food grains—involving as it
did the destruction of pastures and forests—was one of the worst.

"The Mongolian herdsman," I said to the driver when we set
out again the next day, "seems a bit thin on the ground. In fact I've
yet to see him. Why don't you show me one?"

"You'll have to go to Outer Mongolia for that, or the Mongolian
People's Republic, as the Soviets call it," he answered playfully.
"The Chinese can't spread there—there's the Gobi Desert in between." No, he could not show us a Mongolian nomad, but he did
the next best thing, which was to show us an *obo,* that mystic symbol, to a nomad society, of the land's divinity. We came to this
after a long drive in the minibus, and though it was only a heap of
stones on a rocky peak, with a branch stuck on top and shreds of
material tied to that flapping in the wind, still there was something
wild and compelling about it, this dot in the distance which appeared, up close, to be an altar or a fertility symbol, a declaration of
the nomad's claim on this land.

Later, when I returned to the subject of Outer Mongolia, the
driver said that though he didn't like to listen to broadcasts from
there (for "who would, given the anti-Chinese talk?"), he had to
give it a higher rating than Inner Mongolia as far as development
was concerned. By development he meant, of course, the growth
of mechanized industry and the replacement of the horse by the
motorcycle. When he was saying this I suddenly remembered
something Owen Lattimore wrote, in his book *Mongol Journeys.*
He was trying to express that old tension between nomad expansion
and retreat, and he came up with the image of a river. When I came
back to England I looked up this passage in his book; it went like
this:

> You may say again that nomadism has always been like a
> river discharging into the sea. Far up at the headwaters,

deep in the hinterland, the sea was only a legend. In the estuary it depended on whether the tide of the sea were flowing or ebbing, as well as on the volume of water discharged by the river. With an incoming tide even if the river were in flood the water was turned brackish far upstream; on an outgoing tide the saltiness of the sea was weakened even beyond the mouth of the river; but this depended partly on whether the river were strong with heavy rains or weak with drought. Today we have this old conflict of inherent tendencies but also something new; it is as if the immense power of industrialism has built locks and pumps, able to force the salt water inland far beyond its "natural" reach.

Back in Hohhot, we stopped by the grave of Wang Zhaojun, a Chinese court lady who lived in the first century B.C. It was she whom the Chinese emperor, to fulfill the terms of a peace settlement, despatched to Inner Mongolia to marry a chieftain of the Xiongnu, a barbarian nomad people with their home on the steppes. She suffered this sad fate because, exquisite though she was, she had failed to catch the eye of the emperor. Not that he ever saw her; it was only her picture he saw, painted by a court artist whose job it was to portray the harem ladies, these being so numerous that the emperor had no time to interview them all. Wang Zhaojun had refused to bribe this painter, and to spite her he made her out to be rather plain. It was ten years before the emperor discovered the truth, and when, too late, he found out, he had the painter beheaded. Meanwhile the khan died; as for the lady herself, one version of her story has her marrying the khan's heir, while another has her taking poison to avoid committing incest. Hers was exactly the sort of fate Chinese poets liked to write about, and she has indeed been immortalized in verse by Du Fu and Li Shangyin, as well as by lesser poets. To read such verse is to know what the name of Zhaojun evokes for the Chinese: haunting grief, the ever-greenness of a faraway mound, the quiver of a lute, the loneliness of the northern desert, the pining for things south of the border. To these associations the current regime has added another: the ancient forging of ties between the Chinese and Mongolian peoples.

Leading us into a park, our guide showed us a spot marked by a stone inscribed with Zhaojun's name. It was then assumed we wanted to climb to the top of the mound. For the Chinese cannot imagine anyone not wanting to climb to the top of a height when there is one at hand. No hill, pagoda, or tower is safe from the Chinese sightseer, who likes nothing better than to scramble all the way to the summit and look out, never mind that the view is often not worth the effort. Now the Japanese would perfectly understand this; but not the Swedes. Our three, while obediently trooping up the steps, looked perplexed by this exercise, and when we were all down on the ground again, I heard them asking the guide why we couldn't have been given a tour of the city's underground shelters, constructed by the Chinese in case of an attack by the U.S.S.R.

The guide, like many Chinese guides, was good for declaiming the length, breadth, height, and age of historical monuments but not much good for anything else. She was not even well-meaning. She seemed primed to ward off any questions about Hohhot. For sidelights on the city, you do better quarrying the telephone directory. Where else but in those pages do you get such condensed but revelatory glimpses into the monotonies, needs, the very stuff of a city's existence? Hohhot's was a thin book, printed on cheap paper. The inside pages contained a two-page advertisement for birth control, taken out, I noted, by the Municipal Family Planning Bureau. The entries were arranged under headings: Offices of the Regional People's Government, of the Party, of People's Associations (these included the Federation of Trade Unions, Chinese Communist Youth League, Women's Federation, and some learned societies). Next came Culture, Propaganda, Sports, and Education. Last of all came a section headed "Services." Here you will find, each supplied with two or three telephone numbers, the whole gamut of life's needs, as felt in Hohhot. These, in the order in which they appeared, are: Guesthouses, Food and Drink, Photography, Hairdressing, Baths, Rentals (of transport), and Cremation.

Everything had become less easy to take in than it had been at the start, and Takia and I felt simultaneously that it was time to end our first journey. "Let's go to Peking," he said, and his words could not have fallen on more receptive ears. I needed the relief of the big city, and though Peking is only that by Chinese standards, at that moment it seemed—and this is a measure of how far Maoist thinking had got to me—at once soft and sybaritic. For to the true Maoist the city is the symbol of hedonism, the very opposite of the rigors of the Red Base. If he could have had his way in China, there would have been none of that gulf, familiar in all the underdeveloped world, that separates city from country, and the cossetted living of the one would have been overtaken by the worthier ruggedness of the other.

It was in the Peking underground system that I was most sharply reminded of this. Coming into the subway, I found the station strung end to end with clotheslines and washing. I said to Takia, "Ah, now I see how they narrow the gap between city and country —by bringing the country right into the heart of the city." No scene could look more domestic, more like a country woman's backyard. Takia's comment on this was: "You'll know when the Reds have entered Hong Kong; it's when you see washing hanging up all over the Landmark." (The Landmark is downtown Hong Kong's swankiest shopping arcade, the place where the boutiques carry labels like Gucci and Yves Saint Laurent.)

Peking adjusted perspectives, and showed me another face of China. Before taking the plane back to Hong Kong, we invited some friends of friends to dinner at a restaurant. One of them, a young photographer, couldn't come because he'd arranged to have dinner with Marc Riboud. But we had a chance to talk to him, and to see some of his pictures. There was a time, for instance during the shortlived "Peking Spring" three to four years ago, when his pictures might have given that slant on Chinese life and politics that Marc Riboud's do.

"Riboud has a very sure grasp of Chinese reality," he told me, "but I wouldn't dare take the kind of pictures he takes—not now, at any rate, not if I want to stay out of trouble."

Of the others, mostly artists, one had had a poem published in an underground magazine and another had been thought too avant-garde to be safe. Until they got quite drunk, these people gave little away, and during the whole of the dinner not a single political opinion was expressed. Yet I thought I knew who they were; they were people who just missed being dissidents. I could see them hanging around Democracy Wall, that focus of the Chinese dissident movement, where posters once went up calling socialist principles and methods into question, and where humble journals of dissent were distributed and sold, though I could not see their dissent as anything more than merely rudimentary. I may be unjust, and it may be that they only seem pallid to me beside their more sanguine Russian counterparts; still I was not persuaded that it would take all that much to frighten them into docility.

When dinner was over the poet invited Takia and me to his home, a room he shared with his wife in her parents' apartment. We listened to his most cherished tapes. I sat on the bed and watched one of his friends groove to the music of yesterday—the Beatles singing "Can't Buy Me Love," "Hey, Jude," and "Revolution." Takia had brought our host a dozen large bottles of beer and these were quickly emptied.

The poet's young wife, coming to sit next to me on the bed, confided to me a picture of domestic stresses, her voice lowered disconsolately. All that year, she said, her husband had been drinking heavily, going out eight nights out of ten, and sometimes staying away altogether, too sloshed to find his way home. As she spoke she looked at the poet, across the room, but he never met her eye. She continued impetuously to voice her private thoughts: of course she had tried to reason with him, and of course, what with the frustration they all felt in the present political climate, it was perfectly understandable that he should resort to drink. But all the same she couldn't always forgive him—how could she, when he refused so utterly to get a grip on himself? It was so isolating, and she didn't know what to do; all she could think of was to start drinking herself, to shame him into giving it up. He didn't like to see her drinking, but it was just this that made her do it. My feeling, which I refrained from voicing, was that inebriation was her husband's way of getting stoned—Qingdao and Five-Star beer was his feel-good drug, his hash.

The more I saw of these people, the harder it became to resist not only the feeling of familiarity, but the wish to interpret their behavior. They certainly repined against the system, as a card burning draftee repined against the Vietnam War, or any hippie against suburbia and the fuzz. The difference is that there is no escape open to them; they can neither emigrate to Canada nor drop out to Nepal. Yet because, in Peking, the outside world is a little nearer, there is a stronger yearning for going abroad. They ache for escape, and hanker after places like Paris and New York with all the appetite of unfulfillment. Privileged as artists and impotent as rebels, they are quite obviously frustrated. But it is sophisticated frustration, assuaged rather than intensified by their feeling of being on the outside. There is solace in their sense of difference, as they listen to their Beatles. If other Chinese savor of the fifties, these felt to me to be of the sixties, and made me think I had hit upon the Chinese avant-garde, Peking's bohemia. It was a world away from the one I had just left.

In more ways than one Peking was different from Yellow River China. I grew to dislike it, because its citizens disliked me. Along with tourism, knowledge of the outside world, the progression from provincial ignorance to urban awareness, Peking has bred opportunism, snobbery, envy, and hatred. And while I can accept the opportunism and the snobbery, I cannot accept the envy and the hatred. It is something whose manifestations may well be invisible to the European stranger, for he is less of a target than the Chinese who doesn't have to live in China. It is the Chinese émigré who is made to feel the resentment most, perhaps for having had things all too easy. I had never felt as much unspoken recrimination from perfect strangers as I did in Peking. Of course one seldom expects capital cities to be nice to their visitors. There are many contenders, but for sheer hate the citizens of Peking may well take the cake. That finished off Peking for me; and I fled.

Loesslands

*I have come to the end of the world—we are imprisoned by these
loess hills, and with the greatest difficulty can we believe there
is any world other than this. It is the oddest impression.*

—— Robert Payne
in Yan'an, 1947

It was no mere coincidence that after the fabled Long March
ended in a small town in northern Shaanxi in 1935, the communists established their capital in Yan'an. The place, beside the Yan,
the Yellow River stream from which it takes its name, is hugged
by loess hills which insulated the communists from the fierce
hostilities then racking the country. It was here, in cave dwellings cut into the hills, that Mao Zedong thought out China's
destiny and Chinese communism first came to its maturity.

Nor was it an accident that Xi'an, in southern Shaanxi, was
China's first imperial capital and, at the height of its splendor, the
world's largest city. Near where it stands, to the south of the Yellow
tributary Wei, Chinese civilization itself was cradled. Loess, that
easily worked soil which the Chinese call *huangtu*, or yellow earth,
was its seedbed, as it was the ground for the seeding of a new China.

Death and the First Imperial Capital

To arrive in Canton just as the Canton Fair was opening, to be told
that all the hotel rooms were solidly booked, and to find that one's

connection to Xi'an had been canceled, was not an auspicious start to a journey. Yet it hardly bothered me; I was full of unflagging purpose, fresh and accommodating, as one always is at the start of a journey. Takia had been diverted to an ethnic minority festival in Yunnan, down in the southwest, and I was traveling on my own. This in itself gave me a sense of freedom, and I did not doubt that I would get out of Canton that day. The only thing to be thought of was how.

I consulted the railway timetable, and decided on an overnight train to Changsha; there, if I was lucky, I could catch a flight for Xi'an the next day.

Having bought my ticket, and a couple of hours to kill, I thought I would take myself to the Tomb of the Seventy-Two Martyrs at Chrysanthemum Mound, a revolutionary site that is mentioned in every guidebook to Canton. I had to ask my way there when I got off the bus, and was quickly reminded that asking one's way is a chancy business in China, as surmise is often offered as certain knowledge, and everything is made to appear reassuringly near.

The seventy-two martyrs were among those killed in a revolt against the throne in 1911 in Canton. Like many a military operation, the offensive was distinguished by the courage of the fighting men and the incompetence of the organizers, and in the event, only one of the revolutionary units attacked as planned, the others having lost their nerve at the last minute. The two sides clashed in the street in front of the governor-general's offices, but as the government authorities had learnt of the plot in advance and taken appropriate measures, the revolt was swiftly put down.

I had expected to recognize the monument from the photographs I had seen of it—a faintly absurd ensemble of obelisk, proscenium, and pyramid, the whole crowned by a statue of liberty. The east-west mixture of styles is not altogether inappropriate, for just as Marxism had been a prod in the second Chinese revolution, so Western democracy had provided an ideal in the first. Besides, the money for it came from Chinatowns in many foreign countries, and the memorial itself was created out of donations by overseas Chinese patriots, the names of whose adopted homes—Boston,

Hawaii, Singapore, Vancouver, and so on—were engraved across the cornices of the pavilion.

But when I got there, and mounted the steps, I could see that the statue of liberty was gone; and when I wandered a little further, I noticed that other parts of the monument had been tampered with too. There was a tablet inscribed with the names of the heroes, not only the ones who were killed but also the others who had been involved in the plot. When I happened to look at this tablet, I noticed three names standing out from the rest, not because they were larger or more deeply engraved, but because they had been defaced and then freshly restored. The names were three well-known ones: Chen Jiongming, Hu Hanmin, and Zou Lu.

A number of Chinese visitors from some distant province had fetched up beside me, and when I pointed the names out to them, one of them remarked that it must have been the Gang of Four. Although this was rather glib of her, I nevertheless agreed that the defacement was a good specimen of the genre: the mutilation of historical monuments by Red Guards in the frenzy of the Cultural Revolution, the time when the infamous four were at the height of their power.

Chen Jiongming was a revolutionary turned traitor, best remembered for the time he revolted against Dr. Sun Yat-sen, and forced the latter to take refuge in a gunboat on Canton's Pearl River. Hu Hanmin, on the other hand, headed the anticommunist faction that broke with the left wing of Dr. Sun's party, the Kuomintang, and set up a government of its own in Nanking. When Mao Zedong was secretary of the propaganda department of the Shanghai branch of the Kuomintang, it so happened that Hu Hanmin was his boss, and I shouldn't be at all surprised if the two of them didn't get on. Zou Lu was a scholar, the recipient of a doctor of law degree from Heidelberg University, who worked to staunch communist infiltration of schools in the Canton area, and called for the expulsion of communist members from the Kuomintang.

I suppose the names of these three gentlemen had to be blotted out of history because, for all their contributions to the creation of the first republic, they were guilty of some offense against the communist movement. Like the practice of airbrushing disgraced politicians out of group photographs, this bid for historical amnesia is of a piece with the communist historiographical style, with Stalin's recasting of the Bolshevik past and Khrushchev's de-Stalinization of the time before he himself came to power. It is of a piece, too, with the old Chinese predisposition to the bureaucratization of history; the past in China has always been something you go to when you want an example to legitimize current endeavor or prove a present point.

Countries differ in the degree to which history matters in one's understanding of them. We all know about Chinese history, we have all heard of its iron grip on Chinese society. But seeing the present always in terms of the past is not the same thing as cherishing history. The Chinese don't, as a matter of fact, have much of that sense of lost time which I believe is basic to the valuing of history. For one thing they are a people too old to care: in China one is often assailed by a sense of the past stretching and stretching, with its vigor lost somewhere along the way, and its truths too old to be remembered and revealed. For another thing, the past is too much with them. The Chinese live in the same time-space as the one occupied by the ancients, whose deeds jostle for column inches in the newspapers with those of model workers and Third World leaders and whose sayings, transmuted into proverbs, salt ordinary speech like so many catch phrases.

It is those whose entrapment in their own history is the most absolute who can be so prodigal of it, blotting out whole chunks or taking liberties with the rest whenever they pose a difficulty to the prevailing dogma. The Chinese are sometimes said to work on a larger time scale than other people, but this only seems to be a prodigality of a similar sort, and I am disconcerted by those apologists for the Chinese government's record who say "Well, what can you do? Chinese history goes back thirty-five hundred years and communist rule only thirty." As though China could afford to be slow, just because its history is long. I well remember a remark Deng Xiaoping made to Cyrus Vance in 1975, speaking of Taiwan: "We can wait five years, ten years, or a hundred years, but reunification with China will finally be realized." Far from signifying a deep historical sense, the remark suggests that awareness has simply not extended, as yet, to the point of finding in time passing anything to mourn, in present as in future. No wonder "modern" China dawdles in an earlier century.

Even before I arrived in Xi'an, which is full of reminders of mortality, my mind was already running on the subject of death. For if my journey up here could have been more direct, it did give, in compensation, an unexpected opportunity to observe a funeral ceremony.

This was in Changsha, the night before. I'd fixed my plane ticket to Xi'an, and was sauntering through the city, down Cai E Middle Road, when I came upon a table being set up beside the street. The table had a large piece of white paper wrapped around its legs, and on this was written the Chinese character *dian*, for offerings to the spirit of the dead. I stopped then and there, on the pavement, and seeing two young men hanging about, asked one of them if obsequies were going to be performed that night.

"Yes," he said, "in a couple of hours from now, at 8 p.m., to be exact. You can come if you like."

Did it matter, I asked, that I didn't know the family? Not at all; it would be perfectly all right, he was himself part of the family. I declined dinner, which he next offered, and said that I would be back just before eight.

When the time came, it brought a cloudburst and a downpour. The rain came splashing down from the eaves of houses, and all the potholes filled with water. A bitter wind had come up, and in spite of my padded jacket I shivered with cold. But never mind, I thought as I set out for Cai E Middle Road, even if the rites are in the open there's sure to be some sort of shelter.

When I came in sight of the table, I found that it had been placed at the far end of a narrow alleyway between two blocks of buildings, and that a tent had been erected above it. Behind the table a curtain hung, passing for a wall; and from a clothesline strung across this curtain lengths of fabric in different colors were suspended, each about a yard and a half long.

As I saw it first, the whole of it, flickeringly lit by a naked electric bulb with the flex brought in from behind the building, looked like an altar where, in the old days, a votive tablet, bearing the name of the deceased, would be propped up. And it is true that the table, though it lacked a spirit tablet, was decked out as though it were placed in the ancestral temple of yore. It held a bunch of incense stuck into a jam jar, two red candles, three small plates of sacrificial food (apples and cakes), a packet of cigarettes and—in supreme pride of place—a cassette tape recorder.

The deceased, interred that very day, was one Comrade Li Sufang, an employee of the Changsha Municipal Machine Embroidery Factory. This information could be read off the strips of paper attached to a giant wreath of paper flowers surmounting the table. From her photograph, to be seen draped with black cloth among the multitudinous flowers, this Comrade Li appeared a gaunt, bespectacled lady of steely composure. On either side of her likeness were paper rhombuses of calligraphy, and on these I recognized those conventional expressions the Chinese like to use of the dead. "Her voice and visage are with us as if in the flesh," read one. "Her soul wanders in Paradise," read another. There were also rectangles of writing posted onto the corners of the hanging fabrics, and it was obvious at a glance that these bore the names of the donors. (It used to be the case in old China that the most expensive thing about a man was his funeral, and gifts for use by the family or the funeral ceremony were quite in order; indeed they were a way for friends and mourners to help save the bereaved from debt or bankruptcy.)

Near the entrance to the tent sat a group of hired musicians, and although the ceremony had not begun they were already in full swing. I counted three gongs, one large and two small; two Chinese trumpets; two pairs of cymbals; and a fair-sized drum. The musicians, who, with one exception, all looked to be over sixty, did not specialize in any one instrument but would swap them whenever they got bored with the one they were playing—or so it seemed to me. Noticing me, the youngest musician drew up a stool and invited me to sit down.

To one side of the group stood a pile of bricks topped by a wooden board, and on this were laid out a thermos flask, some mugs, a bowl of sugar, a bowl of tea leaves, and a plate of cigarettes. From these the musicians helped themselves from time to time; having no doubt performed at funerals many times before, they could talk, smoke, drink tea, and play their instruments all at the same time. The six of us encircled a stove burning round briquettes, but every now and then I had to move my stool a little further back to avoid the rain that was dripping from the roof of the tent and forming puddles on the floor. Soon after I had sat down the young musician poured some hot water into a mug, generously sugared it, and put it on the ledge of the stove in front of me, indicating that I should drink.

There being no impropriety attached to such questions in China, I asked the men how much they were being paid for their services.

"Two yuan [roughly U.S. $1] a head; we're only amateurs, you know." The man who said this, I learnt, was a cobbler.

"For how long?" I asked.

"Deep into the night," he replied.

"Is that when the ceremony ends?"

"No, we stay up only half the night; the relatives have to keep it up until morning."

"Keep up doing what?"

"Weeping and wailing; for them it's a nightlong wake."

Now it was their turn to put questions to me; and as we were in China, no opening was needed for asking how much money I earned, how old I was, what I was doing in China, and so on.

"So you've come across the border from Hong Kong, have you?" the young musician broke in at one point. "That dazzling world with its myriad temptations." He was repeating a cliché, a variation on the theme of Hong Kong's gold-paved streets, brothel-stuffed alleys, and mugger-infested corners. And then looking into my face, his eyes steady and faintly mirthful, he said, "That place where everything is said to be better than it is here: tell me, do they have services like this there? Do people even die there, or do they go on living forever?"

At this everybody broke into good-natured laughter. Afterward, the young man thrust his gong into my hands, which were outstretched in front of the stove for warmth, saying, "Here, have a go at this." Of course I would not have refused for anything, and greatly enjoyed myself, striking the disc with the sharp edge, rather than the flattened part of the spatula-shaped wooden baton—as I was taught to do. Chinese funeral music is commonly to be endured rather than enjoyed: the trumpets whine, the cymbals crash, the gongs bang, and every player strives for the maximum din with the minimum tunefulness. But my ears grew accustomed to the volume and I even came to like the sounds.

Presently family and friends started to file in, altogether some thirty men and women. As we were no longer in the phase of preliminary proceedings, I handed the gong over and stood up to watch. The ceremony, which began forthwith, goes something like this:

The musician (the only one with combed hair) who gets up and walks to the front of the altar is the master of ceremonies. The people standing before it in the first row are family, consisting of son, daughter, three granddaughters and their husbands. Those in the second and third rows are colleagues and friends.

Master of ceremonies: "Bow once, bow twice, bow three times." Here everyone bends at the waist, straightens up, bows again and again. (A large strapping country woman, I notice, doffs her Andy Capp cap at the start of each of these salutations and slaps it back on at the finish.) Timed to coincide with the end of this performance, an ear-splitting burst of firecrackers rings out behind me, presumably in the street outside.

Master of ceremonies: "The funeral oration." Here a young man, thin-faced, bespectacled, steps forward from the shadows to face the mourners, and in a voice greatly altered from the normal, reads out a speech, holding up a long sheet of rice paper on which black brush strokes may be detected. His speech is rapid, and formal to the point of unintelligibility.

He finishes, and a woman takes over. She is a colleague of the deceased at the Changsha Municipal Machine Embroidery Factory, judging from certain references in her speech. A biography of the deceased lady is rendered, from which it appears that when "those enemies the Japanese" overran the country, Comrade Li Sufang did her bit for the fatherland. This is interspersed with recitals of the departed's virtues, which, had she practiced them as described, would have set her prematurely apart from the living. At certain key points of the speech, recognizable to the musicians and the man in charge of accessory noises, the percussion would strike up and the firecrackers go off, both with the greatest possible noise.

Colleague: "She was an excellent mother, an excellent worker, an excellent comrade." BANG! BANG!

Colleague: "Without the leadership of the Chinese Communist Party, there would have been no new China." BANG! BANG!

And so on. Then another woman takes the floor, and with a formal, but not perfunctory, speech, seconds the views of her predecessor, not forgetting to mention the Party.

Next a member of the family, the son, goes up to the table and mumbles his thanks to everyone for coming. It is a short speech, and in contrast to the others, unprepared. He then retires, and is replaced by the M.C., who, with a sonorousness that can only have come from prolonged practice, begins a dirge. While thus engaged, he picks up three small cups from the altar, fills them with green plum wine, and hands them to the three eldest relatives, who may then be seen pouring the libation slowly onto the floor.

One granddaughter starts to weep, and from where I am standing I can see her shoulders rising and falling convulsively. Another holds back her sobs, but her eyes are bright with unspilled tears. Apart from these two, no one shows the slightest trace of emotion.

They receive sticks of incense from the M.C., as do the rest of the family. Holding these in their hands, the family proceed to pace the alleyway, with the M.C. leading. They go round and round in circles, onto the street, round the back of the tent, to emerge one by one from under the oblongs of hanging fabric. Then they range themselves in front of the altar, with their backs to it.

M.C.: "Bow once, bow twice, bow three times." They do so in unison, but to us this time, the guests and the spectators. At some time before this the tape recorder is switched on, and funeral music heard. One recognizes the music, from having heard it on television seven years before, as that played to accompany Mao Zedong's obsequies, and relayed to all the world.

End of rites, and everyone troops out.

Only the musicians remained, and I asked them, "What happens next?"

"Oh, this is the intermission," one answered. "The family have adjourned upstairs, and should be at their noodles now."

"By the way," I wanted to know, "how could you tell when to go crescendo?"

"The service follows a formula," I was told. What formula? The rites I'd just witnessed, I was to understand, were performed for the soul of the dead according to the Confucian-Taoist-Buddhist mode.

This, I must admit, was something of a surprise. Not the fact that the creeds of the old society survived, after so much deliberate government suppression, for China is notorious for its inability to shake off its past. Nor the fact that Confucianism, Taoism, and Buddhism were here practiced side by side, for I know that the Chinese are little disturbed by the scrambling of the forms of rival persuasions, and like to pay lip service to all the gods, lest they damn themselves by avoidable omission. What surprised me was the easy way my informant said it, as though it should be quite obvious. What could be more natural, his tone implied, when his voice pronounced "the Confucian-Taoist-Buddhist mode," without a moment's hesitation, and anything but in doubt.

"What, with all those invocations to the Chinese Communist Party?" I ventured to ask.

"Why not?" he answered, thinking it neither remarkable nor inappropriate that the Party should be called upon in prayers for the soul of the departed, along with the deities of Confucianism, Taoism, and Buddhism. "They can't all be right, but one of them might be," he said, utterly seriously.

He couldn't have expressed a more Chinese opinion, declining to be purist in the matter of belief systems. Changing the subject slightly, I remarked on the grave mounds one sometimes saw dotting the countryside, observing that the Chinese still seemed to feel strongly about burial and coffins.

"Some of the mounds you see are only temporary graves," he informed me, "dug by the departed's work unit, and not by the family. The corpses lie there until the relatives can come for them; then they are taken back to their ancestral homes, and are properly interred there."

I said I was surprised such practices still went on in the new China.

"Well, not in the city, of course. Only rural folks are allowed to bury their dead, town dwellers have to be cremated, unless you can put up the money to buy yourself a plot in the countryside. They do this, the rich town dwellers—go to all that expense."

I asked him if he believed in the afterlife, but he only laughed, declining to answer. After a moment he said, as most Chinese will when asked for their views on death, "It is fate that determines life and death."

To see how carefully the Chinese considered the needs of the next life and how lavish was the care taken to supply them, one needs only visit the museum of Qin Shi Huang's Buried Legion. This is in Xi'an, at which I now arrived from Changsha.

The Chinese believed that on quitting this life, you should take with you to heaven your family, house, servants, personal possessions, and everything that pleased you while in this world; and since these could not actually accompany you, models were placed in the tombs instead, to later archaeologists' delight. In Chinese communities all over Asia, a relic of that custom can still be seen in the burning of paper houses, clothes, cars, and counterfeit money at funerals, the paraphernalia being sent up with the spirit of the dead in smoke and flames, in a chariot of fire. In the case of Qin Shi Huang, he who declared himself the First Emperor of China, what was buried with him for use in the next life included a veritable army.

Much has been written about this buried legion—about the seven thousand life-size figures of soldiers and horses, the ten thousand pieces of real weaponry—so I don't want to go on about it. But it is undeniably impressive; and if you stop to think about it, what megalomania there was to the conception. What has been unearthed represents only a part of the whole, and remember that we are dealing with the third century B.C., before the days of mass production and American sweep. He thought big, the emperor; one must give him that. And he had made of his departure a masterpiece— not a vain lamentation upon the brevity of life, more like a thrust against time, and against death in its aspects of ending and decay.

The tomb itself lies enclosed in the heart of an enormous tumulus, which on the day I saw it was planted all over with pomegranate trees. It has not been excavated, so there is no telling how much it has been plundered. Beyond stretched the earth, cultivated and green, in whose bowels many more emperors lie entombed. I read somewhere that nineteen of the twenty Tang-dynasty emperors were buried in the vicinity of Xi'an, and I reflected how long it must be before archaeology can uncover those mortuary objects interred, those sarcophagi sealed up and entombed.

One such unopened grave is Qianling, the tomb of the infamous Empress Wu (625–705) and her husband, the Tang emperor Gaozong. Her second husband, that is; she was first married, when aged twelve, to Gaozong's father Taizong, or at least she joined the ranks of his unnumbered concubines. When Taizong died she retired to a nunnery, as was proper, but not before she had caught the eye of his heir, who then improperly married her. Gaozong was a bit of a weakling, and an illustration of what seems to be the law of families: that whatsoever the father is, the son is not.

The site of the tomb, which I visited one morning, is especially fine. It lies under the highest of three hills, and from its top you can contemplate at just the right distance the wedge of clear sky between the other two hills—the shape of peasant straw hats, lying side by side to the south.

Colossal effigies line the so-called spirit way, the approach to the mausoleum, guarding in the imperishability of stone the bodies that are already rotted within. No, not quite imperishable: the heads of sixty-one stone figures had been lopped off, nobody is sure by whom. Qianling has not been robbed, I hear, and if one day it can be excavated without damage to its contents, it should be a sight to see.

All the same, whatever lies buried will only become significant as it is weighted with human association, and one's interest in this place remains the interest in the dead couple themselves. One has every reason to be curious about the girl who came to be called Wu Zetian, or Wu Is Heaven, for she was a combination of good looks, brains, and high energy, and one is always led to wonder, with people so intensely endowed: what do they do with it all? In Wu Zetian's case these gifts were so deployed as to enable her to ascend the throne, and become the only woman in Chinese history to rule as sole sovereign of the empire.

Beauty admitted her to the imperial palace, as it rescued her from the veil; other, more practical talents were useful in steering her path through the harem, that world of women in which preoccupation with power and the darkest machinations for gaining it took first place. Ruthlessness disencumbered her of enemies and whoever stood in her way on the climb to supreme power. If this meant poisoning her own son, murdering her niece, and eliminating other members of her clan, little did she jib at that. (For, as can easily be seen in any family where the slightest question of inheritance arises, bonds of blood, when you come down to it, are much weaker than is commonly supposed.)

All this she in a way justified, by ruling firmly and well. She directed the business of state with the skill and judiciousness of a born administrator. She knew how to use the special abilities of men, without abetting their possibilities for encroachment, and part of her genius consisted in her surrounding herself more and more with able men. In the half century in which she dominated the government, the empire attained to a state of peace, consolidation, expansion, and prosperity; and religion and the arts were far from left behind.

Yet if she is remembered, it is the unsavory side of her image which chiefly survives, perpetuated by many a book, film, play, and recently by a political campaign, in which her name was linked with Jiang Qing's. For the Chinese, who like to look back to older types, thought that with Madame Mao they had another Empress Wu on their hands. Certainly in their vilification of her, Jiang Qing was portrayed as a scheming woman with the ambition and promiscuity of a Wu Zetian.

It was what a fellow passenger said of her, when he and I were chatting on the bus that brought us to Qianling. But while seeing what they had in common, he also observed that the two were ultimately dissimilar. "Jiang Qing," he said, "took her revenge on her enemies by her strength in Mao Zedong, by having what we call a behind-the-scenes backer, whereas Wu Zetian was able to run things in her own right."

He asked me what else I'd seen in Xi'an, and I said that tombs were all I ever seemed to see hereabouts. In that case I must have been to the Temple of Flourishing Teaching, he said. As a matter of fact I hadn't, and asked him to tell me about it. "It's where you'll find the remains of Xuanzang, under a pagoda," he said. "You've heard of Xuanzang?" I had; he was a famous monk whose epic pilgrimage to India in the seventh century formed the historical basis for *Journey to the West* (also called *Monkey* in an abridged English version), a work of comic imagination which stands to the Chinese novel rather as *Don Quixote* does to the European. What's more, he'd been on my mind lately—not because I have any special interest in Chinese Buddhism, of which he was a great exponent, nor because of any feeling for the Tang dynasty, from which both he and Xi'an are inextricable. He had been on my mind because he was a traveler—seventeen years he was on the road—and I was coming more and more to think that I'd never be one. There was a reason for this flagging enthusiasm. It was the other tourists, whom you couldn't help noticing; they were all over Xi'an. Even if, like a Buddhist, I could rise above the world of objects, I could not rise above the world of package tourism, or that sense of futility it makes me feel about my own touring.

Still I went to the Temple of Flourishing Teaching, now that this man had mentioned it. It is twenty-four miles out of town, set on a hill, and when I arrived had just seen off its last busload of native sightseers. I was shown Xuanzang's pagoda by the abbot, who had on a monk's black habit with a triangle of a beige woolly showing between the folds. Almost completely bald, he had an unlined brow and smooth, shiny cheeks. When we were standing about, a Chinese visitor popped up and went straight to the point: "Are you," he asked the monk, "paid a salary by the state?" No, he was not. "Then how do you live?" persisted the inquirer.

"By labor! By farming." The abbot was a little indignant, and his tone implied, "He who does not work, neither shall he eat."

I did not see a single foreign tourist, but you could tell the Japanese had been here in force. They had decorated half a wall of the reception room, where I sat down to a cup of tea with the abbot, with their souvenir pennants, nearly every one of them a memorial to Japanese-Chinese friendship. In fact the Japanese are little given to friendly feelings toward the Chinese, whom they consider hopelessly inferior. Deep down the Chinese reciprocate this sentiment, though with far less reason nowadays than in the Tang dynasty, when they really could teach the Japanese a thing or two, and did.

Apart from making money there the Japanese have no real interest in China. If they show any interest in Chinese culture, this is only because of their interest in Japanese culture, which has so many of its roots in China. If they like to come to Xi'an, I suspect that this is because, as the Tang capital of Chang'an, at the height of its splendor, it was what the Japanese court exactly copied for laying out Nara and Kyoto. It so happened that on my last night in Xi'an, a Japanese girl took up the other bed in my hotel room. She was a secretary, but had quit her job to travel. She asked me if, like her, I was following the Silk Route, the subject of a recent documentary on Japanese television. For her the point of her journey was precisely that: not the fascination of the Silk Route itself, but the vogue which Japanese TV had made of it.

I didn't see her at all the next day, as she had come upon some Japanese travelers in the hotel and was in a headlong hurry to join them. But I did catch still more suggestions of mortality. This is what Xi'an will be to me, a place sedimented with the ancient dead, where you never have to search far before you encounter a funerary symbol. This sounds depressing but is not. For Xi'an is a vigorous city, full of life and traffic and busy humanity. And what I now saw, if decidedly mortuary in intent, was not a bit morbid in effect.

In a large grey building standing to one side of the drum tower, under a line of Chinese characters painted to read "Municipal Theatre Costume Retail Department," there was a door with a curious sign on its lintel. It said: "Funeral and Interment Clothes Sold Here." The door was actually closed, but you could get into the shop by either one of two additional entrances; these had signs which said, "Men and Women's Fashions," and "Theatrical Costumes, Props, and Dance Costumes."

I thought that this was worth more than a moment of my curiosity, and stepped into the darkness of the building. I made for the funeral clothes counter, which turned out to be in the far end of the shop. It was very dark there, but still it was difficult not to see the sign pinned up above the counter, which said, "Burial suits, once sold, are without exception not returnable." I asked to see one.

"Male or female?" inquired the shop assistant.

"Female," I answered, not thinking of anyone in particular.

She took a minute to look through her stock—from where I stood I could see that she was plentifully supplied—and came up with something which I thought you nowadays only saw in the movies. It quite took my breath away, it was so sumptuous—a beautiful ensemble in silk, such as might have been worn by a court lady in the Qing dynasty. The robe was of purple silk, deep as the skin of an aubergine, and trimmed with a border of gold. The skirt, of a heavier silk, was midnight blue and splashed with a phoenix pattern embroidered in gold. (I supposed that the male version would be a dragon.) Together the pieces cost thirty-two yuan, well over half of an average wage earner's monthly salary.

In such finery are the richer dead arrayed when they go to their graves in China. How incorrigible they are, I thought, those millions of Chinese in their baggy blue suits; if they don't dress very styl-

ishly when they are alive, they certainly make up for it when they
die. And the thought came to me that all the chic, all the color, all
the money of China is expended on the children and the dead.

Revolutionary Heartland

These two brief conversations will illustrate the utter anomaly of
my position as a single woman in China. The first was with a woman
ticket collector, at the bus terminus in Xi'an.

"Where are you bound for?" she asked.

"Yan'an, ultimately."

"Visiting relatives?"

"No, just traveling."

"Alone?"

"Yes, alone."

"How pointless!" She almost shook her head at me, it made so
little sense to her.

The other was with a woman who had sat next to me on the
plane to Xi'an. "Aren't you something, though?" she said, looking
at me wonderingly, as though I were a species hitherto unknown
to her. "But why don't you get married? You want to be thought
peculiar or something?"

She conceded it was not unknown in China; she knew of two
spinsters where she came from (Lanzhou), and over the years they
had become freakier and freakier. I then got a once-over from
behind a pair of stern, black-rimmed glasses; she could tell an odd-
ball when she saw one.

I had not expected to be affected by this kind of disapproval, but
it is extraordinary how quickly one comes to mind it, to hate having
the ideals to which this country is dedicated—togetherness and
happy family life—so unchallengeably applied to oneself. One
very soon realizes that it is not only the historical lag, or the pro-
verbial gregariousness of the Chinese, which makes them so abhor
the unfamilied status. It is also that difference which exists between
the West and the communist state in the relationship individual

lives bear to society. To a man in the West, society is that which sets the limits he must not exceed; and in exchange for this he receives the assurance that no one will encroach excessively upon his private life. In a communist state, where someone is always watching, and where the frontier between self and society is constantly effaced, a man is never alone, and thirty to forty years of depriving a people of aloneness must make the very idea of it seem alien and repugnant. Chinese I met never tired of reproving me for my solitariness, saying that being alone was "unnatural." This is perhaps only to be expected, when the only life they know is the collective life.

Now, I was traveling into country where, in spite of the Party's prescription for late marriage, to marry at twenty-four is to marry late. Already in the bus, I could feel this gulf between myself and them, these workers of land who have no inkling how things might be different, and who have yet to be broken upon by the world.

I tried to find out when we would arrive at Huangling, where I planned to break my journey before going on to Yan'an. But one thing I'd learnt about this country: one mustn't think about time, one must take things as they come when they come. "When do we get there?" the driver had said. "Why, whatever the time is when we arrive—that's when we get there."

We were running over fields of wheat and rape plant, past the River Wei; past the young girls with their heads wrapped in kerchiefs against the sand, hoeing or digging or squatting by the roadside; past the petrol station where we all had to climb out, none but authorized persons being allowed in such places; past the town of Tongchuan, where coal is mined and the railroad comes to a stop. And we were climbing to the hills, with terraces of loess falling away below us and cave dwellings which seemed the next thing to mere earth.

Our route wound northward in and out across spurs. The temperature quickly dropped, and I found I had to put on more sweaters. It was raining quite hard now, and the driver suddenly braked to a stop and climbed out to spread a tarpaulin cover over the luggage rack atop the bus. Next to me sat a little boy with one shoe off and a thickly bandaged foot. He remained silent, absolutely silent, from the beginning of the journey to the end. Only once did I hear a sound from him; it was when we were passing the end of the railway line at Tongchuan, and the sound might have been the word "train."

The men around me all smoked and stared dumbly out of the window. But not for long; as soon as I began to make polite conversation they turned to me and grew chatty. They were returning to Luochuan, further to the north than Huangling, so they were getting off later than I. They loved Luochuan; "a great place," they assured me, breaking into wide smiles. (With its dirt tracks and mud huts, Luochuan is not, as I discovered when I passed it the next day, everybody's idea of a great place, but I liked these country people's simple pride in their hometown better than the city dwellers' disgruntlement with theirs.)

We talked about this and that, and presently one of them asked me if we had "walking tractors" where I came from. I replied I understood not, at least I had never seen one until I came to China, where they are turned out by the thousands and used for transport and power. He did not know what to make of this, until his friend broke in with, "It's probably obsolete where she comes from; in America they probably haven't seen one for a hundred years."

From tractors the conversation drifted to railroads, and I asked why there wasn't one going to Yan'an; it was the shrine of the Chinese revolution after all.

"Yes, they did lay the foundations for one," one of them told me, "but that was when Chairman Mao was still alive. After he died there didn't seem to be much point."

"It's hill country around here," his friend explained. "It's poor, and there are no mineral resources to make it worthwhile."

We were talking in this way when a young man walked down the gangway and asked to swap seats with the man next to me. He said I must be from Hong Kong, and he was pleased to meet a compatriot from Hong Kong. I assumed that he had a purpose for changing seats, but it turned out he only did so in order to be of service to me. Did I wish to have anything explained to me about this country? I was not to hesitate to ask him questions. Had I noticed how much cleaner and pleasanter Xi'an had become? It was the new mayor, I was to understand; he had spittoons placed at strategic intervals on the sidewalks and cracked down on any shop that didn't wash down and look after its stretch of pavement in front. He spoke in a voice which had been places; just now he was on his way to Fuxian, on business, but he was afraid he couldn't reveal what his business was, giving me to understand that it was an official secret.

Next he took to explaining things to the peasants from Luochuan. "The lady is a traveler," he explained. It was like this: where she came from people could save up their money and their holidays and go off somewhere, anywhere they chose to. Now China was another matter; in China you couldn't travel whenever you wanted to; "for instance, you couldn't go to Hong Kong even if you could afford it."

The men from Luochuan drank it in; it was all news to them. "Now is that so?" they exclaimed. "You mean even if we had the money we wouldn't be allowed to go to Hong Kong?" No, they wouldn't; but the revelation did not in the least upset them. Perhaps the contrary: whereas a minute before the thought of traveling abroad had never entered their soul, the fascination of the idea now seized upon them.

"But suppose we wanted to go, what'd we have to do?"

The young man told them they'd have to apply for an exit permit.

"And how do we do that?" Their curiosity had been aroused, and they wanted to know if it could be done from outside Peking. When the young man told them that ultimately the decision would have to rest with Peking, they said, "Well I never!" and "Think of it"; and I thought how far we were here from even the world of Peking, with its Democracy Wall, Peking Spring, and those urban dissidents who want lighting out.

Where else but in China would you find people living in enforced isolation and under what can only be called totalitarianism, and not even know it? I felt I had just been given nine-tenths of China in a nutshell—a brief, but magnified fragment of the medieval world; and a shuttered feeling suddenly bore down upon me.

It was 2 p.m. when we arrived in Huangling. I had vaguely expected to find someone there to meet me, but the station was empty, the rain fell steadily, and there was not a soul to be seen. I walked up a street leading away from the station, hoping it would take me to the district headquarters guesthouse, and was relieved to find that it did.

Huangling means the Yellow Tomb, for according to tradition it is here that the Yellow Emperor, the mythical ancestor of the Chinese race and its first sovereign, lies buried. The tomb was too far to walk to in the rain, and I thought I'd leave exploring until the morning. Instead I took a short walk, down a path which was as near as Huangling seemed to come to possessing a main street, watching where I was putting my foot, for mud clutched at every step. I came to a wall with a blackboard on the far side of the street, and when I peered at it through the rain, I was diverted by what I found written upon it.

The message was quite unambiguous: everything should be done, read the text, for the encouragement of inner beauty and the discouragement of outward show. Do appearances matter? No, they do not. Here is an illustration of a misguided and lamentable belief that they do. Recently a wedding was to take place between a driver and a girl belonging to the same commune. On the day, he came to fetch her from her home in his freshly cleaned tractor, which his parents had thought to deck out with a red nuptial blanket. There he was, all spruced up and eager, when there was this terrible outcry from the bride's parents, who would not hear of their daughter going off with the groom unless his parents had properly adorned the tractor with a big red rosette. Such concern for appearances, in the opinion of the local officials, would lead to the neglect of true honest-to-goodness values.

Back in the guesthouse, I was fed, as a lone diner, on beef slices, bean curd with chili, rice, and egg soup. Afterward, feeling the lack of company, I twiddled my way through the buzz of a radio I found in my room. It was a huge affair, built to a prewar design, and from it I got Shaanxi Broadcasting and a litany of the harmful effects of rats on man—specifically on his health and the fruits of his agricultural labor. In a voice as feminine as it was friendly, the broadcaster expressed the hope that the nation might be united in combating this scourge. For the remainder of the evening I listened to this not undiverting program, which I learnt from a closing announcement was called Science for the Masses.

From a wish not to leave Huangling without, as it were, paying tribute to one's ancestor, I went next morning to the Yellow Emperor's shrine on the hill. I found a grove, with old gnarled trees, a temple where several delegations from Hong Kong and Macao had left giant paper wreaths, and a pavilion housing steles. The wreaths carried the inscription: "To the father of our race." The words seemed quite natural; telling the Chinese he was mythical wouldn't have dissuaded them from laying those wreaths. My own feeling was almost proprietary: yellow the river, yellow the earth, yellow the name of this our first king, yellow the land's oldest color, the stamp supreme.

I did not linger at the temple, afraid that I would miss the bus to Yan'an. As to the time this bus was due to arrive at Huangling, no one could advise me. Other people were waiting in the station besides me, some sitting on the bench, some sprawling over it dozing. Against the wall by the entrance two ragged Tibetan men stood smoking, conspicuous in their maroon robes and large fur hats. They caught the eye of a young man with a cigarette dangling from the corner of his mouth, who, out of curiosity or, more likely, boredom, walked up to the taller of the two and asked to see the knife he was carrying.

The Tibetan gave it, and from the corner of my eye I saw the young man swing the knife, then flick it in a sudden lunge at its owner. He was only playing the fool, but I heard the scrape of steel against flesh, and then a sharp, croaky cry. When I looked I saw the dark blood oozing from a gash in the Tibetan's hand, and the young man skulking away. I instantly rummaged in my bag for some strips of Band-Aid, then walked up to the Tibetan and put them into his palm. He looked at me in an uncertain, distant way, then shook his head slowly. After some rummaging in the folds of his robe he brought out a small, dirty plastic bag, and as I watched he took from it a pinch of ash-colored paste and smeared it thickly over his wound.

An hour and a half passed before the bus arrived. By the kindness of a soldier I not only had a seat but a good view from a window. Approaching Luochuan, and for some distance beyond it, I saw the fissured terrain of the loesslands, such landscapes as I had never before seen, of a geology so strange as to be of another planet. Vertical cleavages appeared, of the color of grey cardboard, and steep scoops of earth hugged by cultivated ridges tipped with green and whorled to the pattern of a thumb print. The Loess Plateau, the largest in the world. Into this region the Yellow River cuts a deep, narrow valley and receives almost half its silt. Here, where soil erosion is a scourge of truly alarming proportions, the Yellow perpetuates in a vicious cycle the scouring of a land already denuded, a land slit by gullies and gashed by ravines, where transverse movement is hardly possible at all, and where one is exposed defenseless— to recall the words of Teilhard de Chardin—"to all the great winds of the earth."

Yan'an, reached after four hours' driving, looked at first sight to be an overgrown village with shabby houses flung about a river. You crossed this stream, the Yan, which was completely dry at this time of the year, by a bridge; then you had to follow the road some way until you had passed two intersections and found a turning to your right. At the far end of this turning stands the Yan'an Hotel.

It is very large, and unwelcoming, and when I entered there was not a human figure in sight. For some time I had almost the feeling that I had the place all to myself. I wandered in and out of some rooms, and also went outside the grounds to look, but it was only after prolonged search that I found Comrades Zhang and Cai at their desks. It would not be true to say that they were intent on their business, for it was past office hours, and their business was the official reception of guests—of whom, as my reconnaissance had revealed, there couldn't have been many.

Comrade Zhang was a short, moon-faced, roly-poly man, Shaanxi-Provincial in speech. One felt he was amenable to an appeal to the human, as opposed to the bureaucratic, side of him—an impression that would be fortified in the succeeding days. Comrade Cai was much the better looking of the two, and with his aloofness the more easily recognizable official. I was not hopeful about my stay in Yan'an when I learnt that it was Cai, and not Zhang, who looked after foreign visitors. In the event, however, he took hardly any notice of me, having more important matters to attend to, such as the impending visit of an American journalist. Any claim I had to his attention while that American was in town would have required that I be other than mere Chinese.

I was quite happy to be left alone, and wandered that evening down to the river. Whenever I looked up I could see the Precious Pagoda, that emblem of Yan'an, not only of the town but what it represents: the consecrated shrine of the Chinese revolution, one of the first places in Asia where socialism was lived. Its appearance in a movie used to send a rush of emotion running through the audience, swelling their hearts.

A narrow path lined the riverbank, and on it I found a congeries of stalls. It led to a row of squat, tumbledown huts, and when I stopped in front of one I saw that it bore a sign advertising lamb *pao*, a spicy soup which I knew was a local speciality. I entered this eating house and asked for a bowl. In an instant I had the cook plunging the meat into his caldron and his wife giving me a piece of bread to eat with it. As I sipped the soup I looked about me; an eating house, I have called it, but it was really nothing but a hovel with a rickety table and some stools. In a corner a heap of jumbled rags and flour sacks lay on a bed, if you could call it that, and on this an old birdlike man in a green cap was perching.

When I raised my eyes I found his pupils gazing at me, as his brown fingers stroked a wispy beard. There was somebody crouching at the far end of the bed, and I saw that, in complete contrast to the old man's tired appearance and the flyblown untidiness of the room, it was a person of startling freshness. She looked more than usually tall, her face had a certain angularity, her eyebrows were thicker and her shoulders were broader than is normal in a Chinese girl. But she was handsome, and in the dimness of the room her skin glowed.

I told the cook I liked his lamb *pao,* and all at once everybody started talking. I learnt that the eating place was a joint enterprise of the cook and the old man, and that Ailan, the girl, was the old man's daughter. The father was a retired soldier; as a young man he had fought the Japanese with other Red fighters in the New Fourth Army.

"So you must have known Mao Zedong then?" I was fascinated.

Ailan answered for her father, "Well, yes; he used to go round picking up the cigarette ends Chairman Mao had thrown away and smoke them." She added, "He doesn't smoke now, his health won't permit it"—this to the sound of a racking cough from the father. It was curious to watch the old man as Ailan spoke; for a moment, behind the dull gaze, the spirited eyes of another person looked out, as if the old Red Army fighter lurked somewhere behind that form made tired and frail by age.

I wanted to press the old man for details of his past, but the few words he spoke were uttered so bronchially that I found it hard to understand him. I would have liked to have asked him: the revolution you fought for, what good had it done? But the sag of his shoulders seemed to say: enough, enough; and the eyes once more looked distantly, as one who has long been familiar with the breaking of dreams. Besides, I suspected that, like most men, he was only concerned now with the small things that involved him intimately; with how much a catty of lamb cost, or how many bowls of lamb *pao* they sold that day.

We went on for about half an hour more, but the time was mostly taken up by the cook and his wife putting questions to me, with the direct simple curiosity of their kind, about what life was like in the world outside. Poor as they were, when I got up to go they wouldn't take any money from me, saying I'd eaten so little, and had I not repeatedly insisted, they would have happily fed me for free; this was part of the Chinese kindness.

When I regained the street leading to my hotel, I found it abandoned for the night. I think I was already halfway down it when I discerned a movement behind me in the dark. It turned out to be Ailan, wheeling a bicycle. When she had caught up with me she said shyly, "Father said I ought to escort you. The streets are not all that safe, you know, with all those rowdies." I let that remark pass uncontested, though I could hardly conceive of being anywhere safer than in China, and I had yet to see a real rowdy, instead of the bored unemployed youths to whom she was alluding.

She, too, was without a job, I learned. She was twenty-one, and by her own admission was not qualified for anything, being of that generation which matured in the years of the Cultural Revolution, when everything, as she put it, "was torn to pieces and you went to school not to be taught but to rag the teacher."

"But surely," I said, "even if book learning was out there must have been things you were interested in, were good at?"

"Yes, there was, there is." She brightened up when she said this.

"And what is that?"

"Archery," she said; "I'm very fond of archery." At the last sports meet in Baoji, a city to Xi'an's west, she broke the record for Shaanxi Province. It was in the papers, and she agreed to show me the clippings.

We reached the gates of the hotel, and when we said goodbye I held out my hands to her. Taking them, she asked me, "Would you like company tomorrow; would you like me to show you the sights?" I said I would like nothing better, and we arranged to meet outside the hotel at nine.

Next morning I was early, and so was she. It touched some soft spot in me, to see her dressed in her Sunday best: a black polo-neck sweater, a light blue polyester jacket, a pair of green, flared trousers, and high-heeled shoes. We walked down a long dusty street and finally came to the Memorial Museum of Revolution, our first call.

This was a chill cathedral-like building, where a huge blown-up photograph of Mao Zedong greets you in the emptiness of the front hall, looming out of a wall swathed ceiling to floor in red flags. To my sense an atmosphere of embalmment pervaded this museum, filled as it was with the souvenirs of the Chinese revolution: dead faces staring out from photographs, letters, pages from books, maps of campaigns, a greatcoat once worn by a Red soldier, the pony Mao rode in 1947, which taxidermy had restored with rubber flesh and glass eyes. The halls were made for thronging, but were at this moment sadly deserted. In its vacancies Ailan sought a guide, and at last found one, a diminutive girl whose eyes kept darting to the next glass case, the next display, the next mural of inspirational quotation, the exit signifying the end of the tour. She delivered her piece well enough, of how Mao Zedong, Zhou Enlai, Zhu De, and their ragged army withdrew to Yan'an at the end of the Long March, but the hearts of the young, I thought to myself, are not in the story.

The guide's manner said as much: she was polite, but a little distracted. Hearing her recital, and seeing the empty halls, I thought of all the people whom Mao and his kind had led to this wilderness, then to the promised land that afterward had turned infertile, beneath the sweep of his ambition, which reached further than any man's, and the curse of his longevity, which stripped him of all human suppleness. And not irrelevantly, there came to my mind those words of Jesus to his disciples, "O faithless and perverse generation, how long shall I be with you?"

I stopped before a photograph of Mao riding his pony out of Yan'an, and spotting the indistinct figure of a woman riding behind him, observed to my young guide that it was Jiang Qing.

"Oh is it?" she said, from politeness, and without glancing at the picture. As someone at a dinner table might absently indulge a boring neighbor while her attention was being held by a conversation elsewhere, so did she receive this piece of information. Her lack of concern for Jiang Qing was the measure of her distance from the power politics of Peking and perhaps even from the trauma of the Cultural Revolution. The thought occurred to me that that nightmare—all those stories one hears of people being tortured or beaten to death or made to fill their mouths with ordure—was not real for her. Jiang Qing was not to her what she was to all the embittered actors, writers, film directors, and intellectuals who came in for a mauling because they had once known her as a small-time movie actress in Shanghai—a memory she wanted to close the door on.

When I emerged from the building I noticed the grass they had planted in a rectangle in front of the steps, and the four large Chinese characters picked out in gravel within it. Be Practical and Realistic, they said—a motto to urge one back down to earth, from those dizzying heights of revolution just left behind. One recognized the text as the watchword of the moment, the one they like to quote at each abandoning of all that was most messianic and purest in the Maoist vision, all that dictated putting ideology first and your material concerns last—all that went, in fact, with the tradition inherited from Yan'an. Four little children were scrabbling about the grass, playing. One wore a holster, and was waving a toy gun. At that moment it seemed likely they would grow up looking on the practical side. The characters stood out in the glare of the noonday sun, and seemed to me like an obituary of the Yan'an ideal.

In the afternoon Ailan and I went to other shrines of the revolution, not quite as pilgrims, but not without a certain respectfulness either. The shrines were cave dwellings, places where Mao Zedong had lived; and Wanjiaping, Fenghuangshan, Yangjialing, and the Date Orchard are their celebrated names. That's where he worked late into the night, forgetting to sleep, the guide said; that's the plot he cultivated. That's the stone table at which he talked with the American journalist Anna Louise Strong, and told her "Imperialism and all reactionaries are paper tigers." Comrade Zhu De received his guests here; Comrade Zhou Enlai had his office there; and oh, that's Liu Shaoqi's former residence, closed to the public for a long time, but reopened now that he has been politically rehabilitated. Yes, the guide confirmed, this bed where the Chairman slept, that desk where he wrote his famous essays, those chairs where he sat—these are all reproductions, the originals having been locked away for safety in some repository.

I have a weakness for revolutionary fetishes such as were here displayed. But what would in retrospect signify Yan'an to me were not these revolutionary symbols. On the contrary, for all its specialness in the history of Chinese communism, to me Yan'an retained an intenser feeling of immemorial China than any place I'd seen so far: Those old peasants in their patched padded jackets, eternally squatting; those silent women with their faces of endurance and hardship; those stone breakers sifting building pebble from the bed of the dried-up Yan, as though concrete had yet to be invented—the collective impression which these made on me was of a life lived in the same way since the beginning of time, outside the turmoils of history. These were the same people, I felt, who first met the eyes of the Long Marchers as they arrived, footsore but triumphant, in the shadow of the Great Wall and entered the communist base in northern Shaanxi.

Observing them from the bus taking me back from Date Orchard, one would not have thought that anything as transforming as a revolution had happened. The bus passed these people, and also a hoarding standing back from the road. I read the slogan with which it was blazoned, discerning Mao's handwriting. "Hard Work, Plain Living," it said, and I wondered how that exhortation sounded to those peasants who toiled beside its shadow, who throughout their lives had known nothing else. I had the sense I had caught revolution in an act of erasure, and I suddenly thought I knew what socialist construction was all about. At that moment socialist construction struck me as the process whereby poverty is simultaneously eliminated and induced.

At nearly all of the revolutionary sites Ailan and I were the only visitors, wandering in and out at our leisure. Ailan was anxious that I should not miss anything, every so often pointing to things I might not have noticed. "Here, you see, are the two essentials every Red soldier carried—a sack of millet and a rifle." On hearing I had never had millet gruel, she thought hard about how she could get me some to try. "It's quite delicious, and very easy to make. Perhaps you'd like to take some millet back to England with you, I could easily get you a sack." Once she pointed to a drum in a shop, and said it was what you played in *yangge,* the local folk dance.

She asked me if I'd ever seen it performed, and I said no. But this was not true, as I later remembered; there was the time, far back in childhood and the first years of the new China, when scarcely a week went by in Shanghai without some procession passing our house, with rouged girls in peasant costume dancing the *yangge,* each with one of those drums strapped to her waist, beneath the photographs of Stalin held up high, and the banners proclaiming, "We'll show them, those Americans!" The dance itself became all the rage in Shanghai, and I remember learning to do it myself— three steps forward and one back—not knowing that it was Yan'an agitprop, only that it was the very latest thing in Shanghai.

Ailan was quite the best companion I had met so far in China, and I looked forward to spending many more days with her. I felt that we were, in however superficial a degree, friends. But something held me back, and when, our sightseeing over, she suggested she visit me in my hotel that evening, I was quite dismayed. This was because two days in Yan'an, plus a number of conversations with Comrade Zhang, were already enough to convey the conservative temper of the place, and to convince me that the apartheid between native and outsider, while not rigorous everywhere, was likely to be absolute here. Until she met me Ailan had never had anything to do with people from abroad, and she was not to know that such relations were prohibited in China. I wanted, for her own good, to say no to her, yet somehow I could not bring myself to do so, and that night I found myself giving her tea in my room.

She talked a little about school. "It was a farce. No, that's not it, it was pathetic. All we ever did was to copy passages out of newspapers, and if you caught all the right slogans, you got the highest marks. It's true what they say about us, our generation, that we are all ignorant."

I tried to make her talk about Yan'an. "It seems forlorn," I said, "when you'd expect to see some show of good faith—from the leaders, I mean, the ones who had lived here. I see so little development in the town it makes me feel Yan'an has been ungenerously treated, like something which has outlived its usefulness, and conveniently forgotten. I gather Mao Zedong never came back."

She nodded, then told me that, as a matter of fact, there had been some rebuilding, in the part of the town they call Southern Pass. But it was a flood, and not any government plan, which had occasioned the rebuilding. It was in the summer of 1977, when, after an unusually heavy rainfall, the reservoir up in the hills behind had overflowed, causing the Yan to swell and a flood tide to sweep over the town. Though the water ebbed in an hour, well over a hundred flood fighters were killed, and a whole street in Southern Pass had had to be rebuilt. (Some days later, walking down that street, I came across a house, part of a newish block, which bore on its wall a mark at eye level indicating the height of the floodwaters.)

We then came to talk of the environs of the city, and I questioned her about Nanniwan, a place just under thirty miles to the southeast of Yan'an, and important in the revolutionary memory. It was only a piece of land reclaimed from the wilderness by a division of the Eighth Route Army, but in its image several revolutionary qualities were epitomized: frontier spirit, self-reliance, mutual aid, manual labor. Even Jiang Qing had had to put in six months there, and I had read that when Mao packed her off, he told her that if she couldn't produce all her own food and clothing, she'd die.

Ailan could tell I wanted to go there; "but it's difficult," she said. "Even if you caught the bus it's another twenty kilometers from the station. Coming back, you'd have to try and flag down the bus from Luochuan, as it doesn't normally stop."

I was prepared to give it a try, but after thinking about it for a while, Ailan came up with another idea. "I may be able to do something—oh, it's no trouble, I have a cousin who drives a truck. I don't know how busy he is, but I could ask him to take us. If it can be arranged we'll come and pick you up in the morning." She was giving me a demonstration of the truism that knowing a driver is the one thing that really counts in China, or any place where private car ownership is unheard of.

I was not altogether happy about this arrangement, but I could not tell her candidly what I thought—that though the use of public property for private purpose was common enough in China, it was not a transgression the authorities would wink at, when compounded with the offense of consorting with a foreigner. I thought she could hardly have escaped the authorities' notice, coming to see me at the hotel like that. Yet I did not want to give her any reason to feel that her kindness was being rejected; and there was also the wish, in my silence on the subject of segregation between native and outsider, to spare her her innocence. To give Ailan the least glimpse of the authoritarianism under which she unconsciously lived, I felt, would be to impart a piece of knowledge to someone who was better off without it. I had the scruples one feels when one is about to corrupt another to one's own view of the world at the expense of some hitherto unshakeable certainty of their own.

So I said nothing, and in the end made matters worse. In the morning she called the hotel—the floor clerk summoned me to the telephone—to say that everything was fixed and she would be coming for me at eleven. I waited until twelve. Then I raced round to her father's eating place. The old man was not there, but the cook and his wife expressed astonishment. I asked them, "You're sure about that, that she was coming to pick me up?"

"Quite sure; she said she was going to Nanniwan with you, first thing." No, she hadn't been in touch since then, and they could not tell me where she was.

Arriving back at the hotel, I found the floor clerk hovering in the corridor by the door to my room. She was a young country girl, whose habit of staring with her mouth slightly open contributed to the impression that she was not very bright. She came up to me a little uncertainly, and I heard her say, "That girl who came to your room last night—she phoned to say she won't be seeing you today, she's too tied up at home."

"Yes," I said, almost inaudibly, though I didn't mean to whisper, "thank you." My single thought then, as I shut the door behind me, was: "They got her."

What did you expect? I asked myself. Yet I was angry and distraught, though I knew what had happened was nothing unusual, and something I had prepared myself for all along. But knowing is not the same as accepting, and what made it worse was that it would not do to tackle anyone on the subject, neither Zhang nor

Cai, nor even the girl clerk. I would only make life more difficult
for myself and for Ailan. It was perhaps what I minded most, its
being known and yet unmentionable.

I was haunted by the certainty that Zhang was responsible, but
it was not until the late afternoon of the next day that I received
explicit confirmation of this. I was talking to Zhang in his office,
and when I casually mentioned that I planned to go to the cinema
that evening, he said, "Yes, it's not far. It's opposite the sports
center, you know where that is." I didn't, as a matter of fact, but
I could have, seeing Ailan was an archer, and a habitué. And I knew
that it could not have happened by chance, Zhang's assumption
that I knew where the sports center was.

I was talking to Zhang in his office because I thought of crossing
the Yellow River to Linfen, in the neighboring province; for this
two-day journey by bus, involving an overnight stop at Jixian, I
needed an endorsement on my travel permit. The matter would
normally have been dealt with by Cai, but he was taken up with
an elderly Nepalese gentleman, a book buyer recently arrived from
Peking. Because Zhang was at heart a kind soul, attention was not
entirely denied me, but it was made plain, by his distracted air and
his constant recourse to the drawers of his desk (from which he now
fetched a pen, now a sheet of paper), that there was no question of
it.

I suggested an alternative route, proceeding by way of Hancheng,
where I could pick up a train; but at the mention of this name (which
I only discovered much later was heavily loaded with military
associations), he became silent and embarrassed, as if I were making
a fool of myself, or doing something improper in public. One thing
I did not wish to do was to go back the same way I had come; I
thought it would be too boring. But I also wished now to leave
Yan'an just as soon as possible, and when Zhang proposed that I
did so by flying to Xi'an, I found myself resignedly accepting.

It turned out I had to wait three days for this plane, and a seat
cancellation on it. How was I to pass the intervening days, which
promised stupefying boredom, but must be faced without hysteria?
I resolved to find an anodyne in occupation, walking about Yan'an,

going over the same ground again, and yet again. Each lunch time found me by a kiosk near the main bridge, buying an onion cake from a hawker. Each evening I dined alone, on rice and millet gruel and noodles made from buckwheat; in the way of vegetables, bean sprouts were the best that Yan'an could offer, and these appeared on my table day after day after day.

It was hard to shift the weight of increasing monotony, and I grew to hate the city: it seemed to have made for itself a special kind of citizen, men and women grey as with the dust of ages, their eyes without a spark of interest. In such a mood of repudiation I was bound to miss much that might have been noteworthy about the city; and it is true that of all those hours spent roaming the streets I have only one pleasant memory. It is of a shop, smart by Chinese standards, in Southern Pass. Passing it I was amused to see on its signboard the words "Agency for Film Developing and Artificial Teeth Fitting." In the glass shop window were arrayed framed pictures of chubby babies, two or three sets of dentures, and several single false teeth, and, contrasting bizarrely with these objects, a steaming bowl of buckwheat noodles. As I was standing there, trying to figure out what the noodles did for the window display, a woman drew up beside me; and detecting the look of bafflement on my face, said to me by way of explanation, "I wasn't going to eat them straightaway, you see, and I thought leaving them here for a while would keep the dust off them." You might have thought the window was a larder, instead of the smartest display case in the street.

Another thing about those aimless days in Yan'an: they have given me a new slant on traveling. Whereas at other times I would have abhorred those places where tourists go only to find themselves looking at other tourists, in that unhappy passage of my journey I would have liked nothing better than to come upon another tourist. It was partly the segregation, and partly the feeling that the divorce from any familiar life or thinking was too great. I longed for someone from the outside world to talk to; even the Nepalese gentleman would have served. I discovered we had rooms on the same floor, but for some reason segregation operated here too; the room in which he took his meals was set apart from mine, and when I asked the floor clerk for the number of his room, she denied that such a person even existed. Once or twice I passed him in the corridor, and sometimes he made himself heard in a shuffle down the passage, a light tread, a click of a door.

I thought one day of my first visit to India, years ago, and how the bone poverty bore down upon me. Yet India, desperate as it is, can never crush you as the suffocating cocoon of China could. There at least, the possibility of giving Indian reality the slip exists; there is at least the momentary relief of those hotels which are exactly like so many tourist hotels throughout the world. Here I could not be delivered of China, not for a single moment. More than once I found myself thinking, what in heaven's name am I doing here? And it profoundly unnerved me, to find that I could feel such alienation in a country that was after all my birthplace.

China is one of the last places left where you can truly get away from it all. There can be few countries in the world offering a more complete escape from familiar reality, though perhaps not in the way wished for. Those explorers and voyagers who seek to slip away the layers of their world will find here a deeper loneliness than even they have bargained for. But it won't be the loneliness of the Arctic tundra or the desolation of the scalding desert; it will be the loneliness of being treated always as an outsider.

Without agreeable company, your mind grows narrow and things lose their point. About almost everything in Yan'an I thought unfriendly thoughts. The weather was the wrong sort of dryness; the clear midday sky was too hot; the breeze did nothing to cool you down, it merely carried the loess dust that stiffened your hair. Nevertheless, I was thankful it did not rain, for Chinese pilots and the old Russian planes they fly are only up to taking off in fair weather. And once I actually found my mood softening toward Yan'an. It was when I caught sight of the holes in Comrade Cai's socks—it's always the socks that get me—and it suddenly seemed intensely poignant that this arrogant state functionary should have to wear his socks to a frazzle.

On the day I was due to depart I awoke to a soft rain steadily falling. The night before I had reminded myself, childishly, that at this time tomorrow it would all be over. Now I looked at the sky for promise of sun, and saw nothing there to give me hope. Escape was not to be, not yet. When I came out of my room and walked down the corridor I found the room attendants agog over an umbrella, the sort that opens at the push of a button. They told me you paid fourteen yuan for such an umbrella in Yan'an, more than a third of their monthly salary, and no more than eight yuan in Canton. And they were astonished I could think of flying that afternoon—why, it was raining.

I felt that I was at the end of my tether. I craved company, and finding it to be had the most easily in Zhang's office, went and sat myself there all day. In that time sundry functionaries dropped in, rustled newspapers, stared out of the window, lit cigarettes, chatted—in short, did everything but work. Zhang himself, probably doing his best to avoid me, was seldom in the room, and throughout the afternoon his desk was occupied by a young man who, were I to leave by plane, would have driven me to the airport. That was his sole task for the day, which now the rain had obviated.

In the evening I saw, for the second time, a film called *The True Story of Ah Q*. This is based on a story by Lu Xun, the centenary of whose birth the production commemorates. Ah Q is a village tramp cum odd-job man living in the last years of the Manchu dynasty, and through his story one is initiated into the characteristics of the Chinese, the ones that account in some ways for the state of the country. "Ah" is a common prefix to Chinese names, and "Q," while standing for Quei (Gui), the name by which the man is known in his village, is also an evocation of the queue, a symbol of humiliation which the Manchu rulers forced their Chinese subjects to wear. Lu Xun meant the character to be a composite portrait of the Chinese people, a sort of Chinese everyman, in whose susceptibilities one detects those of Chinese as a whole—their want of honesty and self-awareness.

There is no dignity to Ah Q; if he wins a quarrel, he smugly congratulates himself, but if he loses, he rationalizes his ignominy so that it appears as a moral victory. His story is a chronicle of humiliation: we see tawdry scenes of him being bullied, taken advantage of, taunted, disgraced. To himself, though, he represents all these as a catalogue of psychological victories.

Lu Xun believed this to be very Chinese, and it was what he had at heart when he said, "Whenever the Chinese are confronted with the powerful, instead of resisting they put a good face on their compliance by seeing this as "taking the middle course." Yet once they feel themselves in control, all too quickly they abandon this course for cruelty, heartlessness, and tyranny. . . . Vulnerable, they take to the middle way; defeated, they resign themselves to fate; by the time they become slaves, they are already beyond the point of being able to feel for their own plight." Chinese history, said Lu Xun, is an alternation between two ages: the age in which the Chinese longed in vain to be slaves, and the age in which they succeeded in becoming slaves for a time.

In fact Lu Xun was as bound by his culture as the next man. But it was also what he feared, forcing himself to resist tradition's appeal in order to diminish its power. Of those who are ambivalent about their own culture, few could have felt the dilemma more—between the sense that their inherited culture is impoverished, and the sense, nevertheless, of its ineluctable claims upon their sentiments and habits of mind, claims which, try as they might, they can never completely disavow. "My torture," he once wrote, "is that I have to carry on my shoulders a collection of extremely ancient phantoms; it is a load I cannot shed, and I constantly feel I am being choked under its crushing weight."

Seeing the film, and remembering his words, I was put in mind of a photograph I once saw, taken by a Chinese photo-journalist now living in New York. It is of a Chinese man trudging down a street carrying on his shoulders a hefty wood carving. The carving is of the catchpenny sort that is produced for foreign consumption and purveyed in large numbers to hapless tourists in the Far East. The man's back is arched against its terrible weight. It is the dead weight of Chinese culture, surviving in the factitious and endlessly copied objects of an exhausted art, but surviving nevertheless, having perhaps gone on for too long to stop. Continuity, the Chinese speciality.

Lu Xun had decided on satire as the form for his ideas, and the film failed for me because it presented the story almost as farce. It is true that Ah Q's naiveté lends itself to comic treatment, and this certainly seemed the way the audience could most easily accept the character—they hooted and found it funny stuff—but this wasn't at all what Lu Xun wanted. What he wanted was that the spectator should not be able to tell the character from himself. But for that he would need to have a very different kind of audience from Yan'an's. These spectators took an inordinately long time after the film had started to settle into their seats, and most of them got up and left the cinema, kicking up a considerable din, well before the film ended. I couldn't help remembering something else said of *The True Story of Ah Q* by its author, who died in 1936: "I would have liked to describe a bygone phenomenon, but I fear that my vision may in fact have more bearing on the future."

For the duration of the film my mind was occupied, but I knew this happy state would not survive long beyond the next day, and I resolved to leave Yan'an by bus, even if it meant returning the same way that I had come. Early the next morning I went to the long-distance bus station to buy my ticket to Xi'an; there is one service a day, leaving at dawn, so I had just one more day in this dreary place.

How to occupy myself in the meantime? I wished something would happen; and in time my wish was partly granted. A spanking new Hino coach rolled up the drive, and from it tottered forty to fifty old cadres from Canton. Some were leaning on walking sticks, others were hanging on to the arms of younger men. By degrees I found out who these newcomers were: they were people who had fought with the Red Army in Yan'an during the war, then spread south when the way was open for the communist forces to take Canton. Now they were on the point of retiring, and this trip down memory lane, after these thirty years and more, was by way of a golden handshake from the state. The five or six younger men were their escorts.

I warmed to these people, as one warms to the south after an overlong stay in the north. As expansive as northerners are silent and tense, they said, sure, of course I could go in the coach with them when they went sightseeing. I was hoping to be on hand when they revisited the scenes of their past, curious to see if these induced nostalgia, and was disappointed when the escorts came and told me they had decided to stay in, on account of the rain.

As a gambit to sugar the pill of retiring, the trip was obviously a success. "We'd have still more of these old cadres with us," one of the escorts told me, "if some of them hadn't collapsed from sheer age at the point of departure. Even then it was hard to persuade them to give up the trip. They're really pushing themselves, some of them, but they wouldn't pass up the chance for anything." He was a little scornful of decrepitude, but it being not the habit of the Chinese to be disrespectful to the aged, I noticed that the young man treated his charges as honored old-timers, accepting all of that generation's prerogatives.

Actually age is beginning to lose its clout in China, in the face of the leadership's determination to inject new blood into the bureaucracy, before its arteriosclerosis wreaks more damage on the running of the country. Deng Xiaoping himself had announced that he would step down from all his posts by the time he reached eighty, and it is known what he had said to the Party bureaucrats: "Don't sit on the toilet if you can't move your bowels, make room for those who can!"

Still no one gave up his position—that leverage so far exceeding the power of money, in a society where politics, patronage, connections and string-pulling count for more than anything—without putting up a fight. As one of the old Canton cadres said to me, "I would be less than honest with you if I didn't admit that this move to fill the upper positions with men of youth quite threw me. Oh, I can do without my pay all right, but can I do without my privileges? If money buys power in a capitalist state, it is the other way round in a socialist one. And that's the truth of it. I'm going to hang on, I tell you; I've got my children to think of!" He was right to be anxious: at what greater advantage can you be in China, than to have arrived at the upper ranks of public office?

I'd have liked to hear him reminisce about the war years in Yan'an, but he retired early, saying he had to be up at dawn for his constitutional the next day. I, too, had to be up at that hour to catch my bus, and remembered to arrange for the night duty clerk to let me out by the hotel's front entrance, padlocked for the night, at 5 a.m., and also a driver to pick me up.

When five o'clock came I found myself pounding the door of the clerk's cubicle, and calling to wake her up. Slowly, rubbing her eyes, she unlocked the main door. Ten minutes went by, then another ten when I looked for the driver, who never showed. In travel it is often impressed upon one that the best attitude to have is to expect the worst. But the lesson is seldom well learnt. I was flattened by disappointment. It wasn't as though I could go another way, for there was no other way. This is Yan'an, I thought, suitably ending on an abominable note.

I said ending, though my reason told me I would miss the bus. Yet part of my mind would not, could not accept it. I could not imagine how I'd endure another day in Yan'an; the bean sprouts would be bearable, but the boredom would not. And I started to run.

The light then was only a fading of darkness. It seemed the whole town was empty; it was too early even for the Chinese, still at their honest slumbers. I was so unused to running that I ran crooked, the weight of my bag hurting my shoulder. I knew I should never gain ground enough at my pitiful speed to catch the bus, but I ran on regardless, as you run in a dream through a bewildering sequence, catching now and then the sound of your feet.

For perhaps five minutes I was alone in the street, but then, as the dawn mist began to lift, I caught a glimpse, leftward, of a form emerging from a door—the day's first jogger. I raced across the street, and drawing alongside him, shoved my bag at him, saying, "Here, help me carry this, quick!" If he wondered how he should take this order, as the height of impertinence or mental imbalance, he gave no sign of it, and for a block or two we sprinted abreast.

I knew I'd never make it, though half my brain said I must hurry, hurry. Against the pessimism of reason struggled the superstition that the impossible might happen, a miracle might occur. Meanwhile my breathing had changed to a furious panting, and my legs felt more and more like lead weights, painfully dragging.

It was when my pace had deteriorated to a kind of tottering that I caught sight of him: a boy on a bicycle, coming toward me. With no thought but to throw myself at his mercy, I stumbled up to him. He slowed, and stopped, and I managed to get out these words: "Comrade," I panted, "heaven-sent comrade, will you take me to the bus station as fast as you can?"

Without a word he swung his bicycle round. Only seconds went by as I grabbed my bag from the jogger, lifted myself onto the seat, and rode off sidesaddle down the street. I held my luggage in my lap, and twice I thought I would fall off, so top-heavy was the bicycle, and so fast did the boy pedal. When we reached the station I had only seconds to spare, and to express my gratitude all I had time for was to yell a "thank you" over my shoulder as I made a dash for the bus; I thought I heard the boy shout "Glad to oblige" behind me, but I could not be sure.

In the bus I sat, or was pitched about, for eleven hours, jolted over hard hills. As it got colder I put on more clothes, until I was wearing all the things I had in my bag: two sweaters, two pairs of socks, a padded jacket. I did not relish the prospect of a whole day without food and drink. But my heart sang; because now something was happening, I was away, I was moving again.

Onto the Plain

Compared to other fields of endeavor water works come easily enough to the Chinese, after so many centuries of experience, and the Yellow River certainly offers them plenty of practice. In the provinces so far crossed, I had seen what a benefactor the river could be, providing power and watering arid places. Nonetheless it is scourge as well as savior. In Henan Province, across which it flows immediately after its confluence with the Wei, one can see something of both these faces. One also sees a third: when the river has been tamed as far as possible, and natural calamities avoided, there still remain, interwoven with water's spontaneous violence, all those woes and sorrows born of human failing, mischance, or man's urge to destruction.

Errors and Encounters

I was seen onto the train for Three-Gate Gorge by a Chinese teacher I had chanced to talk to on the bus from Yan'an. Although he told me he was going to stay in Xi'an for a few days, and I had mentioned the name of my hotel, I hadn't expected to see him again. But when I emerged from my hotel the morning of my departure for Three-Gate Gorge, I found him uncertainly lurking outside. His eyes must have been trained on the entrance, for the moment I stepped outside he advanced upon me. He had known better than to look for me inside; he was far less of an innocent than Ailan.

He greeted me warmly, and gave me a moist-palmed handshake. He then carried my bag and rode on the bus with me to the railway station. I didn't know what to make of him or what he was after; the Chinese émigré's terror of being taken advantage of had gripped me. In a month from now, would I be receiving letters from him requesting money, books, or television sets? Did he want foreign currency certificates, or letters smuggled out?

But no, he seemed only to want to talk. As I was early we sat on a bench in the station's waiting room and shared a hard boiled egg I'd bought. He said he was interested in the history of science and was familiar with the work of Joseph Needham, the eminent scholar whose monumental *Science and Civilisation in China* may well be regarded in the future as the greatest historical work Cambridge has produced this decade. "It's terrible, in a way, to be Chinese," he sighed, "and see the best work on your country done abroad."

"China is so backward," he said, "both materially and intellectually, the one causing the other. Poor and blank—that's exactly what we are, just as Chairman Mao had said. Only, he was wrong to think that we're the sort of blank paper on which 'the freshest and most beautiful characters can be written, the freshest and most beautiful pictures can be painted.' We're just blank, that's all. It's been at least a thousand years since we fell off from the peak of our cultural development, and in all that time we have existed in our own decayed world, while the rest of the world has changed. That's our tragedy, the energy running out; we have long exhausted the reserves of our race, and the resources for revitalization."

Yes, I agreed; certainly in China you felt the awful inertia of an old stagnant civilization, against which every bid for change or progress seems to glance off impotent. I said I was tired of meeting people who rhapsodize about the glories of ancient China, when really they have no real sense of these marvels, and invoke them only as a salve for present inconsequence—a false kind of chauvinism. Though it is true that self-criticism comes easily to the Chinese— the visitor is always being apologized to for the backwardness of China—all too many Chinese still believe that the visitor is the barbarian, they are the civilized.

The teacher and I were agreed on the fallacy of the common persuasion that the root of China's troubles is communism, believing, as we both do, that a nation gets the government it deserves. Though the Chinese are indeed hamstrung by the system under which they live, their inability for renewal we supposed to lie in themselves. All that was unhealthy in the old world is allowed to live on. What is the communist bureaucracy but the old mandarinate in another guise? It is an old sanctity which makes a brain worker— that is, a member of the intelligentsia—so abominate manual work; no amount of class struggle could shake him out of it. If communism abets rather than hinders these atavistic tendencies, this is not a reason for thinking that it is a bad thing in itself.

I said that if there was one thing which irritated and saddened me in my encounters with Chinese, it was their assumption that, however inferior in other matters, in the length of their history they were preeminent. "I know I am no better," I said, "bemoaning China's too long past yet finding it a matter for pride. But it's not an evasion for me; I don't retreat from the disappointing present by invoking the glories of the past civilization."

The teacher nodded, "Yet that civilization has been dead these hundreds of years, if people would but wake to it." When I made agreeing sounds he continued, "Why should civilizations differ, after all, from human beings? They are born; they grow; they die."

He presented himself, in talking, as a reflective person, someone who has transcended that innocence which so often narrows the Chinese perception of the world. He seemed almost to have transcended Chineseness, in his capacity for self-appraisal and in his disrespect, unthinkable for most of his countrymen, for Chinese civilization, and not just for the government or its cadres. Yet in the end he could not overcome his curiosity as a Chinese consumer. Just before he put me on the train there came that question I had feared all along: he asked me how much, in truth, did tape recorders cost in Hong Kong? It was the first time he had sounded like a Chinese living under communism.

There was standing room only on the train, and I was relieved it was not long before we arrived at the town of Three-Gate Gorge. The place was clean and, by Chinese standards, prosperous; but it looked monotonous, as new towns do, with a center no more than a block deep on either side of the main street. I checked into the Municipal Revolutionary Committee Hostel, which doubles as a hotel for foreign visitors, and then wandered in a southeasterly direction down the street.

I heard someone say, "Want to buy some gold?" He was squatting on the pavement, a young man who couldn't have been more than eighteen or nineteen. I looked at him with some curiosity, but saw nothing in his manner that suggested more than a half-hearted attempt at touting.

"No, thanks," I said. "How would I get it out of the country?"

"How about antiques, then?"

"No, thanks," I answered, "for the same reason. Besides, I don't have the money. Not all foreigners are rich, you know."

He pulled a face, his mouth rapidly switching from a look of rueful disappointment to a heart-melting grin. I asked him how he'd come by all that gold and those antiques in the first place.

"Oh, family. They're of no use to us, which is why I thought you might . . . Well, you know how it is in China. You can have plenty of money, but nothing to buy with it. Not that gold and antiques are as good as money, of course, especially if you're not supposed to have them."

I wanted to ask how these things managed to escape notice by the Red Guards, or by the authorities, for that matter. But just then a bus drew up alongside us, and the young man made a dash for it, leaving me in mid-sentence.

I resumed my stroll. Spotting an irrigation duct at the end of the road, I traced it, descending a gentle slope. Presently it rounded a corner, and as I followed it I found myself on a ledge cut into the side of a hill overlooking fields. The fields were all enclosed in fences made of entangled twigs and a few pieces of that rarer material, wire. The wattle made me think the fields were private plots. In one of them, a woman could be seen crouched over a row of chives, teaching her little daughter, who was perhaps five or six, to weed. A house stood on one side of the ledge, and in the doorway a middle-aged woman was laying some bricks. It looked very small, as though it had only one room, partitioned into tiny dark cells.

In front of the house, seated on a stool, a younger woman was dandling her baby. I spoke to her, inquiring about a derelict building we could both see in the distance, standing beside a reservoir and looking as though it might have been a temple, with its tiled roof and flaring eaves. She said she didn't know what it was, then called out to the older woman, who turned out to be her mother, and who didn't know either. We then had a Chinese conversation, while she proceeded to nurse her eleven-month-old baby; that is to say, we exchanged information on our place of origin, age, and occupation. She was a doctor, aged thirty, and her mother, who looked far too young to be a grandmother, was forty-nine. They were from Shanghai, and had been transferred to Three-Gate Gorge in 1958, the year after the construction of the dam was begun. A great industrial hub being envisaged on this site, with the enormous kilowattage the dam was designed to produce, great numbers of technical people and factories were to be moved here from manufacturing centers like Shanghai.

I told her I'd been to the Liujia Gorge hydropower station and the Longyang Gorge dam construction site, and had met people there who had started their career here. "Yes," she said, "Three-Gate Gorge is like a great conduit, channeling people all over the country. Not only technicians, but peasants too. Because the construction involved drowning the surrounding valleys, hundreds of thousands were moved from their homes. They've all come back, though, the ones who were resettled in Gansu. The plant is not working at full capacity, as you may have heard."

I had indeed; as I explained earlier, the planners had poorly designed the dam, underestimating the amount of silt that had to be evacuated. The Three-Gate Gorge power plant is something of a white elephant.

Yet it was something that had to be seen, now that I was here. A representative of the local branch of the Foreign Affairs Office took me. We drove for three-quarters of an hour from the town, through terraced yellow earth country; only the loess seemed redder here than in Shaanxi. At this time of the year, before the summer rains, the water of the Yellow River was clearer than I'd ever seen it; and as I came within sight of the sluices the spumy discharge, unburdened of its silt, actually looked bottle green.

At the power station I had a brief conversation with the chief engineer, who to his credit did not make out it was all the fault of the Soviets that the scheme was not working properly. In fact he skirted round the subject, preferring to dwell on the regulatory, rather than the power-generating function of the barrage. One useful function the reservoir performs, in addition to irrigation and flood control, is alleviating the threat of ice floes in the lower reaches of the river. This has been something to fear from the river, as I was to learn in Shandong when I was there—a spring hazard more or less inevitable when the river swings from south to north, so that when thaw begins in the south, the north is still frozen, causing the water as it rushes downstream to be trapped behind a mass of ice. Such blockages had to be unclogged by dropping bombs from airplanes or by artillery shelling.

Though I sensed that an expression of interest in the planning mistakes would not be welcome, I nevertheless asked if the designers had thought to look up what the American engineers had written when they were consulted after the war, and to consider the objections that they had raised. The chief engineer answered no, they hadn't; or at least he didn't know about it.

Three-Gate Gorge took its name from the fact that the river was divided into three streams here, by outcrops of rock called Man Island, Immortal Island, and Ghost Island. From a photograph taken before the engineers moved in, the place looked wild and deserted. That silent, untouched landscape is no more; concrete abounded all around me as I walked the length of the narrow wall jutting out from between the two parts of the dam, one spouting water, the other undergoing repairs. I did not pause there for long, the gale which swept across the gorge was so fierce and cold. Instead I returned to the station, to see if I could still find some traces of Sovietism there. The turbines, I saw, were Chinese, having all been manufactured in Harbin. After a quick search I thought I discerned a Soviet legacy in two lamps, one in the power-generation room, and one outside—great orbs fixed to the walls by curlicued ironwork that would not have looked out of place in a palace in Leningrad.

On the way back to town, I was joined in the car by an elderly, loquacious mechanic from the station, who wanted a lift and plunked himself down in the front seat without so much as a "by your leave." I passed half an hour listening to him as he ran through the train of ills occasioned by the Cultural Revolution, the chief of which, to his way of thinking, being the spinelessness of the generation that grew up in it. Such people believed the world owed them a living. He himself was of the old school: I should have seen him when he first came to Three-Gate Gorge, how hard he worked, what zeal he had, how willingly he made sacrifices for his country. He thought, in my not returning to work for the good of my fatherland, I had failed, if you please, to show the patriotism incumbent upon me.

At this point the driver broke in with a question; he wanted to know if I had any children. When he saw me shake my head in the rearview mirror, he asked me why not. Was it because they pursued a rigorous population control policy where I came from?

I answered no, and added that such campaigns as were mounted in China were not necessary in my country because couples voluntarily limited the size of their families.

That was manifestly a shock. "But why?" he cried.

I offered the first explanation that came into my head, "Well—children are such a burden."

This, I could see, was even more of a shock. To a country odious enough to find children burdensome, horror could be the only reaction.

"All the more reason why you should come back to live in China," he firmly decided. "At least there's nothing in the way of economic hardship here to stop you from having children; it's only a political directive that limits us to one child each. But that's still better than none." To him there was never any doubt that we in the West were to be pitied.

The mechanic nodded at all this, deeply concerned about my bleak, childless future. But then he recalled us to more immediate matters, and asked me what I thought of the hydropower station. There, too, was something to be sorry about, he observed without waiting for my answer. "It's a useless, useless thing—outstandingly useless." A gross mistake, pure and simple. The Chinese, he held, had been led astray by the Russians. This he sincerely believed, and wished me to believe it too. Had he not been told so by everyone? Was this not how the case was presented to the public by the powers that be?

I let it pass. He could no more help believing it was the Soviets' fault, I thought, than the authorities could help pretending that it was, there being no politics without charade, as there can be no bureaucracy without cover-up. It is a game for which the Chinese have a particularly developed taste. Who has not heard of "face," that conceit which instantly overtakes the Chinese when they want to preserve their dignity or conceal facts damaging to their prestige? Lu Xun, the writer I mentioned earlier, makes the point that what characterize the Chinese are "concealment and deceit"; and it is true that there is something hypocritical to their masks of politeness and their rituals, something insincere in their predilection for smoothing things over and for letting sleeping dogs lie. Face-saving is nothing more than a flam, since what is saved is merely appearance. "The Emperor's New Clothes" is a Chinese story, and could have been an allegory of the conspiracy the whole nation engaged in during the Maoist years, when the Chinese people connived with the leadership at the myth of greatness, accomplishment, stability, and unity. The people knew what was expected of them, gave themselves to performing it, and knew that the authorities knew they were faking. Every Chinese I ever talked to about Watergate was convinced that the scandal should never have got out; no point in washing one's dirty linen in public, they all said.

In China many an official has prospered by play-acting; when the government line changes he will simply play a new part. This adroitness is the first requirement of a good communist, according to several people I talked to in China; the definition of a successful

Party member, they said, is someone skilled at the putting on and taking off of masks: the more masks, the better communist.

Every kind of falsehood prevails in Chinese life. Few people can be more at home in the realm of hype and euphemism, where the meaning of anything can be reversed. "You always know," a Chinese émigré in England once observed to me, "when something has gone drastically wrong in China. All you have to do is to see what their newspapers enthuse about; the more extravagantly they praise something, the more you know that that thing is wanting. For example, if they gave you a real-life illustration of a factory and praised its safety precautions, you would know that occupational hazards and accidents have reached staggering proportions." In that respect their language serves them well, for with it the Chinese can perform such feats of circumvention and paradoxical juxtaposition that one who is unaccustomed to its plane of logic can never know what is an aphorism or simply nonsense. (Henry Kissinger was only one of many whom it confused; once, hearing Mao Zedong crack a crude Hunanese joke about women, he read into it a dark meaning it did not have—as a tip-off about the dangerous ascendancy of Jiang Qing.)

In my travels I found that a request to the Travel Service or the Foreign Affairs Office involving the slightest effort of organization was an infallible means of prompting a lie. That the proposed destination is temporarily cut off by roadworks, for example, is a favorite. As the Chinese tend to lie for convenience their excuses are usually quite unimaginative. When asked to arrange for me to visit a secondary school at Three-Gate Gorge, the representative of the Foreign Affairs Office, who despite initial agreement had no intention whatsoever of exerting himself to the extent necessary, came back to tell me it couldn't be done, the school was on holiday that day.

"Are all schools on holiday, or just this one?" I asked.

"Just this one."

I was not to be put off, and asked him why this particular school should be on holiday when none of the others were. He looked at me, then lamely said, "I'm none too clear myself."

"Don't worry," I assured him, "I don't mind looking at an empty school." At this he looked troubled, and I added, hastily pursuing my advantage, "Or can you arrange for me to see a school that's not on holiday?"

He cast about for another pretext, and came up with, "I'm afraid you won't have time. Your train leaves just after lunch."

"No, not really. It leaves at 15:41 hours." I was not to be fobbed off with an earlier train.

I got to see my school in the end, but not before he had further demurred, saying it was difficult to arrange at such short notice, in his discomposure neglecting to recollect that I had put in for it two days before.

The No. 2 Middle School, with fifteen hundred pupils, had crammed classrooms and was short on electricity, but the teachers were charming and the discipline breathtaking. The two deputy head-masters were university graduates, but the head himself was not. He was an affable, long-toothed man whose speech was so burred by country accent that I found him almost incomprehensible. I did wonder why he was headmaster, until I heard the others address him as "Secretary," and realized he was a boss in either the local Party Committee or the Revolutionary Committee. Everyone was perfectly relaxed; nothing had been specially laid on for me; and I wondered why it was necessary for the Foreign Affairs Office man to make such heavy weather of it.

I suppose the point is not that the lying could be avoided, but that it is scarcely thought of as meriting the beating of one's breast. The Chinese masses have passed the point where they can ever marvel to find themselves deceived by their leaders, or to discover that what is doctrinally correct today is not doctrinally correct tomorrow. I had supposed it not to matter, after meeting people anesthetized by the Cultural Revolution, whose response to politics is either cynicism or indifference; and it is perfectly true that many people are incredulous of government propaganda, and since they are not fooled, I thought, it ceases to be false. Yet it is also true that by the time the man in the street has been told for the thousandth time—by newspapers, by television, and even by those popular narrative strips you can borrow for a small fee from street hawkers in every city—how treacherous, predatory, licentious, and greedy are the people of New York and Hong Kong, he is not going to be able to think of these people as anything else.

The train that left at 15:41 was as crowded as I had feared. Near where I stood, there sat three women with two small children, an obese little girl of about six and a not so obese little boy of about the same age. The passengers, like all Chinese on the move, were eating. From time to time the women fed the children with cake and biscuits. The relative sizes of the two children were noted by the parents, and on the little girl's considerable dimensions the mother was congratulated.

She acknowledged the compliment and declared, with an expression of maternal pride made unattractive by complacency, "Yes, my daughter is a great eater; she can eat three *liang* [over 5 ounces] of dumplings at one sitting." (To give an idea of how much that is, I should note here that I manage two *liang* at most.)

The children were nibbling cake with a bored air. Looking at her little boy, the other mother observed, "My son doesn't have all that good an appetite." At this a sudden, piercing cry came from her child; tears cascaded down his cheeks, and he would not be solaced, would not be cajoled to a silence, except by his mother pronouncing, "No, no, you do have a good appetite; you do like your food."

From all of which it will readily be seen the place of food in Chinese life, and how much a good stomach, like an ability to hold one's liquor in some cultures, is a matter for pride. It may also be seen how child rearing practices contribute to the national obsession with eating. I was visited by a vision of a maw, into which food was endlessly poured.

The train was a little late getting into Luoyang. In that city a sandstorm awaited me: clouds of enveloping sand with which the clear skies seemed out of sync, the grains probing one's hair, eyes, clothes. I hurried across the square in front of the station, and was so blinded by the dust that I forsook the bus for the instant insulation of a hired car. I thought, as I was driven to the Friendship Hotel, how this loess dust, carried from the west by the Mongolian winds, and the millenia of silt deposited by the Yellow River, had built this vast plain around me.

Just before I arrived at the hotel I had a glimpse of wheat growing in the middle of an intersection, where in other countries you might expect a flowerbed to have been laid out, being treated with violence by the wind. The hotel, a Soviet legacy, had an unusually hospitable receptionist—which hospitality was expressed in the ushering gestures he made toward the dining room, to which I was to hasten this minute if I were to catch dinner, before even the formalities of checking in.

Looking about me as I sat at a table, I saw a wealth of package tourists finishing their dinner: Americans with their countrymen's look of geniality, generosity, and hopefulness; Frenchmen with their panache and their ability to make the sounds of their language heard distinctly above the loudest din. (I seldom saw Britons traveling in China, and suppose it's either because they can't afford to these days or because as tourists they are more self-effacing than other nationalities, in keeping with their eclipse in the eyes of the world.) I also recognized Renping, a Chinese girl from America I'd shared a room with in my hotel in Xi'an. She had arrived on the same afternoon in Xi'an, and her appearance had saved me from having to share a room with the person next to me in the queue at the reception counter, a middle-aged West German woman, all rolled up trouser legs and tan and hiking boots, posing as a student enrolled in Chinese courses at a university in Taiwan. (This was a popular expedient for getting a considerable reduction in room rate, and until the Chinese authorities cottoned on all you had to do was to arm yourself with one of those student passes mass-faked in some backstreet printing establishment in Hong Kong.)

The delight I both felt and voiced at meeting up with Renping again was sincere, for already in Xi'an her anxiousness to arm herself with a compass had struck a sympathetic chord in my own disabled sense of direction, and endeared her to me. In that respect, at least, we were kindred handicappers.

One experience she told me about when we first met I can very easily imagine befalling myself. She was returning late one evening to Xi'an, after a day excursion to the outskirts, and she was dismayed, upon arriving at the hotel, to find it shuttered for the night. Looking about her, she also saw something she hadn't noticed before: it was a sign by the door spelling out the hours of business. Besides being annoyed, she was baffled, thinking it strange for a hotel, especially such a big one, to close its doors at 8:30 p.m. At the same time she realized that if there was one lesson she had learnt well in her travels in this country, it was that nothing is so implausible that it can't happen in China. Before the ways of this country, she reminded herself, one should stand prepared for any eventuality, however unlikely.

With this thought she started hammering at the door. It was past eleven, she was tired, and badly wanted a wash and to go to bed. She banged loudly, with all her strength, and presently she saw the door slowly open and a puffy-eyed young man peering at her behind it.

"Let me in," she said sharply, "I have a room here."

"Pardon?"

"Look, I'm a fully paid-up guest at this hotel, and I want to go up to my room."

The young man began to rub the back of his head. "This is not the hotel," he said sadly. "The hotel is over there"—pointing to a similarly large building across the square. And then he added apologetically, "We're only the People's Post Office here."

Renping was a student of Buddhist art, and was traveling all over the country inspecting and photographing carvings of the Buddha and bodhisattvas, a line of work quite physically exacting, as many of the relics are to be found in almost inaccessible caves high up in the mountains. She would have had a field day here in Luoyang, whose limestone Longmen Caves are famously studded with statues, if she could have elicited better humor from the curators. But it is seldom the habit of Chinese men to accept that a woman can be no less serious about her work than a man. The head curator had all this time been keeping her at a distance, and though at first he asked her some questions on her artistic aims, he was not interested in real information, and was only concerned to establish that she did not have the multiplicity of authorizations he considered necessary for full access to the caves.

But Renping was not a person to give up easily. Before I arrived in Luoyang she had befriended a young traveler from Hong Kong, and as he was free to wander as he wished, she put it to him—and he agreed—that he wander with her camera into just those caves to which she had been refused entry. She got the photographs she wanted, and though it may be felt that she had done so by an irregular method, I thought her not the less to be congratulated for that reason.

I later met this obliging young man, called Ma, and liked him at once. Though he had been traveling in China for eight months, and intended to continue for another four, he had managed, heaven only knows how, to resist boredom, homesickness, fret, and any sense of futility. He was lean and canny, and his eyes peered at one levelly through his glasses. With his sharp features and narrow frame, he could never be taken for a northerner, but he now laced his speech with many local bons mots, which made him very entertaining to listen to. He had acclimatized himself to this country in a way I could only envy. He was traveling the length and breadth of it on less than five yuan (roughly U.S. $2.50) a day, and he shamed me with his determination to resist exceeding his budget through succumbing to the temptations of a hot bath, a clean bed, or a meal eaten under hygienic conditions.

We were to spend many days in close company, the three of us. As is the way with seasoned travelers thrown together, we would not undermine the intimacy of the road by questioning each other's antecedents. So I never found out what he did for a living. We traveled together to Gongxian, a county town about forty miles to the east of Luoyang, where we saw the tombs of several Song emperors, and the sculptures of five famous Buddhist grottoes near the northern banks of the Yiluo River, a Yellow tributary. The tombs were mounds of earth with a lineup of stone statues, some of animals, others of men, standing lapped by waves of thigh-high wheat in wide, open fields. The animals, paired, were elephants, tigers, rams, horses, crouching lions, and mythical beasts. The men were keepers, officials, foreign envoys bearing gifts, and lumpish generals with their hands on the hilt of their tall swords. Profound unconcern for archaeology, as against the claims upon the land of agriculture, seemed to underlie that landscape.

In the grottoes, my eyes flickered back and forth among sandstone scenes of the adoration of the Buddha, decorations of flying *apsarah* (angels) and lotus flower, while Renping could be heard clicking them all onto Kodachrome. When first dug, way back in the sixth century, these caves had been on ground level, but they are now well below, the river silt having raised the land around them down the centuries.

The life around seemed simple and immemorial. Leaving Ma and Renping to their picture-taking, I strolled over to the Grotto Monastery, found it turned into a primary school, and sat in on one of the classes. The children, all smiles and snotty noses, were learning to write characters—mostly the names of cereals, I noticed. The land round about was planted, so they knew very well what they were learning. The children seemed curiously self-contained, and for their age were extraordinarily silent; no teacher could have asked for better behaved pupils. The teacher was young and modest. This was only a rural school, she said, run by the production brigade (a division of the commune); the money came from a collective fund put up by the peasants themselves, and not from the state or anything grand like that.

If the children were a little older, she told me, their parents would prefer them to work in the fields, so there was not much hope of their becoming scholars or raising their station. I had heard that except in the more developed provinces more than half of the country's teenagers were illiterate, and I asked the teacher if this was true. She said she understood so, nodding absently, as one who did not see herself as having any role to play in the nation's education. I was suddenly quite depressed, feeling there was no simple way to a general prosperity in this country.

When it was time to go, Ma suggested that we stop by a museum not a great distance from the caves. This was once the manor house of a landlord, called Kang Baiwan (Kang Million), whose progeny had fled to either Taiwan or the United States. It was just then being used as the setting for a film, a historical drama. The cast and production crew were all being lodged there, and as I followed the keeper through a succession of archways, courtyards, and vacant rooms I caught glimpses of elegant, epicene men with touches of rouge on their cheeks.

My pleasure in these rooms, in the porcelain dinner sets laid out and the silk gowns hung up, like properties which a stage manager had arranged for the rise of the curtain, originated I know from my bourgeois nostalgia for the cultivation of the old world. Yet at the same time I was not unconscious of how far away, in its privilege and material amplitude, the world of the landlord was from that of the peasantry, whose toil had directly paid for it. And through this I saw, going back in my imagination, the impoverished tenant yielding up half his crops to the manor, the feudal lord taking to himself the tenant's wife or daughter whenever it pleased him, the visiting satraps sumptuously feted by the baron, the peasants going hungry. Can one wonder that the tenants rose up with murder in their hearts?

Now, after the revolution, the two Chinas share the nation between them, the cultivated and the uncouth, the latter far and away the more numerous. To every educated, urbanized Chinese, there are ten people still yoked to the earth and its most ancient claims.

In the countryside around Gongxian, I perhaps came closer to the life of these nine-tenths of the Chinese people than anywhere else in my journey. I owed this to Ma and Renping, who as travelers were far more seasoned than I, and who thought nothing of hitchhiking, and got rides on trucks, bicycles, and mule and horse carts whenever there was opportunity. Thus I came to know the kindness of those country people, and to experience the different modes of transport they used. I remember clinging for dear life on the back of lorries, on roads execrably bad, so that the rattling, hurtling, and helter-skelter bouncing left one indescribably shaken and curiously joyous. And bounding along in that commonest of Chinese means of locomotion, the mule cart, with the driver saying, as he flogged the wretched animal to renewed exertion, "What an ill-fated beast— uglier, stupider than the horse, yet better tasting as meat. Nothing but the most strenuous work for twenty-five years, and then what happens? It's chopped up and eaten!" We were sharing the cart with two country women, one of whom gave her baby suck the moment she was settled, unmindful of the quicklime the cart was also carrying, and with which we were all covered at the end of the journey. She was dried up but fertile, like the Yellow plain we were traversing.

I was to ride such carts again and again, even after parting from my two companions of the road; and that lazy jolting, with the mare snorting and the sun rising to show me that sad and by now familiar countryside, with the brown plain stretching and the pop- lars casting their slanted shadows, remains a memory of the purest happiness.

Playing with a Water Hose

On a late November day I found myself in Huayuankou, whose name means Garden Entrance. Here there had occurred one of those events which it is impossible now to leave out of any history of the Yellow River, namely the breaching of the dykes by Chiang Kai-shek in 1938, in a desperate bid to stop the Japanese advance by spreading a devastating flood in its path.

I doubt if Chiang ordered this lightheartedly, but then I also doubt if it cost him much remorse; it was a strategy necessitated by war, that was all. The formula was nothing new, after all: when the Manchus invaded the city of Kaifeng in 1644, only a couple of hours downriver from here by car, the townsmen defended them- selves by opening the dykes and unleashing the river upon the invaders. Destruction and salvation had always been mingled in this, the dyking of this epic river.

Following such historical precedents, Chiang ordered the first breach to be blasted on June 2, 1938, at a place to the east of Garden

Entrance. But the water was still shallow then, and the gap soon clogged up with rubble. Three days later Kaifeng fell to the Japanese, and all at once eight hundred able-bodied men were dispatched to Garden Entrance, there to dig a tunnel through the levees. Day and night they worked, illuminated by the headlights of a row of army trucks; and when, on June 9, they had bored right through the wall, they raised their guns at the opening, and widened it with sixty to seventy shots.

Come late June and the river was in spate. Through the gap, now a hundred yards wide, the water poured straight out of the river, gathering volume as it met the stream from the first breach to the east. Nothing could stop it now, as it ran in a deluge all the way to the Huai, a river that flows between the Yellow and the Yangtze. It surged over the towns and villages in between, devastating the homesteads, obliterating their crops and drowning the peasants, until not a place was left habitable or arable upon the plain, and people clung to life by eating grass and chewing bark.

Leaving their ravaged villages, 12.5 million people wandered homeless across the flooded plain, their ankles sinking in the sludge, the babies crying, the aged intermittently stumbling, while all about them lay the wastes that marked the passage of the Yellow River waters. Close to nine hundred thousand people died from drowning or starvation.

The water stayed on the land for nine years. The deluge itself was terrible enough, but when the water receded, further effects of the tragedy were to show themselves: the river system dissipated, the soil water-logged and impregnated with salt, the watercourses silted up and the land deeply slashed by gullies.

Now, all of a sudden, Chiang Kai-shek decided that the breach must be closed. He was in the thick of a civil war against the communists then, and, compared to them, was in rather bad shape. His soldiers had lost heart; the Americans were deserting him. To the north, the celebrated communist generals Chen Yi and Liu Bocheng (he who was called the One-Eyed Dragon) were in command. Possibly, by ordering the breach to be closed so that the river might be sent back to its old bed in the north, Chiang thought he had it in his hands to separate the communist armies. With a river thrown between them, he saw General Liu stopped in his tracks, and with the rush of waters back to its former channel in Shandong, he imagined that the communist economy could be disrupted in that province.

All this time U.N.R.R.A. had been intermittently repairing the dykes down by Garden Entrance, but because the peasants cultivating the dry bed abandoned by the river when the dykes were breached in 1938 would be devastated by restoring the river to its old channel, U.N.R.R.A., the communists, and Chiang had all agreed to delay the diversion until resettlement arrangements had been made for them. So when Chiang suddenly ordered the breach to be closed, this was in violation of existing agreements. U.N.R.R.A. realized that, come the high-water season, the diversion would cause the farmlands on the old river bed, all eight hundred thousand acres of them, to be flooded and utterly devastated. Yet, under Chiang's unremitting military pressure, it was U.N.R.R.A.'s supplies of construction materials, food, and engineering skills which helped to repair the breach at Garden Entrance.

To soften the blow to the peasants U.N.R.R.A. had planned to ship dyke repair equipment and relief supplies to Shandong, but Chiang Kai-shek's air bombings made sure that they didn't get that far. When the water level rose, and hundreds of thousands of farmsteads were threatened, the peasants took to strengthening the dykes themselves, leaving their fields when they should have been bringing in the harvest. They were chivvied by air attacks by Chiang Kai-shek's fighter planes; yet so determined were the communist organizers, and so united were the peasants in their rage and anxiety, that all along the lower reaches there were dyke builders at their work, coming back at night if Chiang's artillery harassed them during the day. They were spectacularly fast—faster still if they could but scrape up more food—while women and children took the places the men had vacated in the fields.

In the event, deflecting the river did not staunch the advance of the One-Eyed Dragon's army, and one night that summer (1947) his troops slid across the Yellow River in boats and headed for the very hub of Chiang Kai-shek's power in the Yangtze valley.

Of Chiang's scorched earth policy, Garden Entrance stands as a reminder. The span of the breach there is marked by a pair of dusty pavilions, standing like bookends at the limits of a low splodged wall. They speak of a man trying to tamper with nature— as though, observed a contemporary American war correspondent when Chiang Kai-shek deflected the river the second time, "he were a god playing with a water hose."

Before the pavilions ran a mud track, and on the morning I was there a convoy of laborers could be seen straggling along it, each pulling behind him a cart loaded with earth. Piles of stone marked the path like cairns, and told me better than anything that dyke building was in progress. The embankment was being set further back here, and a railroad, used for freighting construction and maintenance materials for the Yellow River banks, was accordingly being moved back.

A path at the far end led me round the corner and onto the rim of the main construction site. In its half-empty sprawling reaches men could be seen in clusters here and there, some shoveling sand, others drawing carts. They were mere specks in the arid distance, growing blurred and bleached beyond. In a depression lay a straggle of tattered tents, intermingled with goats, pigs, a line of washing, stacks of hay, and a jumble of broken carts and tumbled wheels. There was a slaphappy air to it all.

When I scrambled down the dip, I saw a husky young man with a broad sunburned face come out of a tent wiping his hands on the apron tied round his waist. As I went by I could see into the tent: an electric light bulb, the ground laid with straw, some clothes hanging up to dry, enamel basins and mugs and bundles of bedding wrapped in striped sheets. At the entrance of each tent a rough brick oven exuded warmth and charged the air with the smell of wood smoke.

I realized that the tents were kitchens, and asked the young man what he was cooking for lunch. He lifted the lid of a huge bamboo

basket and pointed to the two hundred and more white buns steaming inside. At this moment an old man emerged from a tent across
the way; and he, stirring a caldron the size of a bathtub in which
a vegetable stew appeared to be cooking, greeted me and offered
me a cup of boiled water. I declined, and he said no more, but he
kept on smiling at me in a kindly fashion as he stooped to prod the
embers in his oven. The same earthy patience was stamped on his
face as on the bare yellow landscape around him.

I was about to go when a lean young man appeared beside us.
He was the supervisor of works, with glasses and an air of the
schoolmaster about him. Without much prompting from me he
proceeded to explain the project. It was all very simple, he said:
they were building the embankment with the very sedimentation
that was raising the riverbed and causing the floods the embankment
was intended to dam back. The earth that went into building that
ridge of high ground had all come from the river bottom, and none
of it had to be lugged up over the bank. There was a boat which
churned up the water in the very depths of the river, making it even
muddier than usual, and a pipe which discharged this heavily silt-
laden flow onto the site. Once the silt had been deposited, and the
water drained off, either to irrigate the surrounding country or back
into the river, you had all the earth you needed to raise your embankment. It all sounded very sensible, very resourceful. But it was
also primitive: this immense undertaking, with all its apparent
success, all its indispensability, remained essentially a pre-mechaniza-
tion enterprise, with barely a truck or bulldozer to help it along.
Apart from the spade and the hand-pulled cart, in all the time I
was there the only pieces of equipment I saw on the site were two
light tractors, chugging over the spoil banks, and fulfilling a function that would have been better discharged by a steamroller.

As if guessing my thoughts the supervisor added that the works
would have been mechanized if a project downstream hadn't needed
the machinery more. In any case, there wasn't any necessity for it
here. They had laborers enough, some eight hundred of them,
mostly peasants who, now that the harvest was in, worked at this
as a sideline occupation to earn some extra income. Depending on

how much they did, a day's labor could bring in from two to five yuan each (roughly U.S. $2.50), and though few achieved the latter figure, this was not a sum to be sniffed at.

I remembered that all of Garden Entrance was reclaimed in this way—with wheelbarrows, spades, and shoulder poles, and perhaps, in those early days of the People's Republic, an inspiriting sense of national purpose too. The formerly flooded area, until reclamation an expanse of sand dunes and alkaline marshland, shows up on the map as an oblong slab tilting southeast from here down to where the overflow found an outlet through the River Huai. Making the area habitable again became at once the aim and symbol of "socialist construction." It took twenty years, and the official chronicles relish the statistical indicators of the accomplishment: so many miles of drainage and irrigation channels dug; so many hectares of swamps filled in; so many tons of grain subsequently produced; so many hundreds of bridges, dams and culverts built; so many trees planted; so many machinery repair shops installed. Even if the methods for achieving all this had not much changed since the time of Chiang Kai-shek, the look of the place, one must admit, is a far cry from 1938.

Down by the desiccated creek that is the Yellow River in autumn, the water lies low and becalmed. Looking across, you see the smooth line of dyke masonry and the flats beneath it extending far and brown. Beside the sedgy bank three boats bob about their moorings. It is an imperturbable, monotonous scene. Against such a background, the gigantic red legends on the revetments, enjoining you to "Control the Yellow River," to "Turn the Curse into a Blessing," stand out the more. All in all, I think, considering the odds against it, the response to these calls is something to be impressed by after all. Primitively carried out though it was, and massively demanding of human effort and sacrifice, still these Chinese have tamed the river more absolutely than any of their forefathers. From now on my journey will follow the four hundred miles of levees they call the Great Wall on the River—a wall which the people hope will stand between them and China's Sorrow.

Course Diversion

*It is not a believer in the old adage that as you make your bed
so you should lie in it . . .*

—— Harry A. Franck
on the Yellow River, 1923

Whenever the Yellow has changed its course, it has done so in
Henan Province, between the cities of Zhengzhou and Kaifeng. And
it was in these two places, too, that I caught some intimation of the
changing condition of China in the early 1980s: a groping up
through the dislocations of the Cultural Revolution toward a transi-
tion to something that is neither socialism nor capitalism, but a
system that the country hopes will work.

People spoke of the economic reforms, believed they were over
the worst, and hoped that it was not too late, that the mistakes of
that "lost decade" could still be unmade. The world that Mao
Zedong made no longer fits, and in the hands of his successors, the
course that he set is being spasmodically diverted.

Free Markets and Cantonese Spivs

Kaifeng is situated at the point from which most changes in the
course of the Yellow River have occurred. Brief as my trip to this
city was, I shall always think of it as one of my most enjoyable. As
Kaifeng was the last stop on the journey I made on my own, there
was perhaps that relief which comes with the thought of things

195

drawing to a close, the prospect of leaving this sometimes hard, often tiring country.

The tourist round was quickly done. From 960 until 1127, when it fell to a barbarian tribe from Manchuria, Kaifeng was the imperial capital of the Northern Song dynasty, a city whose rich, bustling street life you can still catch, by looking at *Spring Festival on the River*, a famous long scroll painting which minutely depicts it. In its prime, Kaifeng was the world's largest city. But of its splendid past only half a dozen relics remain: the Iron Pagoda, the Buddhist Xiangguo Monastery, the Old Music Terrace (also called the Terrace of Yu the Great), the Pota Pagoda, the Dragon Pavilion, and the medieval city walls.

I liked the Iron Pagoda best. Seen from a distance, the reason for its name appears obvious, but the pagoda is not what it looks, for it is really a brick structure, covered all over with brown tiles. There is a small lake to one side of it, and it charmed me to see the pagoda reflected in it at sundown, and the dozen or so women comfortably washing their clothes by the shores. One of these, a pretty girl with pale round knees, had her boyfriend serenade her on his mouth organ as she did her laundry crouched over the water.

I liked the Old Music Terrace least. So named because a famous musician of the "Spring and Autumn" period (between 722 and 481 B.C.) used to play here, it is a dull and unkempt place, with dusty pavilions one much like another to look at, and panels of worn calligraphy engraved on badly scratched stone. The only thing which rescues it from utter monotony is its Yellow River connection: during the Ming dynasty a temple was raised here to commemorate Yu the Great, the man who might be said to have invented flood control in China. He is a mythical figure best known to Chinese children (who can never escape reading about him in school) for his dedication and self-abnegation. In all the thirteen years he worked on the Yellow River he never once went home; though he passed the door several times he always managed to resist the temptation to cross the threshold.

All the flooding by the Yellow drained Kaifeng's vitality, though in early times the river never went anywhere near the city. But since it burst its banks and changed its course, Kaifeng has had the worst of it. The very streets now rest on silt, and I gathered that one of the reasons the medieval city walls haven't been knocked down is that in some places the masonry is too deeply sunk in muck.

There is an easy way to grasp the danger the river poses to the city, and that is to go to Liuyuankou, to the north of the city. There you will see the riverbed raised several feet above the land, and dykes so high that they can only imply the most fearful surge. Kaifeng has made its stretch of the river one of its sightseeing stops: a brown, brooding scene of mud, stone, embankment, and sky, which, once the summer rains come, is turned into a frenzy of churning waters, a terror. At Liuyuankou, you will see at once that it is silt and spate which make the Yellow River what it is, a source of China's sorrow.

But just now the Yellow River was calm, and as I made my way through the city, it was the tame, lulling image of the Yellow River carp which I had on my mind. I went in and out of restaurants, picturing that fish on an oval plate, simmered to a turn in a clear rice wine sauce. But they all looked at me as if I was hallucinating, saying they had nothing whatever to offer—neither fish nor fowl nor even any of the hard floury foods you find heaped on every northern table.

It was seven o'clock, and, in defiance of the notice which declared closing time to be half-past eight, the restaurant workers were packing up for the night. I took their point, having, of course, seen it all before: in Lanzhou, in Xi'an, in Peking, in all those places where what its apologists call job security in the worker's state appears to the bourgeois skeptic as sloth, inefficiency, inflexibility, and the dead hand of what the Chinese themselves call the "iron rice bowl"—the bowl which, because employees can never be sacked, can never be broken.

Though it seemed hopeless I went on trying with a mechanical obstinacy, going from restaurant to restaurant, and succeeding only in adding to my sense of frustration. So there was relief, as well as delighted surprise, on regaining the streets behind my guesthouse, and in coming upon a square where lamps and candles were alight, and in finding the place entirely given up to food vendors. The quest for food, forlorn a street away, was here a piece of cake. For the crossroads, once fallow these long evenings, had been turned into the noisy, thronged, aromatic province of the fast-food entrepreneur. I crossed the square, now stopping at one stall, now at another, until I had sampled all the things that I thought I would like—sticks of barbecued lamb kebabs, bowls of coagulated soybean milk, rice porridge, fried noodles, fermented rice, stewed apples—and more than made up for missing dinner. When I remarked on the liveliness of the scene to one of the hawkers, she immediately agreed: "Yes, Kaifeng's cuisine has always been famous for its snacks."

What also impressed me, moving from one stall to the next and taking the utensils with me, was that the vendors never asked for a deposit on the bowls and chopsticks I borrowed—something new in my experience in China. It made me feel I was being served by men of commerce, in business for themselves and willing to indulge the customer. I couldn't help comparing these vendors to the traders I'd previously met, for instance in Shaanxi and northwest China, who seemed so half-hearted you wondered if the businessman really was making a comeback in China, as he is supposed to do in the new economic climate and the interests of progress. I remember an occasion in Yan'an, when I tried to buy some hard-boiled eggs from a hawker, and found myself waved aside because she'd rather not sell me anything than look for the right change for my one-yuan note.

Of course free marketing by the self-employed is nothing new in China, but whereas in other places the goods on sale might only be a replica of what can equally be found in the state stores, with perhaps an edge in quality, this was the first time I had seen the economic reform embraced with so much imaginative and lively endeavor. Until now it had often struck me what a picture of overall dearth the self-employed in China presented—those bored youngsters sitting by the roadside selling a lapful of peanuts, looking as if they hadn't had a customer all day. But here it was more like the open-air markets in southeast Asia—the mass of stalls that used to spring up at night on the car park in Orchard Road in Singapore, for instance, or the bazaar down by the Macao ferry station in Hong Kong. Until now I had thought sharp businessmen an endangered species in China, where people have become so habituated to state ownership that the hope of a quick return no longer charges the Chinese with as much entrepreneurial energy as it did proverbially.

This of course is an over-simplification, like almost any conclusion reached about China. There are distinct regional variations, and it all depends on where you go in China, and what the historical circumstances are. The Chinese themselves, for example, have a conspicuous and just respect for Canton—the sort of respect a customer will have, say, for a lavishly stocked supermarket. Because of its historical experience and proximity to Hong Kong, Canton has that commercial confidence and know-how which makes it the showcase of economic pragmatism in China. Peking may be the capital, Shanghai may contribute overwhelmingly to the gross domestic product, but it is Canton which Chinese minds conjure up when they try to imagine Progress, Success, or the Future.

In China it is the Cantonese who have gone furthest in the exploration of the "capitalist road." And the full extent of this, shown in the greater play given to market forces, and the energy, greed, roguery, and flash which this releases, came home to me as I was winding up my trip.

I had proceeded to Zhengzhou from Kaifeng by train, and boarded a plane there for Canton. What happened when the plane reached Changsha, its first scheduled stop, could have happened to any traveler on China's domestic airline: one of the engines packed up after takeoff. The pilot swiftly returned the plane to Changsha, and made a heart-stopping landing. There we were stuck for a whole night, while it rained very hard. Next day, as various analyses of the odds for and against the plane taking off again were being made by the stranded passengers, I made the acquaintance of a group of travelers from Canton.

After the austerity of Yellow River China, its hard-worked peasants, frugality, and remoteness from the twentieth century, I very much enjoyed this encounter with coastal China, whose people feel, and respond to, the cut and thrust of the world outside. These Cantonese passengers were lounging in the farthest corner of the airport waiting room, but it was not long before their voices were heard across the room.

"Bloody northerners, they haven't a clue what they're doing, have they?" one of them said.

"What do we do now?" another Cantonese voice asked, sounding as if it was at the end of its patience.

The first speaker, I noticed, had quite a way with him; dark, lean, curly haired, he wore his levi's, authentic down to the faded blue and the frayed hem, like a badge of distinction. "Do you know," I heard him say, "I've been up here three times and I don't find it any easier. My god, they eat dough here; imagine, *dough*! Those stick-in-the-mud peasants."

It is a belief of southerners, as well as a part of the truth, that North and South are reversed in China; South in China is not what it is in other countries, the place where poverty, backwardness, lethargy, and muddle reign instead of teutonic success and efficiency.

The prevailing opinion was that it would be disastrous, if they were stuck here, and condemned to a prolonged diet of the northern staple, wheat, instead of rice. One asked if the rumor that the airline was having an engine flown up to Changsha from Canton was true. "Damned if I know." This was from a man who wore a digital watch and a pair of trousers so flared at the hem that only the tips of his leather shoes were unenveloped. He looked faintly loutish, with smarmy hair and a hint of a moustache.

There were six of these noisily cocky Cantonese. Laughing and swearing, they made the other passengers seem tame and boring. Though I wanted to join in, I hesitated at first, wondering what I should say, and if my knowledge of the dialect—which I should certainly have to speak if I were not to be instantly excluded—was good enough for me to pass myself off as a Cantonese. What I broke in with eventually was, in view of the known unreliability of the Chinese airline, wouldn't it be better if we addressed ourselves to the possibility of completing our journey by train?

It may seem surprising that such a possibility should have been left unexplored until this late hour. It is something that has to do with the difficulty, which everyone knows only too well, of getting berths on express trains at short notice in China. There was also no question of getting a refund on our air tickets without the most protracted, frustrating encounter with bureaucracy. We were also miles from the railway station and it was raining very heavily.

When I spoke the man in levi's gave me a wide, engaging smile; after that I felt I'd been accepted into the group. More than accepted: I felt as if I had been adopted, as a protégée.

The next step was to request that the airline provide a bus to take us into town. This was not well thought of by the personnel; in fact it was not thought of at all. Were we sure we didn't want to wait for the plane to be repaired? They had sent for parts and could fly us out in a matter of hours. When I relayed this information to Lin, as I shall call the man in levi's, he said, "Yeah, and get us all killed while they're at it. I don't trust those engineers an inch."

There followed several hours of waiting, in which we had all the leisure for restlessness and boredom. There was no sign of anything happening, and it was probably a good guess that it would be a matter of days, not hours, before the plane was serviceable again. When it became obvious that no one would buy the airline's story, the staff finally agreed to drive us back into town, those that wanted to go (half the passengers preferred to sit it out). The ride into town felt interminable, and when the bus finally halted, it was a group of tired, bedraggled passengers who climbed out. We were unnerved, what's more, by the prospect of scrambling for seats at the train ticket counters, each ruled, as likely as not, by an unfriendly petty tyrant.

Pedestrians passed us, and I envied them their umbrellas. Nevertheless I thought I had much to be thankful for: if I hadn't teamed up with the Cantonese I should probably be hysterical by now. As it was I rather savored the feeling of having them look out for me.

Approaching the station, I found myself walking beside the dude with the flared trousers and loutish look. He said we were lucky not to have been killed when the aircraft engine gave out; I said we were indeed. When we arrived at the station we went on talking, and there gradually grew a thick sense of confidence, of comradeship even, though Chen (as I shall call him) was not the kind of man you wanted to spend a lot of time with alone. They had all been up north on business, he confided, some for three weeks, others for much longer. When I asked what sort of business he said they were buying materials needed by the enterprises they separately worked for, directly from the suppliers. "They're fixers," I realized: people employed to sidestep the delays, rigidities, and inefficiency of the Byzantine system of central economic management, in which different units at the same level may not deal directly with each other but must go all the way up the line of vertical command.

That explained the handbag they each carried, the black plastic zip pouch they wore with the strap looped round the wrist, which Lin, for one, liked to swing about, to show how heavy with banknotes it was. (Later I learned he was carrying 50,000 yuan in hard cash.) Chen said they closed all their deals with cash—that way you got in fast. They were people very much impressed by money, and the things that money can buy. Part of Lin's contempt for northerners, for example, had to do with their relative distance from the world of expensive goods: "If they only saw what it's like in Canton," he said, "wouldn't their eyes pop . . . the color TV sets, the cars . . . ?"

Chen, I noticed, was wearing fifty-yuan worth of clothes, a month's salary to the average Chinese wage earner. Where did all this money come from? The biographical details, gleaned piecemeal, could have come from a novel. He had an uncle in Hong Kong, and several times over the last ten years he had tried to steal across the border to join him there; the rap was usually worth a stint in jail. Freed, he'd been scraping along, until Maoism was overturned with the fall of the Gang of Four. Under the new policy of rehabilitating former landlords and capitalists, and making restitution of property seized during the Cultural Revolution, a synthesis of a good nose for money and an opportunity to travel for his work produced a lucrative by-product.

He told me how this sideline worked, beginning in the middle.

"There's this woman in Xinjiang [Chinese Turkestan]—I've just been there, remote as it is—whose husband had a million dollars stashed away in a bank in America before the communists took over. When the Red Guards came she buried the evidence—all the documents, you know—under the wall of her house. Now she's dug them all up and has commissioned me to recover the money for her: after all I have good connections in Hong Kong. My uncle, for one, is a man of substance and position."

I saw that to Chen, considerations of legality were no part of this endeavor. If he succeeded, it was clear, at least part of the proceeds would be converted to his own use. Because there is something in us that longs for things to come out right I found myself hoping that this dealer in dreams would pull it off, even when I believed that what ultimately ensured his success was the complementary ignorance of his client. I could well imagine that woman in Xinjiang, whom Chen said was the concubine of a former landlord, dead these many years: illiterate, credulous, completely out of touch, animated only by thoughts of jewelry and riches.

Chen thought he had a good career ahead of him, scouting about for people with bank accounts abroad, and pursuing these along undisclosed avenues. Just now he was planning a big one, he told me. "I'm onto a family in Sichuan Province, the descendants of Chiang Kai-shek's secret police chief. The total take could be a million dollars, *U.S.*" I thought I knew which family he meant, but the idea seemed so fantastic that I waited for him to disclose it. Then the name of Dai Li fell, distinctly; and I gasped.

It is important to an understanding of Chen's audacity to realize that General Dai Li was the head of the most powerful secret police organization in Asia during World War II, and that as a killer of communists he was unsurpassed. Dai Li: that's a name people used to utter to frighten children into behaving, I thought after the first shock. I looked at Chen in astonishment, remembering how Barbara Tuchman, the American historian, had described Dai: "China's combination of Himmler and J. Edgar Hoover." What risks Chen must have run, I thought, dealing with the family of a man like that. It was reckless all right, but he seemed to keep a cool head though, tossing off that name as though he was giving me the name of a dumpling shop.

Once you knew him to be someone operating in the interstices of law, you could not see Chen as anything else: if any opportunity presented itself he would engineer a swindle of one kind or another. I felt I knew the type well, from my knowledge of that brotherhood of yore, the anti-society of drifters, itinerant traders, charlatans, hucksters, and traveling performers, who lived by their wits, beyond the reach of law and conventional morality, in what is known as the *jianghu*, or hobo, walk of life. He was descended, I saw, from that rich line that ran from the medieval knight errant to the secret society or triad member—an underworld man in modern dress.

And true to that tradition, he was bound by a code of loyalty to people of his own kind. That was one reason, I realized, I hadn't been chicaned out of my foreign currency certificates before now, though there had been ample opportunity. I did notice then that he and the others had started calling me Sister, a term of inclusion which implied their readiness to look upon me as one of their own class, to protect me even. They made a point never to leave me alone for long, and were always telling me to look to my money; the way I opened my wallet I was asking to be robbed, they gently reproached me. This was not so much a comment on my carelessness as on their own easy attitude to other people's property, which dictated caution on the part of the owner.

At one point Lin asked me what I did for a living. I told him I was at the moment unemployed, whereupon he said, believing we had certain traits in common, "Been sacked, have you?" He reckoned he had me figured out: a loafer, he must have said to himself.

We were sitting in a row on a long bench at the railway station, idly talking. Chen, lounging on my right, looked pensive after that short exchange with Lin; a few minutes later he leaned forward to say to me, "Maybe my uncle in Hong Kong can fix you up with something, or maybe"—he looked quite earnest now—"you could think of going into business for yourself. You look to me to be the type who could."

"But what sort of business?" I inquired.

Chen pursed his lips reflectively. "Well," he said, "you could go in for import-export. It's easy as long as you know a good supplier. Anybody can do it, and a lot of people do, believe me—making millions." He would like nothing better than to help me with con-tacts; hadn't he been knocking about Xinjiang? "I know a lot of important people up there," he reminded me.

"Is that so?" I got the sense with him that we were rather like a pair of moneychangers trying to think of ways of fleecing the cus-tomers in the market.

"Sure, I even know the garrison commander, and you can't have a better *guanxi* than that." *Guanxi*, or connection, is a sort of magic, and is what you have to have to get things done in China. "You could get a nice business going exporting the best of Xinjiang's local produce to the rest of Asia."

"Such as?"

"Garlic."

"*Garlic?*" I obtusely repeated.

"Sure, garlic. I can't imagine you not knowing about Xinjiang garlic, a smart woman like yourself. It's famous; when you corner the garlic market, you as good as corner it all."

As a matter of fact this was news to me. I didn't then take Chen seriously, and had I not, much later, broached the subject with a dealer in Chinese foodstuffs from Indonesia I chanced to meet on the train to Canton, I would have credited the whole conversation to Chen's fancifulness. As it was, that dealer corroborated Chen's remarks then and there: garlic from Xinjiang was one of the most sought after things in southeast Asia, and whoever was onto a good supply of it was onto the golden goose. We live and learn.

We spent a whole day together, those Cantonese spivs and I. We were hours at the dreary station, wet from the rain, forced to in-action, and yet obliged to be constantly on the alert: it was only by repeated trips to the ticket counter and dogged contrivings that bunks were procured for all—Chen and I on the express from Peking, the rest on the stopping train. I was strung out to the limit, because of not having slept the night before, and because, after a month of traveling in China, my body no longer withstood as well as it did at the beginning the fatigues of waiting, moving, the crazy swings in temperature, the gritty dust, and the shoddiness of everything. I was all the more grateful, therefore, for the kindness of these men, who shared everything with me—their dinner, their secrets— and gave me that sense of security which came of feeling we were all in it together.

Since then I have vacillated about whether these men were sinister, comic, a bit of both, or only to be expected, given the continuities of culture and the recent lowering of barricades in China. I must admit that the last interpretation seems the most persuasive at this point. I had thought such men a vanished species in China; yet here they were, wheeling and dealing for all they were worth. What an anomaly, what piquant irony: these continuators of the Chinese *jianghu* tradition, who in an earlier time would be advancing the cause of corruption and vice—hustling, running opium, or worse, while at the same time upholding chivalry and mutual solidarity—were surfacing once more in China. When I finally parted from them at the journey's end, it was with the twin regrets of leaving their company and leaving an endangered species.

What Mao Saw

In Zhengzhou, in front of the Henan Provincial Museum, I saw a statue of Mao Zedong, his right arm raised, the tails of his greatcoat slightly billowing, standing on a fifteen foot pedestal and overlooking the tops of yellowing maples. It is the size of King Kong, and has that stamp of gracelessness which, rightly or wrongly, I attribute to the emptiness of imported Soviet taste. It is fast getting out of date though. This statue, which must at one time have seemed the last word in commemorative masonry, is now no more than a period piece, and even the convictions of the man it represents, for all their lingering force in the world at large, seem in China itself to be of an earlier vintage. In Zhengzhou I felt acutely that China is losing the vision Mao Zedong had seen for it.

There is a dusty corner of the Monument to the Great Strike of

February 7 which forcefully conveys to me this sense of artifacts outliving their sponsoring ideologies. The monument, consisting of twin pagodas raised at an intersection between the old city and the railway station, is a place every tourist is obliged to see. The great strike took place in 1923, and was a protest by railway men against the banning, by the warlord Wu Peifu, of the founding congress of the United League of Railway Workers of the Peking-Hankou system. In putting down the strike the warlord's soldiers killed thirty-five workers and wounded many others; and in the pagoda, several types of visual documentation record this outrage upon the workers' movement for posterity. There are explanatory maps of the tangled infighting among the warlords in the 1920s; oil paintings; photographs of early communists, including one of Mao Zedong as a clear-eyed young man of twenty-six; and a tableau in sculpted plaster of railway workers, encircling the great leader in blank and perpetual resolution.

On the day I was there the place was swarming with people, and, not wanting to press through the crowd, I had no mind to linger in the gallery at the top for the good view of the city you are supposed to get from there. So I wandered down to the basement, and there I found hardly anybody about, and something very different.

In a cubicle roped off from the main concourse, two large cabinets stood like bookends against the openings, blocking a massive tableau from view. But if you clamber over the ropes, as I did when no one was looking, the stark and almost life-size figures of worker-heroes in a revolutionary stance—bronze hand clutching hammer, knee bent in a lunge—confront you suddenly in the harsh fluorescent light. You will recognize the genre, and may have seen its exemplars in Moscow or East Berlin. Down here the figures are caked in dust, and the ensemble looks like some immense discarded junk, brooding there eerily deserted.

Seeing it, I was reminded of Andrzej Wajda's *Man of Marble*, and specifically of a scene from that film. It is the one in which Agnieszka, a student film maker, discovers the marble statue of a fallen Polish Stakhanovite, an exemplary worker-hero of the 1950s, locked away in a museum storeroom with some other relics of that earlier,

Stalinist time. The discovery intrigues her, and she sets off to re-construct the life of the model worker in film. Inevitably, in piecing together the world of the past, she comes up against the realities of the present—the new wealth and the old hypocrisies. From that mood of bourgeois aspiration and bureaucratic corruption, the sense of revolution has long retreated; and Agnieszka's search, while revealing how it was in Poland in the 1950s, also shows what has happened to it in the 1970s.

It was the feeling of the fifties and sixties that was imparted by this Chinese relic, left to gather dust in the basement, and the idea that no history repeats itself like the history of revolution. The discovery of that bronze ensemble, in its cloistered setting, gave the artifact an almost archaeological interest, reinforcing the sense of a time repudiated. And seeing those figures, looking so intent and solid, I was returned to that earlier, simpler time, when faiths were stronger than they are now, and the attainment of classless society seemed worthy of self-denial and collective endeavor.

I remembered then an item from the memorabilia of that period—a photograph of Mao Zedong, which used to appear on the frontis-piece of books about the Yellow River. It is of him sitting on a hill, his feet shod in cloth shoes, gazing at the river in the distance. It was taken on a hill only a short distance from Mangshan, a low range of hills flanking the south banks of the river to the northwest of Zhengzhou. This is now the site of a pumping and irrigation center, one that Zhengzhou offers as a sightseeing destination, as it is thought to be a scenic spot. Miles of cultivated land are irrigated by the station, and the city itself depends heavily on it for its industrial and domestic water. Yet the place was once unwatered and sterile; and it was not until the winter of 1970, when Zhengzhou's school leavers took to the hoe, under the national rustication program, that the place took on its new look, with locust trees, weeping willows, poplar and pine clothing the slopes.

The once dun Mangshan grew green. Eight enormous pipes had been thrown down the foothills, and a reservoir dug to gather the water; the flow was piped one hundred sixty feet up to the summit, whence it was distributed to the plains around. The sluices were opened in 1972, and since then, so one account goes, the summers have brought forth apples and pomegranates.

All this I knew from reading, but seeing the place for myself proved more difficult than I had expected. I now again had Takia for a traveling companion, and though two heads are certainly better than one, it still took a long time to figure out how we should get there. The bus we would have taken was not running; the Yellow River Bridge was undergoing repairs that day, it seemed, and so far as the engineers were concerned, the traffic across it could go hang. In fact it is not necessary to cross the river to get to Mangshan, for the hills lie to the same side of the banks as Zhengzhou. But the bus was bound for points further afield, and closing the bridge obliged a suspension of service. Nobody had thought to make any alternative arrangements. If there was something cavalier to all this, it was probably because the task of making provision for the repercussions of official decisions often seems to be beyond the Chinese.

Buses were parked this way and that in the sprawling station. While I made inquiries in one corner of it, Takia went off to ask in another. It turned out that there was—one might have known it—a bus going only as far as Mangshan; in other words exactly where we were headed. Nobody I asked had mentioned it. Yet it was leaving a stone's throw from where we were standing, and it was leaving in half an hour. We had discovered this by piecing together the disclosures of half a dozen people, for if there is one thing Chinese informants dislike, it seems, it is to tell you everything at once.

It took just under an hour for the bus to reach the purlieus of the pumping station, but our arrival at this destination was the conclusion of a loud and lengthy dispute. We were approaching a level crossing when our bus was held up by a long queue of lorries in front. We were stuck for a long time, and as the minutes dragged by one or two passengers began to mutter their displeasure. They were quite disagreeable over this, and told the driver she should go on ahead regardless. A number of people at the back of the bus fell in with this suggestion, and became loud in their insistence on moving. Another passenger pointed out that this was folly: the

Yellow River Bridge ahead was closed, he said, and that was why the traffic was piling up; why bother to pass these trucks in front, since the road ahead was blocked anyway?

The driver observed, correctly and prudently, that she couldn't drive on ahead even if she wanted to, the lane being completely taken up with these trucks, none of which was getting through.

"But cars *are* getting through," insisted the opposition, pointing to the vehicles coming in the opposite direction, down the narrow lefthand lane.

To her credit the lady at the wheel did not think fit to follow their example, and I must admit that, seeing the lorries loom up one after another before me, and hearing the throb of their engines, I had my doubts about forcing a passage too.

Presently there was a lull in the traffic coming toward us. Only the driver, even if she wished to, could not now move her bus without appearing to bow to opposition, thereby losing face. Her wish not to give way to the pressure placed upon her by those supposedly under her control obliged her to remain impervious to persuasion. It was an interesting situation, of the kind one might find in sociological writing, or a committee in stalemate. The group has thrown up the usual figures: we have had the aggressive and argumentative member; the member who refuses to budge; the member who advises inaction; silent members who nod and agree. And now, when every side has gone as far as it would go and the time has come to break out of the impasse, very likely a diplomat figure, preferably an elderly dignitary with a gentle voice, will speak up and offer a formula to reconcile the opponents.

I couldn't see him from where I was sitting, but that tone of quiet authority and conciliation, breaking late into the debate, at a moment when everyone was more or less ready for it, was recognizable to me at once from my knowledge of Chinese disputes. He addressed himself to the driver, and all he said was, "Why don't you give it a try?" But it gave her the necessary let-out, for any misgivings she might have felt at risking face were forestalled by the man's obviously superior social status, which made her submission an honorable rather than a humiliating thing. He must be a cadre, I thought—at the very least. At the instant we resumed our progress the bus was rocked with a shuddering shout of "Victory!" by the passengers. But it was my private belief, as we swerved out and passed the line-up of trucks, that no one was more relieved than the driver.

We alighted. Up close, the green of the terraced hillsides looked ragged; the slopes had not been planted for some time. A path led us up a steepish incline, and from it we could see the terraces rising over us to our left and right, unshaded for the most part, and pre-dominantly taupe in color. Here and there openings in the hillsides led to what might be cave dwellings; but I could see no sign of life, either there or in the surrounding country. We decided we were going up the wrong incline, and turned round to find our way back to the beginning.

We saw then that there was another approach, by flights of steps flanking those giant pipelines, leading up to the crest over which the river water is pumped. A small park with a fountain is laid at the bottom, and a pair of pavilions perched on the hump to en-courage the impression that this is a scenic spot. One enters here quite a different kind of environment, but the higher one gets up the slope and the wider one's view of the countryside, the deeper is the suspicion that this place is only a showcase, a green and watered enclave encircled by acres of brown. Below you, down the splaying hillsides, the terraced arcs are lined with firs and poplars. Away to the right in the distance, the Yellow River Bridge and its companion —one carries railway lines and the other lanes of roadway—stretch until faded into haze. But turn to your right and round a corner, and you will not fail to notice the difference: all around the slopes fall sandy, and bare, and brown.

Yet it remains true that agriculture depends entirely on irrigation here in Henan Province, where up to eight months can go by with not a drop of rain falling. The river is not only a living presence; the province depends on it utterly for its lifeblood. To transform its floods into irrigation, to make it provide insurance against Henan's notoriously unreliable rainfall, was a first priority of the regime that came into power in 1949. In the river, many of the obstacles and potentials of national construction were seen to be trenchantly represented; and it was here, in that famous decree, that Mao Zedong had called for the mastery of the river. "The work on the Yellow River," he pronounced, "must be done well." These words, inescapable here in their red mounts across the facade of the pumping station, were to leap out of the page in boldface type whenever they appeared in print.

Nowadays one tends to brush aside such slogans, forgetting that the Chairman's inexhaustible *Quotations* had once galvanized a nation into action. Of their kind they are actually quite memorable. Classic phrases like "Political power grows out of the barrel of a gun"; "Imbalance is normal, balance is temporary"; "The atom bomb is a paper tiger"; and "Doing is itself learning" have laced the vocabulary of an entire generation, not only in China but universally. Yet the impression they now make is of a failed talisman, something that turned out to be a dud.

Some such weary thought, I must confess, crossed my mind when I came down the hill. A park was laid out at the ground level, and wandering about it, I reached an opening into a circular fountain. There, cross-legged upon a stony plinth, above a bed of stones protruding from the water, sat a statue of a woman with a baby in her lap. She is a lumpish lady, dressed in what the present-day Chinese imagination supposes to be classical costume. No doubt against every intention of her executor, there was a ridiculous aspect to this unfortunate effigy, which struck me as the earnest product of somebody's mistaken idea of plastic art. But she was there for a purpose, I found; she and her baby were an emblem of the Yellow River, which, as the Chinese never tire of telling you, is the cradle of Chinese civilization itself.

You have to admit that it is not much of an emblem. Yet even as it struck me as crude, as ludicrous, it put my mind in a historical frame, and reminded me of the context to that injunction of Mao Zedong. Mao's call for the work on the Yellow River to be done well, I now recalled, was no more than the reiteration of an ancient charge, one handed down the centuries by "hydraulic civilizations" all over the world, from the Egypt of the Pharaohs to the China of the dragon throne. No less than these ancient rulers, Mao was conscious of the importance of managing water.

Mao had felt himself equal to the challenge not merely of government or other human institutions, but of nature itself. I thought again of that photograph, of him sitting on a bluff near here with his hands resting on his knees. In half a dozen books published up to the seventies, there are awestruck references to the occasion marked by this picture: his inspection of the Yellow River from Mangshan in October 1952. In it his face, seen in profile, is turned toward the river, which we can see had only one bridge then. He looks a homely sort of figure, not like a great man, but what he is gazing at seems important, from the homage he pays it with his eyes. He is looking at the river, but he is seeing something beyond it too. Whatever one may think of the picture, or of socialist iconolatry, there is no question of protesting his historical quality—the sort that comes from an unshakeable conviction about an idea, or a nation.

Approaching the pumping station on the bus, I had glimpsed a sign upon the flank of a hill; it read, "From this spot, on 31 October 1952, Chairman Mao ascended the hill to inspect the Yellow River." At that point I had not yet climbed the hill above the station, and I had wondered what Mao had seen from his spot. I now knew, from the small distance between his lookout and mine, that it must have been pretty much the same view. Yet it became necessary for me to see it from his vantage-point—not out of curiosity, but from some vague notion of pilgrimage, which I now found quite irresistible. At any other time I would have scoffed at the idea, but just then it was as if I couldn't turn my back on it, not if I were to render a plausible account, to say that I had tried to understand.

I didn't have very much time, for we were catching the 2 p.m. bus, and that was due in a quarter of an hour. But I set out anyway, thinking I would go as far as I could in the time. To my dismay it turned out to be much further than I had expected, and I had to turn back before I reached the spot. This sense of coming so near without arriving at what I sought nagged me though, and I asked the bus driver, when he finally showed up, if he would stop there for a few minutes while I went up and had a look.

He said he would be at the terminus for some minutes, and if I wanted to go on ahead in the meantime, he could pick me up on his way through. I knew it wasn't anything, but I was grateful to him for not thinking me a nuisance, breaking his familiar routine with demands; and I set off as fast as I could in the direction from which I had just come. Along the way I saw those people who are always to be found in the outskirts of a Chinese city—laborers employed in the fields, aged loungers squatting beside the road smoking. Foolishly I stopped to ask one of them how far I was from Mao Zedong's lookout post; he neither knew nor cared, though he was a local, and of an age to have straightened up once at the mere mention of the name. And I was reminded of my surprise of the evening before, when, telling us all about Mangshan, the young bartender at the hotel had scratched his head and wondered which leader it was who had gone up in person to survey the river.

If it had once been a landmark, I could see at once when I got there that it was no longer so. The loose slopes were banked with stone walls, solidly mortared and surmounted by a parapet. The plaque was there, tilting crookedly against a wall, the paint on it chipped in several places, and the rust creeping up at the joins. In front of me I could see the river in the distance, and all along the road below, trucks were coming to a halt with their loads. Behind me the path led to a clearing, but I was shut off from it by a padlocked gate. Peering through its grilles, I could make out a row of what looked at first like red brick houses, roofed with the grey tiles of Chinese tradition, and opening through arches decorated in an English dogtooth design.

In fact they were only facades, leading into caves whose names were carved in emerald niches above the doorways: Cave of History, Cave of Mangshan, Cave of Glory. The scene was not without color, but under that leaden sky, and with that shuttered air, the impression it made on me was of the pallid sepia of an old photograph. There were brown reeds sprouting from between the tiles on the roofs, and in the flowerbed, a straggly bamboo strained to hold its own against a tangled undergrowth.

Forgotten or repudiated, how many faiths have been buried here? That clarion call, the injunction to best nature, all those barrages and hydroelectric power stations, those hundreds of culverts, si-phons, sluice gates, reservoirs, and pumps tripling or even quad-rupling the area under irrigation, the dykes getting higher and thicker, the mass mobilization, the sense of nationhood, of elevated purpose—all that immensity of actions, far from inspiring awe, nowadays produces any number of shrugs. "Which leader was it now, who came in person to look over the river?" "Who knows where Mao Zedong's observation post is?" History has moved on, discarding the Maoist certainties an earlier generation was weaned upon, and now the people are left cynical and dejected. The earlier dynamic has fizzled out, and in this era, when the myths by which men lived no longer serve, no idol remains to the people.

To an incalculable degree the country has been changed by Mao-Zedong-Thought, that seductive ideology that is part tribalism, part occultism, and part Marxist theory. Mao had led the Chinese people in a truly astonishing enterprise, in the pursuit of a destiny which he persuaded them to desire with all the ardor of romantic youth. Yet now people prefer to forget it. And these sad looking cave-houses with their air of lonely neglect: what an image they were of that familiar phenomenon, the waning of ideologies and the passing of power.

I was there only for a few moments. Then I slid down onto the ground and waited for my bus. Seeing it clatter up seconds later, I flagged it down with relief. We were two hours getting back into town, caught in the traffic that had been thwarted from crossing the bridge over the Yellow River. Throughout the journey I stared out of the window, absently. Outside there was a complete foul-up, with motionless trucks pointing this way and that, each one trying to edge in. In my boredom I thought back to the river; and how, lacking rain, it had dwindled, exposing shoals.

But sitting there in the bus, hemmed in by all that traffic, it was not so much the river itself that I best remembered, but what came over the loudspeaker as I was making for its banks. It was after my descent from the Mangshan heights, when I was walking past the pumping station and down to the river: quite suddenly, there came from overhead, following a broadcast of news, a burst of music from the soundtrack of *Snow White and the Seven Dwarfs*—first the chirpy "Hi-ho! Hi-ho! And Off to Work We Go," and then the sweetly wistful strains of "Some Day My Prince Will Come." As if to signify the distance China had come, from the world of Mao Zedong to the world of Walt Disney; or perhaps not so much the distance that lay between these fabulists, as the things that the two had in common.

Railway Junction

Standing as it does at the junction of the Peking-Canton and Long-hai (Gansu to the coast) railway lines, Zhengzhou links the country north to south and east to west. In the old days it was a place of lust and lawlessness, where all trains were obliged to stop for twenty-two hours, to give passengers time to visit the red-light district and the opium dens. It was badly shelled by the Japanese during World War II, but the city has now been physically and morally transformed, its bomb sites replaced by red brick workers' apartments and machine tool factories, its prostitutes and drug peddlers superannuated, its horrendous dust and loess laid with plane trees and poplars. The price of this cleanup was a certain characterlessness though, and Zhengzhou is a rather boring city—in fact a bit of a dump.

As the China Travel Service, which often does not know on which side its bread is buttered, will be the first to tell you, Zhengzhou has little to offer the tourist. Of guidebook comments on the place, I like none better than Evelyne Garside's in her *China Companion* (1981): "Little of note took place in Zhengzhou between the Shang dynasty [16th to 17th centuries B.C., when it was founded] and the construction of the railway at the beginning of the present century." Yet in the Soviet-style hotel where we were staying, elderly American package tourists could be seen sitting down to dinner every evening. For us it was the first place we'd come to for a long time where you could read something of the outside world, for the hotel had a supply of *China Daily,* the English-language newspaper published in Peking, albeit of issues two to three days behind. Often a sense of isolation overcomes you in China, and you feel yourself so cut off from the rest of mankind, in the fastness of something so distant and fossilized, that if the world should come to an end you would not even know it. I felt this in the evening of my arrival in Zhengzhou, for, picking up my outdated copy of *China Daily,* I read that Brezhnev had been solemnly buried, when all this time I had not even been aware that he was dead.

We had come for the river, and the Yellow River Exhibition Center was our first port of call. We had been told Zhengzhou was distinguished for this place, which incorporates numerous visual aids to a rudimentary understanding of the river, from clay models gushing with water to photographs of areas transformed by its control.

Of the two curators who admitted us, the one who showed us around was the less sympathetic. She told us, as she whizzed us through the frosty echoing rooms of exhibits, that the author Han Suyin had visited no less than four times, and also many important Americans and Europeans. I couldn't catch half of what she said, for she seemed very anxious to hasten the tour to an end, and delivered a great deal of information in double quick time. In a way I don't blame her, for I too would want to get out of those chilly halls as fast as possible and retire to tea and warmth in the reception room. All the same I thought her manner a shade more huffy than strictly called for. On arrival at the center we had asked if we might visit the Scientific Research Center of the Committee for Water Conservancy, a setup falling within the same bureaucratic division as the exhibition center. And it was probably our audacity, as non-scientists, in requesting this that had so annoyed her, and prompted that remark about Han Suyin. We were without even those qualifications that American nationality might have given us. We were properly abashed, and when the tour ended, and an array of books and souvenirs were brought out for our inspection, we bought far too many badges of the Yellow River in self-extenuation.

Afterward we wandered at random about the city, and stumbled upon a Muslim quarter lying athwart the site of the ancient settlement on which present-day Zhengzhou stands. Here a city was founded some four thousand years ago, and traces of that ancient habitation remain: sections of the surrounding ramparts, graves, bronze foundries and pottery kilns, and pits dug for storage. Now it is the hub of a Muslim community showing some autonomy (there is a district Hui government of sorts there) and resistance to Han acculturation.

We looked for a mosque, and found one in scaffolding at the end of a dirt lane. We were received most hospitably by an old caretaker pottering about in the courtyard, overlooked by painters and carpenters renovating the roof. The architecture of the mosque is entirely Chinese, and only the few pallid turbans, left on the floor amid the shadows, confounded the impression of a Confucian or Buddhist temple. We peered into a room where dead bodies are brought to be prepared for burial, but all I could make out was a slab fixed on legs in the gloom. This is the bed where the dead are laid out and washed; and over to the left of the courtyard, barely recognizable amidst the planks and the scrap, is the coffin in which the corpses are taken to be buried. The coffin is never interred with the corpse, but brought back here to be used for the next body.

Low roofs of weathered grey tiles, held up by dozens of curving round beams, hung over broad pavements and dusty streets. Every now and then a framed tasseled signboard with Arabic writing appeared on a wall, and through the open door beside it you could glimpse some figures crouched in the half light, stirring the noodles publicized by the signboard. A local speciality appeared to be a spiced roast chicken, red on the outside like tandoori chicken, but waxier; four or five men were selling it on the sidewalks, from those wheeled carts that you see all over China. Half of one cost us the colossal sum, by Chinese standards, of about one U.S. dollar. I had assumed the vendor had roasted the chicken himself; not so: he gets his supplies from the mosque, where their preparation com-

plies with religious standards of hygiene. Another cart we stopped
at had a caldron of boiling water sunk into a cabinet, with only its
broad bamboo rim showing. Stewing in a crescent around the rim
were dates and pears simmered to a glossy brown softness by the
blanketing steam. The signboard, a framed picture of a yellow
teapot, of the bulbous shape of an onion dome, and with its lid and
spout tapering like minarets, simply proclaimed (as credentials
enough) *Islam,* spelt out in the three different ways possible in
Chinese: Yisilan, Hui, and Qingzhen.

There was quite a bit of petty trade here. My attention was
caught by a large old woman, sitting upon a sidewalk near the
crossroads, hawking babies' cloth shoes of rainbow colors and of
the lavish workmanship that great poverty combined with copious
leisure produces. All were different, with the uppers adorned in
embroidery and fluffy embellishments, and the toes stitched to look
like the faces of cats and tigers and other indeterminate animals.
"I am eighty-five," she chuckled, lifting her unclouded eyes from
her needlework, "and I make these because, well, I have nothing
better to do." I saw that she had a huge goiter and an indefinably
gentle face. Her shoes sold for almost a song—about twenty cents
a pair—but even that proved too much for a passerby, who stopped
to ask the price and then walked huffily on.

To people from the capitalist West, the apparently unrewarded
expenditure of time and effort such as was suggested by those shoes
is sometimes disturbing. The life of that old shoemaker, with all
those hours of slow sewing and waiting on the pavement, would
dement the modern mind with boredom. She had ample leisure,
it is true, but in the West the leisure classes are those who rush
around pursuing interests and distractions for which they can somehow never find quite enough time. The poor must experience time
differently from the rich; they have more of it and it hangs heavily
on them, and this despite all the time-consuming menial chores
they have to do. Emancipated by servants and labor-saving devices,
the rich are yet ensnared by their possessions and their urge to fill
each moment with activity and meaning. The leisure of the poor
comes of their unemployment in either production or consumption:

they have more time because they work less, both at their jobs and at maintaining standards of eating, clothing, cleaning, and entertaining.

Two other things remain with me of my stay in Zhengzhou. One was the Yellow River carp we had ordered for our dinner on our last night at the hotel. It is the region's most celebrated dish, cooked with quite the most imaginative disregard of the tradition that decrees fish as a savory. Its name, Carp with Baked Noodles, it owes to the fact that the fish is served blanketed with a floss, spun to a gossamer crispness, which I decided after the first taste could only be sugar. The result is an exquisite tactile sensation, each mouthful popping and dissolving at once. But the dish, though impeccably cooked, is too remote from anyone's culinary experience to be true, and it would take a palate less conservative than mine to accept without some reserve a fish dish that is more like a pudding than an entrée. Takia, who disdains all things sweet and is moreover a Cantonese with that people's discrimination as regards the cooking of fish, never touched it at all after the first mouthful.

The other thing I remember is trying to get sleepers on our train out of Zhengzhou. To begin with, enquiring about their availability at the railway station, a business that would have taken perhaps two seconds in Tokyo, four in Hong Kong, one minute in New York, and ten minutes in London, took a full thirty minutes in Zhengzhou. At first the signs seemed to be in my favor: there were only two people in front of me in the queue at the counter, and none of them had complicated queries. But when it came to my turn, and I moved forward to peer into the guichet, the lady behind it decided to pick up the telephone and dial a friend for a chat. Since she pretended not to see me, I knew better than to interrupt her, for this would only rouse her ire, an eventuality not conducive to my cause. I could tell from her expression and the tone of her voice that it was an agreeable heart-to-heart talk, going on and on in quite total disregard of the queue lengthening behind me.

Everyone waited. Presently, unable to bear it any more, a woman at the far end edged forward and indicated that I should cut in. Just as I was figuring out how many more minutes this was likely to add to the telephone conversation, quite without warning the lady hung up. But when I made ready to fall upon her, she turned round to her colleague behind the window and proceeded, with some indignation, to go into every particular of some event which had earlier befallen her, protesting at its injustice and requiring her auditor to agree with her.

No end could now be envisaged. I could feel the queue getting restive, and was feeling pretty irritated myself. "What's going on? What's she up to?" I heard another woman say. "She's unbosoming herself to her colleague," I called down, when I realized the questions were addressed to me. Immediately behind me was a young gentle member of the People's Liberation Army, and turning to him in mock despair, I said, "Where I come from this would seldom happen. Holdups, inefficiency, yes; but not this. Tell me, since I don't know how best to react, what do people here do in such a situation?"

"Nothing," he replied ruefully, "except to exercise patience." How Chinese, I thought, to be so strong on fortitude, that quality which makes them take the unendurable lying down, and is the very opposite of the critical attitude that begets discontent, whose fruit is rebellion and change. The Chinese are truly their own best reasons for their country's backwardness.

Her long litany of grouses exhausted, the attendant decided to notice me—no doubt sooner than she intended, for she still seemed very disgruntled, and turned to me with an air of doing me a great personal favor. From her I gleaned the following information: no, there were no bunks left, as I might have known of course, had I been less doggedly over-optimistic.

No, the station master couldn't help. Nor could the head conductor, when the train pulled in: to get a sleeper you'd have to put your name down at the registration desk on the train itself, over there in that wagon. Oh yes, there might be one or two left, you never can tell. But I'd never get in, the door is completely blocked, I said, helpless at the sight of the boarding passengers thronging the carriage. At this the head conductor turned his head, signaling the end of conversation.

There was nothing for it but to board. As I tried to mount the steps, the crowd, whose reaches in front I could not see, crowded closer, suffocatingly close, and at my back I was aware of the mass half lifting me up, and also of their luggage pummeling me and their elbows gouging my sides. And in my ears the train ringing with "Get a move on!" "Go on!" "Don't push for heaven's sake, it's futile!" The minutes yielded no motion, for the door and the aisle were completely clogged. I saw neither in front, behind, nor around me, hemmed in as I was on all sides and unable even to lift a hand to wipe the perspiration off my face. I thought in despair: I will never get through this, never. Then a belligerent, excited face flashed into mine, rudely bawling at me to get out of the way, and a body, flinging itself this way and that, by some miracle advanced itself a little and made the way ahead penetrable also for me.

Now the conductress could be seen, sitting eyes downcast in her boxed-in cubicle; both the eyes and the cubicle were a barricade against the crowd. She was flipping open her registers. I braced myself for irascibility, as I croaked out my request for bunks in all timidity. But to my surprise she responded not ungraciously, and asked to see our tickets. Takia, pinned to an edge of the compartment further down the line, handed these over across the heads of the intervening mob. I passed them on to the conductress, then heard her say, "But there's only one set here." My harried search for an explanation, yelled across the crowd which threatened at any minute to roll over me, only drew from Takia, helplessly crushed and rattled himself, the sharp retort that I had the tickets. This was not true, and I realized, with something like a sickening in the stomach, that they must have been lost in the stampede. Any thought about looking for them was patently worse than useless, in that constriction of arms and legs and feet, where it was a wonder we still breathed. And I, submitting to the wretched moment along the line of least resistance, burst embarrassingly into tears.

I bought from the conductress another set of tickets to replace the one we had lost, and also an extra one for our bunks. But the struggle was not over yet, for now the moment approached when we must fight our way down the aisle to get to our sleepers, four or five carriages down. A man behind me, impatient to advance himself, lifted up my bag, which was hampering progress, and passed it down the line above our heads. Agile, he dived straight into the crowd, refuting the evidence of his eyes, which might have suggested inaccessibility. I felt the aisle stretch ahead of me like an impossible trek through a bristling, teeming jungle of creepers. A sense of unreality overtook me, as compartment after compartment was negotiated, their aisles cluttered like tangled tropical under-growth with the rows and stacks of belongings, plastic, canvas, cardboard, and cloth. The train, clanking forward, hurled me against this seated figure and that, as did the crowd pushing and shoving behind me. I ceased to care whom or what I trampled on. In fact nobody cared: we had all become savages, and those we knocked against or otherwise hurt as we lurched about seemed a race of snarl-ing, cursing monsters. I was quite without compunction, and if anyone should reproach me for jabbing him, over my shoulder I would let fly, in keeping with the belligerence I had grown like a shell, in which to weather this occasion.

My eyes continued to stream. This provoked uncomprehending stares, from people who saw in my plight no shadow of theirs. Indeed they seemed to see an altogether different condition: the overcrowding was disagreeable, yes; but no more than what they often had to put up with. Seeing their incredulous stares, one's impression could only be of a people immensely long-suffering, inured to a level of overpopulation no other could withstand. I heard one murmur to another, "Do you think she's foreign?" How to explain, indeed, such overreaction, so uncalled for a show of tears?

The overpopulation of this country was constantly brought home to me on my journeys, and this was only one occasion among many. When, the terrible tussle over and we were sitting back with joy and exhaustion, I reflected back upon the experience we had just undergone. It struck me forcefully then, the colossal disproportion of available goods and services to the number of people in this country, the ordeal just undergone serving to demonstrate a hideous excess of life, of needs, that overflows all interstices as jungle creepers obscure every chink of available light. This teeming multitude crowds out the good, making civility, humanity impossible. That was one reason we were such savages back there; courtesy and consideration were qualities we had to exclude from our behavior in order merely to get by. One countered the situation with brutality—or in any case the situation brutalized one, which amounts to the same thing.

All that night I lay half awake in my bunk, across from a heavily breathing woman cultural worker from Nanking, my mind straying among several confusions—the city, the train, the river, the crowd, and bits of remembered reading all knotted by the sleeplessness and darkness into a ragtag tangle through which there nevertheless pierced one distinct image. It was an image of rats. There had come uninvited to my mind those Norwegian rats such as psychologists experimentally raise in congested conditions in their laboratories to discover the effects of extreme overcrowding. I once had to write a paper about this, and I remembered now what I then related: that when animals are made to live in much closer contact than is normal for that species, their relationships degenerate into a kind of "behavioral sink." Female rats neglect their young; male rats go on a rampage, falling sexually upon other rats or clamping their teeth on one another's tails, not letting go until the tail is torn off. The stresses bring on all sorts of physiological disturbances, so that the rats' reproductive systems, glands, and organs become deranged, and the rate of their mortality heightened: one way of population control.

Whenever overwhelmed by doubt or disappointment in China, I always tried to think of how it was in the past, to temper my judgement and get the perspective right. Besides, one is encouraged to think in before-after terms in China. Some years ago a well-rehearsed recital by some oldster of the wrongs done to him by the old society, and the dramatic improvement in his lot brought about by the communist revolution, was an inescapable part of every package tour. The Chinese don't bother much about this now, and to us visiting compatroits at least, things are more or less allowed to speak for themselves. Anyway, which overseas Chinese doesn't have a relative somewhere in the country, who will reveal what goes on under the surface? In contrasting the present with the time before the revolution, I am willing to be guided by the contemporary witness, the travel memoirs that come one's way through the years. In this case I was heartened by the fact that there was little similarity between my experiences and those of W. H. Auden and Christopher Isherwood, when they came through Zhengzhou in 1938, as described in their book *Journey to a War*.

It is true that they were traveling in wartime, when conditions may be expected to be at their worst; but even so what came across was misery of a still blacker kind. In those days Zhengzhou was as ghastly a hole as anyone could expect to see. At the railway station, they were set upon by half a dozen coolies, who sprang out of the darkness to grab their bags. Their Canadian companion punched one hard on the jaw, explaining that the coolies were not really porters, but thieves. As for their train, to quote from their account of a ride further down the line from Zhengzhou: "The carriage roofs, as usual, were black with passengers. On every journey, we are told, two or three of them fall off and are killed. At the last moment, dozens of people tried to clamber on to the train, and were beaten off with sticks."

Every third person Isherwood saw seemed afflicted with trachoma, or goiter, or hereditary syphilis. And from an American doctor working in China he heard of growths and tumors and polyps that were endemic to the place, and caused their sufferers to look like freaks. I saw someone like that on this train, and it thoroughly unnerved me. The poor creature was crouched disregarded in a corner of the coupling, and my first glimpse of him instantly brought to mind the Elephant Man of the book and the film, for his face was knobbly all over with strange red protrusions, and his eyes and mouth showed only in the cracks between the bulges. He was a terrible sight, so sad and unsettling that I was seized at once with pity and repulsion. Yet I told myself that in an earlier time I might have seen half a dozen like him, and a difference in quantity *is* very often a difference in quality.

The Past Revisited

By the time the Yellow River flows into Shandong, the last province it crosses before debouching into the sea, bits of it have been left lingering in other places. We stumbled upon a bit in Xuzhou, down in Jiangsu Province, left over from a previous century. It is a bed the Yellow has abandoned for an outlet through the Shandong Peninsula.

Shandong is famous for many things, not the least for its sons and daughters. Its most infamous daughter is undoubtedly Mao Zedong's widow Jiang Qing, one of the Gang of Four, now safely out of harm's way in a comfortable lockup in Peking. Its most famous son is of course Confucius, whose tomb may still be visited in Qufu. Confucius, in a manner of speaking, is still alive and well in China, for all that he lived over two thousand years ago; the tenacity with which his ideas have persisted into the twentieth century is evidenced by the vehemence with which they were repudiated in the 1970s— a vehemence matched only by that with which his fellow provincial, Jiang Qing, was castigated a few years ago.

China is like that, always feeding on its past. It is as if it hobbles into the twentieth century trailing all its previous centuries behind it. The pattern which was set in the past seems to hold fast for good: go where you will, it will find you out and follow you. Here, in Xuzhou, the old course of the river lies in wait; there, below the mountain summit of Tai Shan, an ancient world, a world that Confucius saw, lies spread out in wooded glades, harboring desires and fears that are forever old.

An Abandoned Riverbed

Maps of the geographical history of China are blotched with the shifts in the course of the Yellow River, from the great deflections which sent its outlet flowing from the north of Shandong Peninsula to the south, to the great change of 1048, which moved its outlet to the north once more. Eight centuries ago, the lower Yellow was linked up with the Huai, and the two waterways debouched into the Yellow Sea as one. For 675 years, until their summer flood crest broke the dykes at Tongwaxiang (in eastern Henan Province) in 1853, the lower reaches were channeled through Xuzhou.

Today, the crook of the old channel still dictates the shape of the city, swinging in a wide angle through its northeastern corner. It was the first clear bit of the river we'd seen so far—clear because superannuated, I suppose. The stone embankments ran down to the channel at a gentle slope, and up and down the water's edge, crouching women could be seen at their washing, with sleeves rolled up and sticks to beat their laundry. Some of them had soap, and the suds spread a white floury lather over the water.

Walking along the river, you couldn't mistake Xuzhou for anything but an industrial center, with black smoke belching from its factory chimneys. Dwellings were strung out under this pall along both sides of the river, old crumbling quarters with red blankets airing on clotheslines and newer apartment blocks faced with balconies and pale green shutters. The houses, factories, and apartment blocks all stood on their own reflections. It was one of those cloudless, windless days in November, and I spent the afternoon wandering about the causeway and the bridges, absurdly pleased with the discovery that for once the river ran clear.

Halfway up the river embankment I watched some men digging a pile of stones. A green and yellow shed stood in the midst of this rubble, its sign reading "Yellow River Dyke Administration Station." A man in a beige overcoat seemed to be in charge, and he told me, between deep puffs at his cigarette, that they were strengthening the embankment against anticipated floods. The old course empties into a lake, the Hongze, he said, and downstream it links up with the Grand Canal.

The Grand Canal, that engineering prodigy, on a par with the Great Wall and without parallel in the world of its time, was to China what the Mediterranean was to Egypt and Constantinople. It was the funnel of trade and tribute from south to north, and its flow of grain and booty enriched court, nobility, and army. Cut in the seventh century by vast detachments of conscripted laborers, both men and women, it ran eleven thousand miles from Peking to Hangzhou, and was the longest canal in the world.

Flooding on the Yellow River used to silt and block the Grand Canal, disrupting the grain shipments to the capital, and when the river shifted its course in 1853, the canal route's importance dwindled rather. Near the junction of the canal and the Yellow River there was a system of feeder lakes which stored runoffs from the river and released them to the canal when its flow needed boosting, a technique known as "borrowing from the Yellow River to aid the Grand Canal."

But the river crossing kept silting up itself and the canal, and it proved impossible to regulate the flow in this way without provoking grievous floods. Nor was it much good complaining to the Yellow River Conservancy, the organ thrown in with the grain tribute administration, for efficiency was not a general trait of that corrupt body, whose officers could help themselves to one of the largest budgets in the empire. By the time the river shifted its course the administration of the river and canal was cracking.

What the conservancy represented in detail, the state of the empire exemplified as a whole. Public services deteriorated. Dykes fell into disrepair and granaries into ruin. Secret societies proliferated. Peasant revolts spread, precursors of the Taiping Rebellion so soon to break upon the land. In 1853 the flooding reached catastrophic proportions, and the Yellow River turned round and flowed north.

And now, in Xuzhou, a strip of water lingers to attest to the old bed. Dyke building goes on still, as arduously as ever it did. Up there by the bend, a second team was erecting levees with stones it would take two able-bodied men to lift. Homely girls, a shade more diligent than the men, were heaving and digging and bending their backs to the dying rays of the sun.

When it was nearly dusk, and long purple shadows fell slanting across the banks, a crowd collected by the river, and over the hunched blue shoulders you could see a storyteller in a cloth cap stand up to speak. He had hooded lustrous eyes, and he worked these with practiced effect, along with his jaws. He spoke in a rhythmic way, a traditional mix of colloquial and literary styles, adding emphasis with the flat of his hand: the confident possessor of an inherited art. "He's the best storyteller in the province," recommended the man on my right. A woman, taking up a collection, accepted the equivalent of seven U.S. cents from Takia, though he had offered considerably more. Too thoroughly enrolled in capitalist consumerism, we hadn't realized it was a standard charge, and that you didn't give at your own pleasure.

At that hour of fading light, the river was a metallic blur, and the right bank alone was animated, with hawkers filling up the spaces between the trees with trade, selling chives and fish and poultry. I bought candied translucent haws impaled on a stick. The woman who sold me this sweetmeat suggested that entrepreneurism rides again in China, for she had alternated the haws with kumquats glacéed in sugar, a variation on traditional form, even a sales gimmick. People were arriving at the bridges—seven or eight spanned the river—shopping and exchanging gossip. An old woman carrying a child approached me timidly, attracted by my camera. She was perhaps a little over sixty, though she looked older, with the deeply creased cheeks and watery eyes of those who cannot escape disease and the heat of summer. How much would I charge for a picture of her grandson, she asked, taking me for a local portrait photographer, that most popular of trades in China. I explained I wasn't one, but I doubt if she understood: you could not own a camera without its being the tool of your trade.

I was frequently thought of as a local in China, and just as frequently as a sort of visitor from Mars. Either way the mistake is a comment on their closed world. Here, very soon after I was mistaken for the one, I was taken for the other. It was when I was about to cross the bridge, and noticed two girls of about eighteen peering at me from the other side. They were fair skinned, and friendly faced, and when I went up to them they lost no time in admitting that they had followed us from the other end of the river. Everything seemed to amaze them: they touched my jacket, exclaimed over my shoes, and wondered if I'd be thought plainly dressed where I came from; they had heard women were glamorous and heavily made up "outside." They had sweet natures, were unbelievably ingenuous, and hid their faces when Takia raised his camera.

"The only foreigners we ever saw were Japanese, tourists changing trains at the station," one of them said. "What strange looking people, not attractive at all. When we saw you two we didn't think you could possibly be Japanese—you didn't look nearly so frightful."

After a while they vanished, over the bridge and into the crowd. We continued our walk and drank hot tea at a stall, and I tried, rather hopelessly, to find out when it was that the river changed course.

"Ah, it would be before the devils came," said the man sitting with us at the stall, for whom past time was clearly marked by the Japanese occupation. Unprompted, he began conversation on other subjects. We liked Xuzhou? It *was* a good place. He'd never been out of it himself. One would not care to live anywhere else. "What a place!" he kept on insisting. What a place for providing you with all you'd ever want. He made the cornucopian plenty sound incontestable, in this place where women washed their clothes by the river and beat them with a stick.

Propped up in a half-reclining position against the still sun-warmed wall, the tea seller smiled at everyone as though holding court, twice shifting her swollen old bulk on her precarious stool to lean forward and top up my glass. She had folds and folds of skin and padded covering and I was surprised her smile did not reveal toothless gums, she seemed so old. She never said a word, but just kept on smiling as I brought the subject round to the year the river shifted its course.

"Yes, it was before the devils came. It was a long time ago. You like Xuzhou? Best place in the world, I tell you."

This sort of talk—unhurried, limited, yet quite pleasant for all that—continued until night descended in a sudden smother. We dined in haste on a baked sweet potato, with a whiff of charcoal embers still clinging to its floury fibres, for we wanted to take in a movie before our train left.

At the Cultural Palace Cinema, a misnomer if there ever was one, they were showing *Rickshaw Boy*, and for once we managed to get tickets. The film is, of course, adapted from Lao She's famous novel, that allegory of the fate of modern China. It is the story of Xiangzi, who dreams of owning his own rickshaw and marrying a good woman (in that order), and the wretched breaking of that dream. Like most Chinese stories, it is inexorable in the way it piles on tragedy after tragedy: he is seduced and coerced into marriage with a woman he does not love; she is disinherited by her father; she dies in childbirth; a woman he might have loved kills herself; he loses his hard-earned rickshaw; he is tricked out of his money; he contracts VD and at the novel's end is sick and thoroughly broken in spirit.

Left-wing critics see it as exposing the old society in all its repellent degeneracy, but the book is not really an ideological document. Still its author was alive to the futility of individual endeavor in a society like China, where men were not free to shape their own destiny. Speaking actually of an earlier era, his term for China was "individualism's blind alley"; and it was left to Lao She himself to prove the truth of these words in even our own time. One night in the summer of 1966 he was found dead in a lake in a corner of Peking, having either drowned himself or been thrown in after the Red Guards, those nasties enlisted into thuggery by the Cultural Revolution, had beaten him up. They had laid into him, even though he was already sixty-seven and failing in health.

In America, where the English version of the book was something of a best seller when it came out in the 1940s, they changed the ending without the author's consent to a happy boy-gets-girl one, possibly to square with the strong belief in that country that men *are* masters of their destiny. I doubt if it would ever occur to the Chinese film maker to make things gentle for his audience, only more dire. I came out of the cinema trailing gloom. It wasn't any comfort to tell yourself that such things happened only in the old society, or in the time of the Gang of Four, for that matter.

We found we still had time to eat before departure. In the vicinity of the railway station there were two or three places, none of them enticing. We decided on a Mohammedan canteen—a dirty, dismal hall, but slightly less so than the others—and had a bowl of plain noodles soused in ladlefuls of chili sauce. All through the meal I was conscious of three little boys wandering about the tables and gathering whatever was left uneaten in the bowls—not a spectacle conducive to a quiet linger over one's food. Two of the boys would wolf down every morsel of the leftovers, but the third, the eldest, ate nothing at all. Nobody in the restaurant paid the slightest attention to them. I was halfway through my bowl of noodles when I beckoned to the eldest boy to take it from me. Yet instead of tucking in himself, he picked up the bowl and gave it to one of the smaller boys, who fell to it at once with relish. I realized then that the eldest boy was the one who looked out for the others, and it crossed my mind that way back in the old society, beggar solidarities were organized under ringleaders or beggar kings.

At the entrance to the canteen, a bakery booth was putting out rounds of bread, as large as pizzas and as filling. Leaving the canteen, Takia stopped at the booth and asked to buy one. The vendor sent him back to the canteen to get a ticket for it; this he did, pushing his way through the tables once more. Then as he was making for the door he hesitated a moment to thrust the ticket into the eldest boy's hands. I had walked on, but as I turned round to look back at the restaurant I saw the boy, behind, step out into the doorway; he was standing there, a dark shape against the light, and I could see that he had brought his hands together in front of his breast in the traditional gesture of thanks.

Still a little early for our train, we knocked on the door of a soft-class waiting room to get out of the raw night. A woman with pale eyes and a bewildered look in them came out of a side door, checked our tickets, and stood aside to let us in. For all the scruffiness of its exterior, the room was quite luxurious inside. I don't mean really luxurious of course, but one's standards fall rapidly in China. One end of it was taken up with amenities for washing: a tap and sink, an enamel basin on a wooden stand, and beside it a table with a kettle and four or five thermos flasks on top. The other end, bathed in a naked fluorescent light, had half a dozen maltreated armchairs; a begrimed once beautiful rug; and a cupboard, empty but for some old copies of *People's Daily*. Seeing me wash my hands under the cold tap, the woman came forward to pour—what heavenly luxury—a whole flaskful of hot water into the basin. The room was unheated but one did not freeze, and the mere fact of having several chairs to oneself gave a disproportionate sense of ease and comfort.

And I owed it all to a small lady at the Old and Young Soldiers' Transportation Service Planning Office. Arriving at the station that morning, and knowing all too well the difficulty of getting sleepers at short notice, we had braced ourselves for the prospect of sitting up all night on the train. Still we had tried at this counter and that, though we had little faith in our success. But it happened that a clerk at one of these counters mentioned the planning office; and though she mentioned it casually enough, when we heard it we knew it was more than a labyrinth of rooms and corridors, of sluggish factotums and impassive clerks. It was China in uniform, and thus master and arbiter of our fate.

I located the office in a lugubrious block at the back of the station, and I barged in to find a very short lady in charge. When I saw her my earlier bravery deserted me rather, for I found her quite terrifying, and it was plain her colleagues did too. She was clad in subfusc grey, had two cigarettes going at once, wore her hair in a short-back-and-sides, and when she barked into the telephone, she might have been a brigadier bellowing marching orders. It was obvious at once that if anyone determined the life and death of our hopes for a good night's sleep, she did.

Sleepers? "Yes, sleepers." Where from? Ah, England. I hastened to show her my passport, but there was no need: she was already barking into the phone and inducing submission. One had an impression of cigarettes lit one after another, of eyes narrowed against the smoke in an impatient grimace; one had the impression, that is to say, of power.

Did it have to be hard class? Would soft-class sleepers do? There were two berths to be had from those set aside for the People's Liberation Army. "Yes, yes, they would do very well indeed." In that case we could have them, she said. I renewed my warm thanks when I wished her goodbye; and it was extraordinary how, from being the formidable powerhouse of a moment before, she all of a sudden became the gentlest of matrons, patting my back softly and saying I wasn't to worry.

And now it was time to board. The guard allowed us into the station yard ahead of the other passengers. An overhead bridge led us to our platform, and as I mounted the steps I could see the other passengers, a vast shadowy mass, waiting in ranks of four or five below in the yard. Disembodied voices were giving orders from loudspeakers, urging stragglers into line and to move in good order to the train. On this long, dense column the lamps threw a cold, unfocused light, so dimly that the figures in the queue were discernible only in amorphous shapes, like bundles. The scene was bleak, and might have been the spectacle of refugee repatriation, or of war. When I was halfway across the bridge I heard the loudspeakers give the order to move. At first only one or two people strode past me ahead of the procession; but when I descended by the ramp that led down to the platform, the crowd around thickened until, quite suddenly, I found myself caught in an irresistible advance. I knew we were moving from the thud of our feet and the pressure behind me; and for some time these were my only sensations, the rumble in my ears and the propulsion in my back. Of the platform or the train I could see nothing, for I could not raise my head enough to look about me. I was carried forward as though attached to the men around me, and when their pace slackened I helplessly careened against them in the darkness. Then the inexorable movement began again: if a hundred men had gone there were another hundred on their way.

All might have been well if we could have continued in this way as far as the train. But just then someone near the front broke rank and started at a run down the ramp. And inexorably the stampede began, men thrusting away from the column and tumbling into the platform, fighting to get to the wagons first. The press of people surged upon me with frenzied disregard, lurching, pushing, shoulder to shoulder in a dark confusion. My baggage became entangled with the men, who as they rushed past brought swinging blows against my chest and back with theirs. When I flattened myself against the parapet to let the crowd pass I could see them swarming like insects over the wagons, some of them shouting against the babel, some of them pushing their bags through the windows. I could almost feel in myself the crush of one body against another, as each struggled to get through the door first. And all the time more men were streaming onto the platform.

Then there came a slackening in the rush of people; the passengers became fewer and fewer. I reached the platform to find Takia waiting at our carriage. We boarded. That night I could not be sure if I slept, but it was bliss just to lie there, to feel the jolt of the train's progress, until, gathering speed, it lifted tiredness and anxiety from consciousness. Meanwhile, in the bunk opposite, Takia slept soundly, with the long, deep snores of the monumentally calm.

Where Confucius Found the World Small

On a fine day, it is said, you can see the Yellow River from the summit of Tai Shan, or Mount Tai. I didn't on the day I was there, and I don't believe you really can, for the river lies too far away, and I always find that all you ever see from the top of a high mountain are other mountains.

But what mountains! On the peak, in front of the shrine to the Jade Emperor, there stood a tablet attributed to China's very first emperor. It is called the Wordless Stele, for there is nothing written on it that you can see. It is only because thousands of years of weather have effaced the original inscription, but most people prefer the more fanciful explanation, which is that a poet, when he came up here to compose the epigraph, and saw the mass of the ranges unfolding there, was robbed of his words in wonder, and left the stele blank as a sign of the mountain's inexpressible splendor.

This is of course the classic effect of height: that it shuts one up and cuts one down to size. There once was a tablet which bore the legend, "The Place where Confucius Found the World Small." For it seems that when the Master, whose native state of Lu lies across the southern foothills, came up the mountain and looked down, he was awed, and discovered the empire to be small. As children we had to know the passage in the *Mencius* which relates this, and to think of it as a lesson in humility, together with the analogy Mencius uses to illustrate the point: "Just as it is difficult for water to come up to the expectation of someone who has seen the sea, so it is difficult for words to come up to the expectation of someone who has studied under a sage." The stele can no longer be found, but there is a vantage point for viewing Confucius's native state, a terrace inscribed with the name Zhan Lu Tai, which I like to translate to myself as "Here's Looking at Lu."

Landscape viewing is of course a particularly Chinese aestheticism. You recognize the predilection at once, from landscape painting and the landscape garden, where the eye can follow and linger with pleasure over the painted pathways of a scroll, or the shifting vistas of a winding stroll through a traditional garden. Climbing Tai Shan can give you much the same sensation as walking in such a garden, for it is all rock, and trees, and prospects.

But there is one sensation the mountain offers that is missing from the garden or the painting, and this is the sensation of sky. On my walk up through the brilliant light of Tai Shan that day in November, the sky was always part of the scene, and I thought that the maple leaves would not look half as red, or the pines' silhouettes quite as dramatic, if there hadn't been all that blue sky to set them off.

It also feels like all steps. Not everyone who has been up it is aware that it only rises to a height of fifty-eight hundred feet, but few are likely to forget the seven thousand rock-hewn steps you climb to reach the top.

The first stage of the journey is easily done. To reach it from Tai'an, the town at the foot of its southern slopes, you can travel by car, taking what is known as the Ring Route. But this takes you only as far as the halfway point, and beyond this stage you must plod up the eighteen flights of stairs to the top on foot. It is not a particularly strenuous ascent, and nowadays no one would think of being carried up in a sedan chair, but you can still arrive at the summit pretty puffed, and your leg muscles will ache for days afterward.

Up I went with all the others, the trippers with their staffs and the porters with their shoulder poles, between the cliffs falling away on either side, from monument to monument, inscription to inscription, up landing after landing, until at last we emerged at the South Gate of Heaven, and at our feet the valleys of the Yellow River lay endless and hazed. The gate is perched upon the tapering Great Dragon Gorge, and somewhere up there a hermit used to play his drums, the sound echoing around, behind and above, bouncing off the mica, quartz, and feldspar.

Tai Shan was holy to the Chinese, who devoutly worshiped here down the centuries, from the ancient emperors offering sacrifices to the Earth and the Sky, to the humble pilgrim invoking a blessing by the gods. Of China's five sacred peaks it is geologically the oldest—about 7 billion years, one source says—and the most exalted. Its very name is synonymous with consequence: "Though death befalls all men alike," goes a favorite Maoist quotation, "yet it may be weightier than Tai Shan or lighter than a feather. To die for the people is weightier than Mount Tai, but to work for the fascists and die for the exploiters and oppressors is lighter than a feather."

At the summit there is a shrine dedicated to the Jade Emperor, the supreme Taoist deity. The goddess of dawn, Bixiayuanjun, or Princess of the Azure Clouds, has her temple to your right as you clamber up the stairs above the South Gate of Heaven: an ensemble of halls and pavilions, whose pink and yellow impact is undeniably forceful, coming into view on a high terrace among the clouds, encircled by peaks around. The princess is the daughter of Tai Shan itself, for the mountain is divine; and recalling this point is the Stele Carved on Cliff, an immense rectangle of rock, rising thirty feet up in a cleft beneath the summit, on whose face is engraved an inscription composed by the Tang dynasty emperor Xuanzong when he came to perform his sacrifice here twelve centuries ago. At first sight the cliff looks like a massed jumble of characters, for Xuanzong's inscription is attended by many others, but the emperor's epigraph, running to nearly a thousand characters, each measuring seven by eight inches, stands out gilded from the rest. The text is headed "Memorial to Tai Shan," and it expresses sentiments properly self-deprecating and at the same time charismatic: "I am troubled by my lack of virtue; I am ignorant of perfect reason . . . I know not whether I have committed an offense against the gods or the people and my heart is tossed on the floods as though I were crossing a great river. . . . I deployed the power of my six imperial armies; I made the nine regions tremble with fear; the colors and standards were raised up; horses and soldiers silenced; and what majesty! What spectacle! What pomp! In this way did I arrive at Tai Shan, and all was as it should be."

Xuanzong was responding to the mountain like so many emperors before him, sacrificing on it with rites and extolling it with epigraph. As the rainmaker was to occult religion, the emperor was to the Chinese conception. But his responsibilities were ethical as well as metereological, and both weal and woe, the glory of his reign and the abundance of the harvest, hung heavily on his doing the right thing. In him divine right and earthly obligations were always fused, so that if the rivers broke their dykes, or the rain did not fall, this was enough to occasion sacrifice, or penitence, or even dethronement.

But nowadays most Chinese who come up here ask for no more than to see the sun rise over the ranges, the stock experience of mountain travel. Tai Shan is remarkably well organized for this kind of tourism, considering how everything has to be carried up on the backs of porters, including even water. It has an adequate guesthouse for foreign visitors and high-ranking Chinese at the summit, and a somewhat less adequate one for everyone else. A fledgeling free economy offers other conveniences: booths selling dumplings and Shandong pancakes, and benches to sit on while you eat them; teahouses shaded by roofs of matted pine leaves and trellis; popsicle peddlers who charge progressively more the higher up you get; and even portrait photographers to snap you against that scenic pine hanging over the cliff. Here and there, in the clefts of hillsides, you see the low crude huts of highland dwellers, those who live by picking and selling medicinal herbs—ginseng, Chinese cornbind, Solomon's seal, gromwell.

Judging by dialects and accents, my fellow visitors had come from all over China. Some were here because they had a day or two to spare from the official business or conference which brought them to the area. Many of them, especially tanned octogenarians, it seemed, chose to shoot up here for their constitutional. Up and down that steep path people trudged and loitered, some singly, some in pairs, but many more in groups of five or six (for the Chinese are gregarious in travel as in everything else). There was a writer and painter, suitably sporting that fashionable mark of the Chinese intellectual, the long grey scarf with one end thrown over the shoulder. There were some young soldiers propping up a grand old officer. There were three Canadian girls from Saskatchewan whom I recognized from the hotel in Tai'an where we stayed the night before. There was a party from a quartz-watch factory in Shanghai, loud in the recognizably Shanghainese way. There were dozens of porters, some of them mere boys, toiling up the stairs with their pole-loads of everything needed at the top, from bottled beer and orange pop to sacks of grain and building materials. Most disconcertingly of all, there was a seventy-six-year-old lady who, moving more briskly than I on her tiny bound feet, kept flashing toothless and encouraging smiles in my direction. It was a jaunt long promised her by her companion, her middle-aged son, whose filial piety was demonstrated by the unremitting and lavish attention he paid her, and by his inability to find in this any cause for either self-pity or self-satisfaction.

Takia and I arrived at the top in the middle of the afternoon. At the office where we went to confirm our room at the guesthouse, booked the night before by our hotel in Tai'an, we found a large man (another grey-scarved intellectual) making imperative gestures at the receptionist and demanding half a dozen rooms for himself and his colleagues. "All university lecturers," he loudly insisted, repeating that prestigious job title three or four times, "come all the way from Jiangsu Province to attend a conference in Shandong, taking the opportunity to see your famous sights . . . " I found him quite overbearing, as he kept butting in when the receptionist was trying to make out my chit, but I could sympathize with his anxiety to get into this guesthouse, and not the inferior one down the road. Still it was somehow appalling, the way he was so baldly pulling rank. But this is what counts in China, rank and the ability to exploit it. The system itself encourages it: the functionaries and factotums have this dreadful gift for putting the most courteous client on the offensive, and yet are only waiting to be won over by a display of vocal exasperation or seniority status.

Until this happened the receptionist was muttering something about being full, but as the professor knew, and knew that the receptionist knew he knew, this was entirely a matter for altercation. In this they were honoring an idiom of Chinese social behavior in which, through game playing and ritual, a relationship or transaction is cast in terms of one person's occupational standing relative to the other. Had the encounter between the receptionist and the professor taken place elsewhere, in New York say, or in Hong Kong, their relationship would most likely have been cast in terms of the business at hand; one is there to provide a service, the other as a client, and neither would require of the other that his social status or professional authority be recognized, seeing these as extraneous to the matter, as indeed they are. But in China personal qualifications always have to come into it, no matter if this is damaging to efficiency, or a queue is forming. Later, making my way to my room, I noticed the professor and his friends installed in rooms down the same corridor.

Takia and I had a picnic on one of the peaks, on a ridge that, at that hour of the afternoon, allowed us to face the sinking sun. In the shadows it was very cold. A man, a northerner but a member of the party from the Shanghai watch factory, sat down on the ledge beside us and proceeded to take off his socks. Then we all looked, the three of us, at the panorama, grand with the hills falling away all around.

Yet in all that splendor, there is one point on Tai Shan, and one only, where the eye of the beholder senses that it is arriving at some climax. It is at the point, best approached by walking up from "Here's Looking at Lu," where, topping the scree and the thistly slopes, one sees before one the arc of a wall breaking like a wave upon the crest.

The wall is very old and tumbledown, its facade looking scabby from the paint flaking off. One section has completely crumbled, so that the smooth roll of the lines of the masonry over the rising and falling ground tumbles all of a sudden to a stop. The symmetry is abruptly disrupted, but at the point just before this happens, the eye is stopped by the perfect sphere of a moon gate framing the sky; and suddenly all the essentials of mountain, light, and gradient are concentrated in their due proportions. Without the wall and the moongate, the view would lose half its grace and harmony, for there would be nothing to throw the sense of height and spectacle into grander relief, while at the same time scaling it down for the eye.

Afterward we went for a walk, and passing below a makeshift cafeteria, were invited into the tent behind. Our hosts were the kitchen staff who lived there, with the cooking paraphernalia and provisions littered about them. The eating area was in front, the kitchen behind, and the beds and bundles of clothes squashed up somewhere in the middle. It gave a sense of want and hardship, but our hosts were cheerful enough, greeting us with smiles and cups of tea, and an almost careless flow of genuine hospitality.

Dinner was in the guesthouse dining room, seconds after the sunset. The cold made it necessary to seek out some hard liquor. We found bottles of Chinese spirits in the one general store hereabouts, after coaxing the guesthouse receptionist into opening it up for us. A swig of those spirits gave the usual devastating shock, but did one a power of good. We shared it with the three Canadian girls from

Saskatchewan, for they had been placed at our table. They were two nurses and a radio journalist, taking a year off to travel in the Far East. The conversation was mostly about the places they had visited—Japan, Shanghai, Qingdao. Their open-mindedness, their obvious readiness to enjoy themselves and face everything calmly and sensibly, made them very agreeable. Like most young people who consider themselves travelers rather than tourists, they felt themselves under an obligation, wherever they went, to do everything as cheaply as possible. As Takia said, the matter was a point of honor with them, crucial to their respectability as travelers. They had all caught colds, and hadn't had a bath for three days, but it didn't make them glum, and they still preferred the individual struggle to any conducted tour.

Back in our unheated room, provided with two beds and two enormous padded overcoats, it was clear that this was going to be as cold a night as any of us had feared to live through. I fetched some water from the communal pail at the end of the corridor, but took only enough to clean my teeth, remembering that every drop had to be carried up here on someone's back. To keep warm Takia agreed to give half his bed to me, and I only managed to fall asleep huddled against him under a mound of blankets, fully clothed, and with a large quantity of Chinese spirits awash inside me.

At break of day there was no escaping the statutory viewing of the sunrise, for an electric bell rang loud and long at five, and the Chinese, who believe that sightseers should be sightseers, would not have you pass up any guidebook experience. Traditionally the sunrise is watched from the Summit for Contemplating the Sun, a place where the rocks level out to a terrace, but we chose for ourselves a platform jutting out from the summit on which the Jade Emperor temple is perched. The path there was dark and uneven, and there was so little light at that hour we had to keep our eyes to the ground. Men and women hurried past us, their hands tucked into the sleeves of their padded overcoats, chattering excitedly and clearing their throats. There was almost a sense of companionship in the air; it was perhaps the overcoats, which topped whatever we had on underneath and made us all look alike. An enterprising woman had set up a stall and was selling hot soy milk and deep-fried dough sticks in the cutting wind.

We reached the top. Takia set up his tripod. By and by others joined us, and proceeded to indulge in their morning habit of bringing the night's phlegm up from the throat. With all that hawking and spitting, the magic of the moment faded rather. The sun appeared at six-thirty exactly: pop, it sprang up, and transported us from a blur of cold and shadow and black figures to a world of color—orange-pink and white along the rim of sky, and beyond, above the paper shapes of hills, the subtlest lilac and blue.

Breakfast followed, and was of large helpings of hot goat's milk, tea, and a tasty gruel that might have been maize. We started back down at eight, and already there was a large number of porters heaving up with sacks, walking singly, except for those who had to carry boulders for the mountain-top construction works. Looking down, you saw these slabs, slung from poles on ropes, moving painfully up below callused shoulders—a scene straight out of the building of the pyramids. The stone staircase seemed interminable, full of steep turns and landings, but one soon learnt to tread down the steps sideways, and not to press the feet down too hard. There were gateways, arches, and epigraphs, and a few of Mao Zedong's poems engraved on stone, including the one—absolutely my favorite, because so characteristically cocksure—in which he grandly dismisses the first Chinese emperor, the Han, Tang, and Song emperors as so many unlettered boors, and Genghis Khan as someone who knew only how to shoot at eagles, and tells you that: "For truly great men / You have to look to today." There were tawny views of tree-covered slopes—beautiful, but charming me less and less as the stairs went on and on.

At the foot of Tai Shan, one thing I found quite interesting was the tomb of the warlord Feng Yuxiang, who died in a fire on a Soviet ship in the Black Sea on his way home from a trip to the U.S.S.R., only a year before the People's Republic was created. He was one of the more progressive warlords, whose army, based in the north, was supplied with arms and advisers by the Russians. From a much published photograph of him in uniform he looks a generous mixture of uncouthness and defiance: his eyebrows bushy, his beard improbably thick for a Chinese, his nostrils flared like a bull's, his mouth a slash, showing uneven teeth. The ingredients of his personality are almost too unlikely to be credited. He was a Christian who baptized his soldiers with a hose and taught them to sing hymns like "Hark the Herald Angels Sing"; he so loved ice cream that on the Sundays he was prevented from dining with his American missionary friends, he sent his soldiers over for his share; and it was he who, to mark his disapproval of drinking, presented the warlord Wu Peifu with a rare porcelain goblet at a banquet and filled it with water instead of wine. Two of his exhortations to his soldiers were: "Do not smoke; do not drink," and "Plough land, weave cloth, read books"; and on top of their other duties, they had to learn two new characters before every meal, and their wives and daughters had to do the same.

He lived at a time when every kind of intrigue, military factionalism and double-crossing was part of the political climate. He himself was capricious in his allegiances, sometimes siding with Chiang Kai-shek, sometimes opposing him. On the whole his countrymen thought well of him, and in an opinion poll conducted by a paper in Shanghai in 1923, he was voted second in popularity to Dr. Sun Yat-sen. One gathers that under his command irrigation and land reclamation projects were launched and training courses for law enforcement and public health conducted. To pay for it all he must have tapped the large revenues he got from the opium tax, that pie in which every warlord or power had a finger. The side of him that most appeals to the current regime is that he threw his weight behind labor unions and the left wing of the Kuomintang; and this is no doubt why his monument now stands so solidly at the foot of Tai Shan—all steps and granite and gilded inscription.

But for me it is to the side of this massive memorial, in a rough black headstone set in stone blocks in a declivity, that the spirit of the man is best caught. It is the gravestone of his first wife, raised in 1953 by their five children, two sons and three daughters. Feng Yuxiang has been characterized by one historian (Jean Chesneaux) as a nationalist who combined a "Protestant progressiveness with a Confucian morality." And here is the manifestation of it: the woman he had married was the Chinese secretary of the Y.M.C.A. in Peking, but his daughters' names, all highly unusual ones, suggested the Confucian belief that women were required only to be demure, and any inclination to expertise, assertiveness, or hauteur was antithetical to virtue, and not to be encouraged. Their names, which struck me the more for having about them the cultivation of their inventor, were Not Capable, Not Aggressive, and Not Arrogant.

We had left our luggage in the hotel in Tai'an before our ascent, and had booked a room there for when we came down from the mountain. I cannot now think how I managed to remain so calm, but when we arrived at the desk after our descent and the receptionist informed us that the place was full, that he had allotted our room to a Japanese guest, all I said was, "You can't do that."

In the Chinese ordering of foreign visitors, the Japanese as a nation come somewhere below the Americans and Europeans, but they are undoubtedly several notches above us overseas Chinese. The Japanese guest hadn't even arrived, but this did not alter the fact that of the two of us he had the superior claim to the room. As for the receptionist, he was not in a quandary exactly, but felt rather as if, given that a practical solution had to be figured out, this was it. So when I tried to talk him out of it, invoking the quite un-Chinese notion of first come first served, I could conjure nothing out of him but the intimation that that was my problem, now that he had solved his.

I must say that that fazed me for not a few moments. But in an inspired move, Takia thought to lean over and steal a look at the booking chart. This led him to the discovery that, though there indeed were no rooms left, this was true only of our price category. At the top of the tariff there was a vacancy; and this, a deluxe suite, Takia promptly presented to the receptionist as a way out of his perplexity. The receptionist was only too ready to accept our proposition, but not in hearty agreement with us that the deluxe suite should be had for the price of the previously booked room. Much Asiatic haggling followed—all this while a row between a Hong

Kong guest, who reckoned he had been overcharged, and another receptionist, adamant that he had not, was growing louder and more heated beside me. Unlike this fellow guest I have neither taste nor flair for haggling, and I never get any satisfaction from winning a round, only sometimes a sense of suspense defused. I find the game both boring and wasteful, and as far as I can without risking my position, I avoid it where I see it coming. In this instance it was unavoidable; and when it was over, and we got the suite at a price we could afford, the most I could feel was a sense of weary relief. Said Takia, coming from a world where half your contracts are won by good public relations, "If I were him I'd have done a swop and given the suite to the Japanese at the lower cost." In China one is always meeting people whose not knowing which side their bread is buttered on or whose blindness to the main chance makes them very likeable, if exasperating and tedious to do business with.

The room was vast, and got up like a showpiece in the stuffy style of Chinese five-star comfort: four thermos flasks instead of the usual one, plush curtains, drapes, sofas, bedside lamps, carafes of drinking water and glasses, cupboards, desk, coffee table—all set in an expanse of thick blue carpet.

In the bathroom the plumbing looked as if it was up to extended use. I thought with pleasure: here I could be extravagant with water, unencumbered by thoughts of the mountain porter's burden. I turned on the hot water tap, then the cold; nothing happened, and I was seized by a sense of childhood desolation. The hotel was completely out of water, and when I flicked the light switch I discovered it was out of electricity too.

Of course things can't be what they seem, I hopefully thought. I went to the desk on our floor to procure relief. The clerk, when I found him, said there never was enough pressure in the plumbing system to begin with, and as for the electricity, that was a matter for the municipal authorities, not the hotel. He thought the water would come on at 7 p.m., and was over-optimistic, it turned out, by four hours. I felt an attack of flu coming on and the absence of any resources to deal with it. The rest of that story consists of throwing up the sponge and taking to bed.

To the Mouth

At the Yellow ferry crossing at Luokou (or, as some call it, Lekou), the river was the color of milk chocolate. To the right of the river-bank, on Luokou's side, an iron bridge could be glimpsed through a mist. A truck, bristling with worn cloth shoes and soles caught in an enormous net, destined perhaps for recycling, was plunging into the hurly-burly of the ferry landing, followed by dozens of asses pulling two-wheeled carts. I noticed some men and women below a ramp, coaxing their small children to perform the morning stunt of moving their bowels.

To our left, there was a scalloping of dykes, with stacks of what seemed to be large stone blocks on top. The blocks were neatly grouped and numbered, and later I learned that they were for throwing into the river when it is in flood, and if the dykes look as though they are not going to be strong enough to withstand the floodwaters.

Luokou had been important once, probably because it stood at the head of a navigable section of the river. Now it straggles under the lee of the embankment in an attitude of dejected torpor, its houses mostly scruffy, and ringed around by smelly ditches, its streets dusty, and its dogs pitiably thin.

In what looked like a demolition site, a massive concrete structure, recognizably a political slogan wall and a descendant of the memorial archway of yore, sported the watchwords of an earlier era: "Get Going and Go All Out," and "Grasp the Key Link in Controlling the Yellow River" (the latter a variation of that more general slogan, "Grasp the Key Link in Class Struggle and Bring About Great Order Across the Land"). The structure, mottled and faded, looked preposterously out of scale amidst the shambles. But as I continued

247

my journey, the image of that large wall, standing there in that dereliction with its slogan half effaced, kept coming back to me as an expression of the modesty of a reality that is so much less momentous than our plans and so much duller than our dreams.

Shandong and its Capital

When we arrived in Ji'nan, the capital of Shandong Province, a stranger alighting from the same train, who must have overheard us asking for directions, came up to us and volunteered to guide us to the nearest hotel. He did this in a spontaneous and kindly way, and we quickly accepted. Following him, we found ourselves after only five minutes at the Shandong Hotel; but when we tried to get a room there, the receptionist made it known, but not in so many words, that the place was for native Chinese only.

The stranger, being a visitor to Ji'nan himself, did not know where else we might be lodged. But he said his cousin would; what if we waited here, while he went round to fetch him? Takia and I wavered, thinking we would put him to too much trouble, but he wouldn't take no for an answer, and hurried off. Within a quarter of an hour he was back, with his cousin wheeling a bicycle. The cousin shook hands genially, and said that the Ji'nan Hotel was no distance at all, and if we'd like to put our luggage on his bike, we could all of us walk there.

The streets were deserted, though it was only eight in the evening. But the air I breathed in felt thick, and laden with soot. We walked through pools of darkness, past many trees. After his initial friendly greeting the cousin was silent, but then there seemed no pressing necessity to make conversation. His kindness was not a bit the less for his having nothing to say to us—quite the reverse, in fact. It took about twenty minutes to reach our destination, and when we arrived at the gates of the hotel, I was almost embarrassed to thank my two guides, so much did this seem to belittle their kindness. Takia invited them in, but would not commit the indiscretion of insisting, for it would only make them nervous to enter a hotel for foreigners where their presence, if not exactly forbidden, would certainly be frowned upon.

Of the hotel, a group of buildings lying in a walled-in compound, Takia observed, "Chinese houses are always built back to front." By this he meant that the best accommodation in China is almost invariably found in the block furthest from the gate, the reverse of the West, where it is usually the better looking part of a building that faces the front entrance. Here, at the Ji'nan Hotel, it was the quarters at the back that housed the visitors from abroad (in other words, people who matter), while those in front were for native Chinese. In this the hotel perpetuates an old Chinese custom, which required a household to be ordered so that the lowest ranks occupied the rooms nearest the entrance, and the highest (the patriarch and his first wife) lived right at the back—a living arrangement prompted by the need for protection from the dust, smells, and noises of the street, as well as its evil spirits and thieves. Throughout China there are public buildings which, whether they be factories or important government offices, the repository of culture or the bastion of Party politics, can be seen from the street to have such an accumulation of broken odds and ends in front as to make their courtyards resemble nothing so much as a rubbish dump.

Our motives for being in Ji'nan were mixed: we had come partly to see the place and partly to arrange for our visit to the Victory Oilfields, on the Yellow River estuary one hundred fifty miles to the northeast. As a Hong Kong-Macao Compatriot Takia could go there without a permit, but this was not so for me. The first thing I did the next morning, therefore, was to apply to the China International Travel Service, which had an office in the hotel compound. The officer who received me was handsome, brisk, and much too suave to be a Shandong indigene. He had stationed himself behind the reception desk in the hotel lobby, and delayed me only a minute to wash his hands of me. It was Comrade Zhang, of the Overseas Chinese Travel Service, whom I should see.

I didn't know whether it was a good thing to be demoted from the International category to that of the Overseas Chinese: my national standing with the Chinese Travel Service, I found, was a fluid thing, fluctuating according to individual official and convenience—theirs, not mine. As a Chinese I could travel about more freely, but as a British national I could be whisked about in large cars and trust to my wishes being taken seriously. It was with some uncertainty, therefore, that I awaited Comrade Zhang, who had to be summoned from another part of the building.

As I sat there waiting for him to turn up, three Americans, two men and a woman, came in accompanied by their Chinese guide. One of the men, the younger of the two, was almost certainly from New York; he was smooth-shaven but bore the signs of a lapsed jogger. The other, who wore plaid trousers and had a florid face, was a big man with the gruff voice of the shy. The woman was very short, but held herself erect in the full consciousness of dominating, her plump fingers gripping a cigarette. I thought as I took them in: was there ever a threesome less at home than in the Ji'nan Hotel; and I wondered why they were not at the Nanjiao, the luxury hotel with the indoor swimming pool and air-conditioning.

There followed then a conversation which, had I heard it reported or written up in a book, I should scarcely have credited as true, so neatly did it tally with your most facile stereotype of the American abroad. Yet my ears did not deceive me; here was the New Yorker addressing his guide, saying plainly, "Are we going to get American food in Yantai?"

I took it that Yantai, on the coast, was the next place on their itinerary, and held my breath as I awaited the answer.

But the older man broke in before it came. He said, with a mixture of pained patience and hopefulness, "We're sure to get it in Shanghai. No problem with American food in Shanghai."

The guide, to whom it must have been a great mortification that the chances of his charges getting American food in Yantai were even more remote than in Ji'nan, asked, somewhat unnecessarily, "You want American food?"

"Yes!" shrieked the woman, stubbing out her cigarette and jingling her multiple bracelets. "Yes, Yes! Three times a day—breakfast, lunch, and dinner!"

Comrade Zhang chose this moment to walk in. One look at his

face, behind whose blank expression I immediately recognized the functionary in fear of decisions or deviating an inch from the official line, and I decided that my request must come out sounding as preposterous as the Americans'. I could only think, with sinking heart, here is the perfect bureaucrat, who has prospered by the subordination of individual initiative to general procedures. The spiky haircut, which you could see in spite of the cloth cap, went with the rest of his appearance, as did the grey in which he was clad.

When I asked, just like that, to go to the Victory Oilfields, he covered his surprised objections with a veneer of forbearance, "That's not the sort of place you can just drop in on, unless you have relatives there."

He proceeded to explain—a predictable explanation, an administrative explanation, given in a tone which clearly implied, "You're violating normal procedure, and no good could ever conceivably come of it." I think the position was as follows: if we were an organized tour, or a technical delegation, then it might be considered reasonable for permission to be granted and arrangements to be made. The proper channels were not here but in Peking, and two to three weeks was the normal length of time for such applications to be followed through. But as it was—no relatives, no authorization, no special expertise in oil technology—I had not a hope in hell of going to the Victory Oilfields.

For several minutes I unhelpfully stuck to my guns; for several minutes Zhang stuck to his. We were going round and round in circles, he wishing to dismiss me, I thwarting that wish. By obliging him to repeat things which were already perfectly clear, I knew I was causing him ill humor, but I would not call it a day; I could not come so far without seeing the Yellow River off to the sea.

We went on like this for several more minutes, but then he reverted to the most unassailable argument of all—"It's the regulation"—and I knew that there was nothing more to be said; he was bringing the interview, already greatly overextended in his opinion, to a close. That's flat, he was saying, though not in so many words.

There was no question of protesting this, and though I had begun to say something, my voice had trailed away. When I retrieved it

I muttered, more from ruefulness than from any fervor, "It is natural, after all, for a returning Chinese to want to see the socialist construction of her fatherland."

I had, in all innocence, uttered the magic formula. I cannot imagine what procedural wheel I had unwittingly turned, but all of a sudden he was altering the tone of his voice. "Well—yes," he stunned me by saying, "I'll see what I can do." If he phoned the oilfields management today, they could be ready for us in a day. The intransigence was off, and it must be because it was no longer a matter of granting a tourist a travel pass, it was a matter of a compatriot's unequivocal right to glory in the accomplishments of her country. He asked me for my passport, and when he returned it the next morning, radiating friendliness, he told me that my travel permit had been appropriately endorsed: "preferential treatment," he called it, "seeing as you're a compatriot."

The future of my journey thus assured, I set out to see the sights. I thought I saw more old women with bound feet here than in any other province in China. "It's true," said a young girl I chatted to on a bus, "Shandong people are still quite feudal."

This girl, fair skinned and stocky, was from Qufu, Confucius's birthplace in the part of Shandong that used to be called Lu. As befits the home of Confucius, Lu is incurably conservative, and in this it poses a contrast to Qi, the northestern region producing the greater proportion of Shandong's entrepreneurs, seafarers, agriculturalists, and, above all, emigrants.

Shandong has contributed greatly to the Chinese diaspora. The reason was partly the proximity of the sea, and partly history. During the Manchu reign, fear of Russian expansion into Manchuria prompted the court to encourage its Chinese subjects to settle there; large numbers went from Shandong, both as seasonal labor and settlers, and the tradition seemed to have continued. In the early years of this century Shandong provided a large contingent of indentured labor to ease the shortage of unskilled workers in South Africa. And during World War I Britain shipped nearly one hundred thousand men from the Shandong port of Weihaiwei to engage in noncombat work behind the lines in France, and hundreds of these now lie in graves in Chinese cemeteries not far from the River Somme. Thus Shandong spread its wings across the world.

Spreading *its* wings, the Western world came to Shandong in the last century, and stayed on its soil for many years. In varying degrees the British, French, and Germans all had designs on the place, and even now the coastal ports—Weihaiwei, Yantai (Chefoo), and Qingdao (Tsingtao)—bear a strong European imprint. Qingdao, especially, still remembers its two decades under German sway in its famous beer, a brew which, as the most sought after in the country, may well be the Germans' best legacy to China.

But Ji'nan never came under the control of Europeans. A special foreign commercial settlement, laid out in the early years of this century to the west of the city walls, above the geological depression which underlies the city's lakes and springs, was as close as it ever came to the foreign concessions and privileges of the so-called treaty port. Nevertheless, whether left by missionary churches, consulates, the British-American Tobacco Company, the Deutsch-Asiatische Bank, or the Mitsui Trading Company, solid Western-style buildings are still to be seen in the city.

"It's better that Chinese places should remain Chinese," the girl from Qufu was saying. But she was not talking about Ji'nan, where she was a student of medicine, but of Hong Kong, whence she supposed I had come. "The British government—Mrs. Thatcher—was quite wrong about that; Hong Kong is an inalienable part of the territory of the People's Republic of China. And it's only a matter of time before we become reunited with our compatriots there."

She then asked me, "Would you rather it were sooner or later?"

I replied that the people of Hong Kong would rather it were never.

As soon as I said it I regretted it, for my answer clearly caused great distressed astonishment to this young, wide-eyed, well-meaning girl from Shandong.

"Is that true?" her mouth opening a little.

I said I understood so.

"But why?"

I said something about the people having doubts about the safety of their capital, and added that a lot of it was fleeing Hong Kong already.

She gave me one of her wide-eyed, puzzled expressions. "But it'll come back, though, won't it, sooner or later? They are Chinese after all, the people of Hong Kong. Surely they'd find Chinese rule more acceptable than British."

I said it wasn't so much a question of British versus Chinese rule, as a matter of socialism versus capitalism.

But she didn't really understand (and who would in her place?), because at the mention of the two systems she asked me which I thought was the better, socialism or capitalism.

"What do you think?" I asked.

She gave out, bless her unquestioning soul, something like a hosanna. "Oh, socialism, of course!" And she looked as if she was irradiated by some inner joy.

Presently she asked me if I thought China very poor.

I did.

An expression of great artless earnestness crossed her face. There was now a trace of trusting conviction in her voice, "Things will be better, now that the Twelfth Congress of the Party has met."

Afterward, when we had alighted, there was, for her, a pleasing moment when she stopped at the entrance of a public building and pointed to the half dozen men sweeping behind it. "You see these men, they're all high-level officials. Yet they are sweeping the courtyard. I bet that's something you don't get in a capitalist country." The men didn't look to me as if they swept floors everyday, but I was glad I found it possible to tell her I was impressed.

Since she was headed for the opposite direction—she had only walked with me as far as that building to point me in the direction of Leaping Springs—we parted at this point. Leaping Springs is one of Ji'nan's chief sights, so called because it once spurted bubbly jets of water, but she warned me I'd be disappointed in it; Ji'nan's springs had mostly run dry. It used to be that you only had to push a stick into the ground and a fountain would gush out, such is the geology beneath the city, which once boasted seventy-two springs. But, she told me, the air-raid dugouts had changed the course of the underground water, and it was also said that imprudent industrial construction had affected the geography. As it turned out she was quite right about my disappointment: there might have been a gurgle or two at Leaping Springs, but the pond was licked by algae and had a woebegone feeling.

Looking, nevertheless, for something to fasten my interest on, I paused in front of a pavilion commemorating a twelfth-century poetess. Li Qingzhao, whose technical virtuosity has been compared to Edith Sitwell's, was a native of Ji'nan and is China's most celebrated woman poet. Her verse is exquisitely intimate with the sentiment of chilly nights and nostalgia, that melancholy which is born of past joys, and two of its best remembered lines are about leaves and flowers: "plumped up green, pinched red / favored willows, pampered blossoms."

"Let's see some flowers," I suggested to Takia. We'd heard that there was a chrysanthemum show on at Pearl Springs, so I settled for that. The chrysanthemums proved old, for the show was nearly over. The springs were chiefly remarkable for what the organizers, with a touching attempt at decoration which, well intentioned though it was, seemed to me to have hopelessly misfired, had placed upon them: two slightly down-at-heel dragon effigies made of grass, each floating on what might be a sampan, draped with a powder-blue plastic sheet. Between them bobbed three or four pink and orange objects, looking twee and what they were: plastic fish and swans. But the decoration was not something to be dismissed; it suggested that the organizers did try, one had to give them that.

The sky, which had hung dull like pewter, cleared of its clouds as we left Pearl Springs, and I was determined to discover beauty in Ji'nan, soiled as it is by industrial waste and swelling population. It must have been lovely once, I thought, willow shaded and running with canals. Something of this loveliness remains at the Great Clear Lake, which we visited next. It lies at the northern limits of the old city and covers, in its three-mile extent, about a quarter of that city's area. We hired a boat, and it took us around the lake's shores, stopping at an island from which the water, in its crystalline whiteness, seemed dissolved in its own transparency. At the edge of the water curtains of willow hung, joined to their reflections. On the island it surprised me to find hardly anybody about, so accustomed had I become to finding quiet corners pullulating with humanity in China. And it was just this emptiness which heightened my pleasure.

Southerly beyond the hills, I knew, rose the cliffs of the Thousand Buddhas. There, carved on a rock face, could be found a multitude of statues, figures of the Buddha ranging from a few inches to four or five feet in height. Though hidden from us now, the boatman was convinced you could sometimes see the cliffs reflected in the water, just as the novel, *The Travels of Lao Can*, has described it. Resting his gaze on the nearest hazed rise, and perhaps recalling that book, he quoted to us a couplet which says what the place was like: "Lotus on four sides, willows on three, / One city of hill vistas, half a city of lake."

As the boat glided forward, now and then the flashing sickle of a fish leaping out of the lake could be made out, slipping its sheath of water as it shot up. The sight seemed an unasked-for extra, when the sky was so right, and I had the place so much to myself. The light was soft as we disembarked, and there was a sense of willows everywhere.

Victory Oilfields and the Estuary

We started out for the Victory Oilfields, from where it is but a morning's drive to the mouth of the Yellow River. I read somewhere that Shandong would be two humped islands if the Yellow's alluvial deposits hadn't linked it to the mainland, creating a peninsula. This peninsula is lapped by the Bo Gulf to the north and the Yellow Sea to the south; and the Victory Oilfields are what you pass as you make your way northward to where the river comes down to the sea.

A train took us to Zibo, where we were to pick up a car. Zibo produces textiles and hideous pottery, and as a town is built to the standard Chinese design—blank concrete boxes repeated down identical streets. We had lunch in the guesthouse there; and though it was only eleven, I noticed that the other people in the dining room were already halfway through their meal. They were a group of Japanese men, all young and all in uniform. The waiter, who described the Japanese as exporters of yesterday's technology, said they were here because their machines were; in Zibo's textile factories, I gathered, installations of Japanese manufacture increasingly burgeoned.

Then we were on our way. Much slowed by the traffic, heavy with trucks, horse and mule carts, it took us two and a half hours to arrive at the oilfields. For miles we passed alongside heaps of downy cotton, spread out by the side of the road to dry. Through the mental association of cotton with silk, it occurred to me that the name of the province, as it was spelt in the days before the new romanization, had passed into English vocabulary: Shantung, a word meaning soft, undressed silk, a variety spun by worms fed not on your common or garden mulberry, but on the leaves of oak. Seeing the cotton, I did wonder where they could have grown it all; the land looked too barren, from alkalination, for life. For at least half an hour we drove past lonely stunted trees, all of them leafless, and many of them dead.

After the cotton came pipelines. This was before we drove past the township of Dongying, and after we crossed the Xiaoqing River, a Yellow affluent. The driver drove quite well, avoiding collision with creatures domestic and mechanical, all of whom took a proprietory view of the road.

We were met at the Victory Guesthouse by a man and a woman who introduced themselves as Director Zhao and Comrade Wang. I was immune to Director Zhao's smoky glasses, which hid his eyes, but Takia later said they gave him the creeps. Comrade Wang, in whose company we were to spend the next days, was competent but only mildly earnest, I was relieved to find. We seemed to be the only people staying at the hotel, and when we were fed dinner that evening, we ate in an empty echoing room. It was hard to see what the underworked hotel staff found to do, until I noticed them all crowded round the TV after dinner, enthralled by an English language teaching program. The guesthouse seemed well run, but though completed only a few years before, the building was already showing signs of deterioration. Whenever we had a bath a big puddle would form on the floor. When I remarked on this Takia said, "That's China for you—they can lay an oil pipe all the way to Nanking, but can't put in plumbing that doesn't leak."

"Tell us what you'd like to see," Director Zhao had said to us soon after our arrival, "and we'll do our best to arrange it." This was a familiar invitation, and from experience I had learnt it was seldom meant to be taken seriously. But this turned out to be one of those rare instances in which you ask for five things and actually get six. I never thought that he would agree to our going to the estuary, a restricted area, without demur, but when we brought the matter up, quite tentatively, and without meeting his eyes, Director Zhao said, "Of course; we must in that case arrange for you to visit Desolate Isle—perhaps for you to spend the night there." I knew from having studied the map that this was a place on the Yellow River delta, somewhere between the last stretch of the river and its abandoned channel to the south. Here, then, was the chance to get to the river mouth itself. Here, offered with what casualness, what disregard for travel passes or restrictions, was just such a chance as we would have wished to have. What more could possibly have been asked?

The trip was to be two days hence. In the meantime I was introduced to oil extractors, derricks, diesel engines, storage tanks, oilmen and oilwomen. When Comrade Wang showed me the oil extractors, she said that the machine was a modified version of the conventional type; it was more economical of energy and building material, and it was safer. I was impressed, the more so when I learnt that China exports oil extractors to the United States.

A discovery which surprised me, but which the people at the oilfields took as a matter of course, was the large number of young girls at work on the wells. Though the drillers on the rigs were all men, many of the wells were under the charge of all-women work teams. I was shown round an oil-extraction station by a member of one such team, a well inspector for whom the word was peaches-

and-cream. In her smile was mingled such ingenuousness and candor that in the West she would have passed for a fifteen year old.

"It used to be," Comrade Wang informed me, as we watched three men drill a well, "that girls worked on the oil rigs alongside the men. But it proved a bit too rough for them—you have to do the drilling in all weathers, you know—and now they mostly take the lighter jobs." One such job was operating and maintaining diesel engines. This was what a girl, looking as unlike a mechanic as was possible, was doing as I came down from the derrick. She wore a blue cap, and Wellington boots caked with mud, and when she walked over to talk to us, her slender body undulated slowly and with such femininity it might have been a movement of veils and bustles and skirts. Unlike the first girl she was shy, and reluctant to talk about her work, but she seemed to take pleasure in being photographed by Takia. Something extraordinary was the way she faced the camera, with a pose and carriage of head so completely studied she might have been a fifties movie star, skilled at showing her assets to best advantage. We might have been on a film set, instead of an oilfield, from the way she bore herself. Far from thinking this inappropriate, I could not help approving of her, as though hers was an attitude deliberately struck against this masculine world of oil, this complex of pipelines and towering structures repeated to the horizon, in a landscape where all was dull and grey, with nothing soft or bright to break the monotony.

We were shown a factory where diesel engines, such as the one this girl was manning, were assembled and repaired. Here again, one felt strongly the presence of women: on the shop floor the number of female workers far exceeded male. What particularly struck me was a blackboard, on which were spelt out the names of workers, with little flags drawn under them in red chalk, denoting the number of good points each person had won for "completion of production quota," "good attitude," "conscientious study," and so on. Reading the heading above the chart, "March 8 Competition Board," I realized that it was named after the International Women's Day.

In another respect, Victory Oilfields was like no other setup I'd previously encountered. Whereas in other countries it would be surprising to find planting intermingled with oil wells, here it seemed to be the norm. You could see harvested grain stacked in the very lee of the boreholes, striped with the hard shadows of rigs.

Comrade Wang explained: "If it hadn't been for the wells, this place would still be wilderness, but once the oil started flowing, the farming got going as well. Since 1966, when the first families moved here, land reclamation has been undertaken at Victory Oilfields."

And now that two of the land's most life-enhancing fluids were tapped (namely petroleum and Yellow River water), industry and agriculture, workers and peasants, could go hand in hand, the way Maoist thinking had always wanted them to. Hydrocarbons and self-sufficiency in rice: that's the Victory Oilfields in a nutshell. When we were introduced to the leader of the May Seventh Production Brigade (May 7, 1966 was the day on which Mao Zedong urged Chinese cadres to reeducate themselves through manual labor and study), she quoted to us a saying attributed to the late Premier Zhou Enlai; it goes "Integrate industry and agriculture, town and country, for the benefit of production, and the convenience of living."

I was told plans were afoot to develop livestock breeding here, and I saw, besides the odd sheep nosing about the boreholes, a not very successful stab at forestry. This was a small plot on the edge of a reservoir, planted with willow, poplar, and the Chinese scholar tree. The oilfields, Comrade Wang told me, offered good conditions for agriculture: the families of those employed by the industrial complex provided the labor, and you had investment and technical know-how on tap. I inquired conversationally about the mechanization of agriculture, and Comrade Wang showed this to me, pointing at a threshing machine made by one of their own factories, which at that hour of the day was not working. Wheat ricks stood all about; tilting her head at these, Comrade Wang said, eyes brightening, that they had had a bumper harvest that year. The machine looked primitive, but its value can scarcely be discounted, seen against the prodigious physical labor by which so much Chinese agriculture is effected.

Seeing it, I was reminded of an evening I once spent in Qufu. I was watching Roman Polanski's film, *Tess of the D'Urbervilles*, dubbed into Chinese. This in itself would have struck one as droll, but what made it even droller was that the audience, far from finding Nastassia Kinski or the love scenes interesting, started to murmur and nudge each other in excitement only when a threshing machine appeared on the screen. At the sight of the machine seizing the corn and instantly whisking out the grain, the man sitting next to me in the cinema drew a sharp breath, so novel and intriguing did it seem to him, so much was nineteenth-century Wessex in advance of Shandong Province in the mechanization of agriculture.

Still, there was something comforting in all this, in simple rusticity blurring the hard edges of industry. But something was wrong, beneath the show of domestic self-sufficiency. I had accepted the outer appearance, and had not detected the hint of breakdown within. This was left for later discovery, one I made by reading the *People's Daily* on the day of my departure. There, on the front page, was an article about the Victory Oilfields, exposing its shadier underside, a hotbed of theft, embezzlement, wastage, misappropriation, and diversion of state property. "Evil practices and unhealthy trends," the paper called them, and set forth the details: the 150,000 tons of crude oil misappropriated every year, the hundreds of cases of larceny uncovered, the 100 million cubic meters of natural gas wasted, the number of illegal oil-refining furnaces discovered. . . . The matter is now under control, the paper observed, thanks to the cooperation between the district and oilfield Party committees. The culprits seemed not to have taxed their imagination much, but had simply exploited outright the opportunities created by poor management. But one could be sure of how little of the ideological rectitude of an earlier period was left in them. Those disciplines, so strictly enforced once, seem no more than the chains which, once broken, only make the wearer rampage the more. It made me think of a row of dominoes stacked slantwise on top of each other, and then set a-tumbling by pulling the first one out.

Just before we left for Desolate Isle I fell ill. The guesthouse doctor, a woman from one of the coastal ports, took my temperature and diagnosed tonsillitis. I did feel seedy, but was anxious to avoid drugs for fear of side effects. She therefore refrained from prescribing Western medicines altogether, and gave me an assortment of Chinese ones—pills of antelope horn, bezoar, and gentian violet. By the time we came to start out on our excursion, I found that I was quite well.

We started early, and crossed the Yellow River by ferry a little after eight. Including the driver, there were five of us; Comrade Wang had produced a local photographer to keep Takia company, and we were also joined by a laconic young man I had not seen before, and whose presence on this trip was never explained.

The day was overcast, and while we were sitting at lunch, at a small oilfield on Desolate Isle itself, it began to rain. "It can't be helped," said Comrade Wang, "it's that cold wave from Siberia." The same cold wave that had brought a sudden change of weather in every place we had passed through in Shandong, and seemed indeed to be dogging our steps. We had run smack into it in Penglai, a pretty town on the other side of the Bo Gulf from the Yellow River outlet which we had visited after Ji'nan. Now, peering through the car window at the dark clouds overhead, I remembered how the heavens gaped that day, and how the rain fell, so absolutely that the covered motorized tricycle we were riding slithered, and I had almost the sensation that I was gazing at the world through a mirror. I remembered how Takia, getting off the vehicle, tripped and fell head forward, pitching himself and his camera bag into the squelchy, cloying mud.

The scene outside our car window was wholly familiar to me: the sky lowering over the uneven road, and the wind turning oblique a section of the rain. We were crossing one great level stretch of land, on which stiff grasses made up the scenery. A dreary, marshy, wasted land, mile upon mile of it, netted at its furthest end by the delta of the Yellow River. The entire landscape looked blanched, the yellow and brown of the reeds falling away into a liquid grey. I liked this forlorn place, the darkened sky and the water making its way through a vacant land, without form or visible limit, where no man has yet shaped the earth.

It was still raining when we came to a halt, and looked out at long last upon the estuary. This broad flow which ended here had swept with it the mud of an immense country and the ice of vast uninhabitable regions. But seeing it was as much of an anticlimax as it was bound to be. The river had never looked so indistinct to me, and as my eyes ranged over the shallows, and rested on the dead crustaceans washed up ashore—tiny crabs, and the big fat prawns which Takia said were called pissing prawns—everything seemed to lose color and outline.

A hut stood at the edge of the water, and in it I found a handful of fishermen standing about a black caldron. They were stewing some fish, using a fire fueled by what looked like tar and was in fact a dollop of Victory crude oil. The oil set me thinking: they used to drill just off these shores, out there in the Bo Gulf. But an accident had happened; an oil rig had collapsed and seventy-two workers had died, and all because bureaucrats in the Petroleum Ministry had refused to attend to storm warnings. Quite a scandal it was, and a minister had lost his job.

Now there was a desolation to these shores, from which the drillers had departed. Seen through the veils of rain, the river looked lost. Above, the sky formed a second river, rolling up with its own brown sludge. There was no way of telling sky from river and river from sky; there was just this muddy haze, like fate itself, or the way things happen. Somewhere out there the river lost itself in the sea, but again it was difficult to tell where. I began to miss a sense of conclusion, and looked about for something to give my journey its seal of completion. I did not find it until, looking out toward the sea, I spied the shapes of three sailing boats across the water—the first sails I had seen on the Yellow River, and marking a horizon for me.

Epilogue

I remember one hot day when a party of us were crossing the hills in chairs—the way was rough and very steep, the work for the coolies very severe. At the highest point of our journey, we stopped for ten minutes to let the men rest. Instantly they all sat in a row, brought out their pipes, and began to laugh among themselves as if they had not a care in the world.

—— Bertrand Russell
in China, 1920

I do not know exactly what [Russell] is driving at. I do know one thing: if the porters had been able not to smile at those whom they had carried, China would have long since been out of its present rut.

—— Lu Xun's comment

If, as a traveler in Japan, you are asked one question more than any other, it is this: "What do you think of Japan?" It is not a frequently asked question in China; the Chinese have too little need to find themselves different for that.

I never was asked that question, or at least not in that form. But suppose I were, how many impressions I would have to take into account! Which would figure more—the poverty, the congestion, the blackened cities, the depressingly shabby streets; or the snowy peaks above the Qinghai steppes, the fields turned gold by ripening grain, the lotus buds thrusting above the ooze, silence and sun settling behind the Tengger dunes? How much impossible balancing of profit and loss there would have to be. Between, for example, those ambitious reclamation and water conservancy projects which make you realize socialist construction is not merely a watchword, but something to be taken quite literally; and the loss of those things which had a kind of aesthetic value: manners not yet coarsened, the mellowed elegance of patricians, the rustle of patterned silk and the emanation of secret joys from a painted lady, the flamboyance of festivals, the artist creating alone, the celebrated cuisine whose traditions are nowadays more consummately preserved in Hong Kong.

To that composite image of China, would I have to add what I'd heard and read, or could I just go by the look of things? Would I have to superpose upon the awesome image of dams and dykes the equally awesome image of those hideous labor gangs, by whose terrible endeavor these artifacts were brought into being years ago? And would I have to remind myself that we have yet to see in full flower those seeds of error and disaster embedded in past years even in the good?

Which of my several moods in China, from wild impatience and sudden softening, to absolute detachment and utter dejection, would most deeply color my judgment? Which emotion would live longer—the rage I felt at seeing a man run after a packed bus, catch it only just in time, clamber on, only to find himself brutally pushed off it by a passenger ramming his elbow into his ribs; or that feeling of being moved beyond words by the kindness of people who would share with me their last steamed bread?

My answer would also vary, obviously, according to which time scale I took. For are you not told all the time that if life in today's China is no picnic, it was still worse under the former regime? A fair evaluation of what this government has made of China would indeed have to take into account what it had inherited from the past. Yet how to be fair; how much weight, for example, to give to the persistence into the new China of that classic Gansu image of people wearing no trousers, and how much to the disappearance from Shanghai streets of those beggars starved and frozen to death? Which do you count as present faults and which past failings? To what, for example, do you attribute the cultural sterility that confronts you everywhere in China: to the socialist habit of seeing art on an organizational and mass scale and of crippling dissentient individual creation; or to the impoverishment, long ago begun, of Chinese inventiveness and energy, and the degeneration, from way back, of ancient civilization? You can no more measure the alloy of hate in any love than say what deep-rooted malaise lies at the bottom of present stagnancy, or how far back in the drying-up of the artistic wellsprings goes the contemporary aridity.

Which is the inner China, bred in the bones, and which the outer, veneered on the skin? How do you square the opinion of those who believe totalitarianism to be unnatural to the Chinese with the plentiful evidence of it in their past? Then is it the innate qualities of the Chinese themselves that make for them the deepest sorrow that they can suffer, turning them into such ideal material for totalitarian rule—supine, long suffering, incurious, ready to marvel to find their government not unduly corrupt or cruel, to find (as Lu Xun puts it) "a master deigning to accept them as his people—no, not even that—deigning to accept them as his cattle"? Is what they say about the Russians true also for the Chinese then, that they have a talent for oppression and being oppressed? Is it just communism, or is it that communism feeds on those weaknesses that lie in the Chinese themselves?

When you see Chinese laughing and enjoying themselves in the midst of so much reason for unhappiness, should you be cheered that they can show such fortitude, or should you be saddened that they can be satisfied with so little? Do you see them through Bertrand Russell's eyes, or through Lu Xun's? The stoop of those shoulders: do you see an invitation to blows being rained on them, or do you see something more positive, a stoic discipline to withstand those blows? What was it about the Chinese that induced them to believe in, listen to, connive at even the worst excesses of the Maoist vision; was it their fear or their hopelessness, their inertia or their peasant resignation, which begot such credulity and pliancy, such self-serving conformity?

What, ultimately, is the sorrow of China? The inundating waters of the Yellow River, or the emperors' misrule which led to the dykes falling into disrepair? The misrule that led to the collapse of the dykes, or the servitude seconding that misrule? The honoring of virtues befitting dependents and slaves, or the inability to escape the past that reduces the possibility of a future?

All these people, the millions still proliferating, like plants in a jungle, crowding out the light. How hard they must struggle, just to stay in the same spot; for to give way an inch, only an inch, is to let others roll over you like a flood. China sorrows, crushed by its own people, for whom so little can be done because they are so many.

The "weathermark" identifies this book as a production of John Weatherhill, Inc., publishers of fine books on Asia and the Pacific. Editorial supervision: Michael Ashby. Book design and typography: Miriam F. Yamaguchi and Michael Ashby. Production supervision: Mitsuo Okado. Layout of illustrations: Yutaka Shimoji. Composition of the text: Korea Textbook Co., Seoul. Printing of the text, in letterpress: Shobundo Printing Co., Tokyo. Printing of the plates, in monochrome offset: Kinmei Printing, Co., Tokyo. Binding: Makoto Binderies, Tokyo. The typeface used is Monotype Bembo.